REGULATING POLLUTION

Regulating Pollution
A UK and EC Perspective

CHRIS HILSON

·HART·
PUBLISHING
OXFORD – PORTLAND OREGON
2000

Hart Publishing
Oxford and Portland, Oregon

Published in North America (US and Canada) by
Hart Publishing c/o
International Specialized Book Services
5804 NE Hassalo Street
Portland, Oregon
97213-3644
USA

Distributed in the Netherlands, Belgium and Luxembourg by
Intersentia, Churchillaan 108
B2900 Schoten
Antwerpen
Belgium

Hart Publishing Ltd is a specialist legal publisher based in Oxford, England.
To order further copies of this book or to request a list of other
publications please write to:

Hart Publishing Ltd, Salter's Boatyard,
Folly Bridge, Abingdon Road, Oxford OX1 4LB
Telephone: +44 (0)1865 245533 or Fax: +44 (0)1865 794882
e-mail: mail@hartpub.co.uk
www.hartpub.co.uk

British Library Cataloguing in Publication Data
Data Available
ISBN 1 84113–094–4 (cloth)

Typeset by Hope Services (Abingdon) Ltd.
Printed and bound in Great Britain by Biddles Ltd
www.biddles.co.uk

To my Grandparents

Preface

Part of this book stems from my PhD thesis entitled *Pollution Control and the Rule of Law*. (The PhD was undertaken at the University of Sheffield and awarded in 1995.) However, many of the chapters contain wholly new material, and the thesis-based chapters have been reworked so significantly that it would be hard to trace many of them back to their original form. The principal aim of that thesis was to compare different regulatory instruments in terms of what I labelled there as the "rule of law" values of accountability, equity, effectiveness, certainty and efficiency. Although I remain convinced by the efforts of the Sheffield school to discover a public law conception of the rule of law,[1] I am now less convinced that all of the above administrative values can properly be included in such a project. Thus, while chapter 6 of this book contains a similar analysis of regulatory instruments, this analysis takes place within the framework of "legitimacy" rather than the rule of law. Indeed the legitimacy of pollution regulation is a thread that runs through much of the book.

Inspiration for writing this book also came in part from the inaugural session of the environmental law section of the Society of Public Teachers of Law (SPTL), held a number of years ago. It became clear to me at that session that there was an increasing need for environmental lawyers to step back from the ever-increasing mass of environmental *law* trees in order to get a better picture of the *regulatory* wood. Much of the writing on UK and EC environmental law hitherto has been black letter or doctrinal in nature—understandably given the need to provide an account of this mass of new law.[2] Only relatively recently have rather more theoretical, inter-disciplinary and contextual studies begun to appear,[3] which no doubt reflects the increasing maturity of environmental law as a subject. And of course environmental law is not unique in this respect—it is only recently that EU legal scholarship has taken a more theoretical turn.[4]

I make no apologies for the focus on pollution rather than environmental regulation. Although some will no doubt be disappointed that the book is not broader in scope, I readily confess that I am not an expert in nature conservation law and policy. Furthermore, while there are some regulatory issues that are common to pollution and nature conservation, there are also many

[1] See I. Harden and N. Lewis, *The Noble Lie: The British Constitution and the Rule of Law* (London, Hutchinson, 1986); I. Harden, "The Constitution and Its Discontents" (1991) 21 *British Journal of Political Science* 489.

[2] This is not to deny the utility of such an approach. Given that much of my own work is traditional legal scholarship of this kind, it would be strange if I claimed otherwise.

[3] See e.g. T. Jewell and J. Steele (eds.), *Law in Environmental Decision-Making* (Oxford, Clarendon, 1998).

[4] J. Shaw, "European Legal Studies in Crisis? Towards a New Dynamic" (1996) 16 *OJLS* 231.

differences. To give nature conservation the attention it deserves would have required further detailed explanation which, besides being beyond my capability, would have broken up the flow of the text. That said, many of the arguments presented are equally applicable to both fields.

Aspects of the secondary title also require some explanation. The book is in part a study of what one might call regulatory federalism, which seeks to examine pollution regulation in a system of multi-level governance. In this sense, regulation within the UK and regulation by the EC must be seen as part of one system. However, while the book is not technically a study in comparative law—since this normally involves a comparison of separate systems rather than separate levels of one system—there is inevitably a comparative element involved. In examining pollution regulation at EC level and at UK level, it is difficult to avoid this.

As for terminology, the use of EC rather than EU should by now require little explanation—at least for lawyers and political scientists. Since Maastricht, the European Union (EU) has technically consisted of three separate pillars. One of these is the European Community (EC), and since environmental policy comes within this pillar, it is technically correct to use the term EC when referring to it. However, when referring to the overall geographical area, or to the process of integration, the term EU will be used.

Rather more problematic is the use of the term UK. My initial decision to use this term was based on the fact that the United Kingdom (UK) remains the responsible Member State as far as the EU is concerned. Furthermore, on a much more practical level, "a UK and EC Perspective" seemed a much more pithy title than "an English and Welsh, and EC Perspective", or even "an English and EC Perspective". Besides which, this is *not* a book solely about English law and policy. Some chapters (such as chapter 3, which covers devolution) inevitably consider the whole of the United Kingdom. In others (such as chapter 4 on legitimacy), I have made a point of covering the UK because the institutional comparisons between England, Wales, Scotland and Northern Ireland are interesting and instructive. However in a number of the other chapters, if I touch on the situation of countries other than England, it is only in footnotes. I sincerely hope that this is not taken as a disregard of the position in other parts of the UK. The reasoning behind it is much more practical—to do otherwise would have made the chapters concerned rather unwieldy.

I am grateful to the Law Department at the University of Reading for granting me research leave during the autumn term of 1999 to enable me to complete this book, as well as to colleagues who took on my teaching and administrative responsibilities during that period. I am also grateful to the ESRC, from which I received funding under its programme "One Europe or Several". Chapters 3 and 5 in particular can be seen as part of this programme.

On a more personal level, I would like to thank colleagues and others who have provided useful leads or read drafts of some of the chapters, including Richard Bellamy, Tony Downes, Rachel Foster, Duncan French, Jennifer

James, Andy Jordan, Patricia Leopold, Donald McGillivray, Chris Newdick, Tony Ogus, Mike Purdue, Ian Sainsbury and a number of public officials. Needless to say, the responsibility for any remaining errors is mine. I also owe a great deal to Simon Ball—an inspirational supervisor who died a few years ago. Last but not least, I would like to thank Anna and Daniel for being so patient and for all their support during the writing of this book.

Contents

Table of Cases

Table of Legislation

Statutory Instruments

EU Secondary Legislation

Treaties

1

Regulatory Essentials

WHAT IS REGULATION?

Regulation is an elastic concept. At its broadest, the term is used to refer to any governmental rules which seek to organise or control behaviour.[1] On this view, traditional criminal laws on theft and so on might be regarded as regulation. However, this definition is too broad in the context of a book on pollution control. A somewhat narrower focus sees regulation as a "sustained and focused control exercised by a public agency over activities that are valued by a community".[2] The emphasis on "valued activity" has the advantage of including most pollution regulation (where, for example, manufacturing industry is a valued activity), but excluding traditional criminal law[3] (theft not being a valued activity). However, it has the disadvantage of excluding some non-valued activities that are covered by pollution regulation (for example the deliberate fly-tipping of waste by individuals), and may also include some non-regulatory criminal laws such as fraud (where business is valued but fraud is not). Similarly, while the emphasis on "sustained and focused control" captures the essence of the continuing relationship found in most industrial pollution regulation, pollution regulation also includes control of "one-off" activities (fly-tipping again). And finally, the definition, in stressing the role of "public agencies" also excludes self-regulation, which is an alternative means of delivering regulatory goals. A more appropriate definition—and one which is sufficiently broad to encompass European regulation—may therefore be: control exercised by a non-police public body over the activities of individuals, firms or Member States in order to achieve defined goals; or control by firms of their own activities to achieve such goals.

However, while the above definition captures the general sense of what regulation involves, it misses out the separate stages of the regulatory process. This generally starts with programmes or "policy" in a broad sense, which may then be translated into legislation. This legislation will then often have to be supplemented by administrative rule-making and discretion, and any obligations imposed will need to be monitored and enforced. Pollution law and policy, at both Community and national level, are often conceived of in regulatory terms.

[1] C. Harlow and R. Rawlings, *Law and Administration*, (2nd edn, London, Butterworths, 1997), p. 295.

[2] P. Selznick, "Focusing Organisational Research on Regulation" in R. Noll (ed.), *Regulatory Policy and the Social Sciences* (Berkeley, Cal., University of California Press, 1985), p. 363.

[3] A. I. Ogus, *Regulation: Legal Form and Economic Theory* (Oxford, Clarendon, 1994), p. 1.

EC pollution regulation involves the setting of policy priorities by way of the environmental "action programmes".[4] Community legislation—typically in the form of directives—may then be introduced to implement this policy.[5] Monitoring and enforcement then takes place to ensure that Member States are complying with their regulatory obligations in these directives. At national level, pollution regulation consists of White Papers and other government policy documents, giving rise in many cases to primary and delegated legislation to implement this policy. This is then often followed by administrative rule-making and application, as well as monitoring and enforcement of the activities of firms and individuals.

Social and economic regulation

Having defined regulation in general terms, it is then traditional to distinguish between social and economic regulation. Economic regulation involves governmental control of monopolies and competition to ensure that consumers do not face unreasonably high prices and poor quality goods or services.[6] In contrast, social regulation involves control of the socially, rather than economically, undesirable behaviour of individuals and firms. Pollution regulation, along with health and safety, is regarded as a classic example of social regulation. Of course social and economic regulation are invariably closely connected. On the one hand, economic regulation, which prevents economic abuses, will have overall social benefits; and economic regulators may be required not just to control prices and quality, but also to ensure that specific social objectives are provided for.[7] And on the other hand, social regulation has economic consequences for firms and consumers: pollution abatement equipment is often expensive to install and maintain. In the case of the privatised water companies in England and Wales, which enjoy a natural monopoly, social regulation is explicitly considered in the context of economic regulation: the companies are allowed by the economic regulator[8] to raise prices by a given amount in order to pass on some of the costs of social regulation (on drinking and bathing water) to consumers.[9]

[4] Commission of the EC, *Towards Sustainability: A European Community Programme of Policy and Action in Relation to the Environment and Sustainable Development* [1993] OJ C138/1; D. N. Pocklington, 'The Role of Environmental Action Programmes in the Development of EU Environmental Legislation' (1995) 7 *Environmental Law and Management* 221.

[5] Although there is an increasing reliance on non-legislative "soft law" instruments such as communications.

[6] See T. Prosser, *Law and the Regulators* (Oxford, Clarendon, 1997), pp. 5–6.

[7] Such as universal service.

[8] The Office of Water Services (OFWAT), headed by the Director General of Water Services.

[9] OFWAT, *Setting the Quality Framework* (Birmingham, OFWAT, 1998); Environment Agency, *A Price Worth Paying* (Bristol, Environment Agency, 1998); DETR, *Raising the Quality* (London, DETR, 1998); OFWAT, *Prospects for Prices* (Birmingham, OFWAT, 1998).

WHY REGULATE?

There are both descriptive and normative answers to the question "why regulate?" Normative theories that tell us why we ought to regulate pollution fall into two camps. On the one hand, there are environmental ethics, which provide non-economic justifications for pollution regulation; and on the other, there are welfare economics, which establish a normative economic theory of regulation.

Environmental ethics

Anthropocentric theories within environmental ethics would claim that we should control pollution not only in order to protect human health, but also to protect nature because of its instrumental value to humans in providing drugs, food, recreation, spiritual and other benefits. This can be described in either deontological or utilitarian terms: either we should control pollution because humans have a "right" to a clean environment; or regulation should occur because human welfare is likely to be increased by a clean environment. However, this is only to consider the present, and anthropocentric theories also contain an inter-temporal element. The anthropocentric version of sustainable development suggests that we should control pollution because we should leave the environment in an acceptable condition for future generations of humans. The 1987 Brundtland Report definition of sustainable development—"development that meets the needs of the present without compromising the ability of future generations to meet their own needs"[10]—is a classic example of an anthropocentric interpretation. So why should we control pollution for the sake of future generations? Again, one can answer this on both utilitarian and deontological lines. With utilitarianism, welfare maximisation can be read as including a need to maximise welfare across all generations, now and in the future. Deontological theories, in contrast, posit that we owe moral duties to future generations (who may therefore enjoy rights).[11] Both of these are essentially the same as arguments made for controlling pollution in the present, only here they are being applied to the future.

Next there are theories which extend the scope of moral concern beyond humans so as to avoid "speciesism". Some theorists extend the moral community only as far as animals.[12] On this basis, pollution should be controlled

[10] World Commission on Environment and Development, *Our Common Future* (Oxford, OUP, 1987).

[11] Although as Alder and Wilkinson note, not all duty-based deontological theories envisage the creation of rights corresponding to duties: (J. Alder and D. Wilkinson, *Environmental Law and Ethics* (London, Macmillan, 1999), p. 131.

[12] For a rights-based theory, see T. Regan, *The Case for Animal Rights* (London, Routledge, 1988); for a utilitarian theory, see P. Singer, *Practical Ethics* (2nd edn., Cambridge, CUP, 1993).

because the health and welfare of animals may be affected, and either animals have rights to a clean environment just as humans do, or their welfare will be maximised by living in a clean environment. Other, "biocentric" theorists extend the moral community still further to include all living organisms such as plants, insects and even viruses. Since it is difficult, if not impossible, to bring these organisms within traditional utilitarian or deontological ethical theories,[13] biocentric theories have tended instead to rely on an axiological or "values" approach to ethics, claiming that nature has intrinsic and not just instrumental value.[14] They stress that all living organisms are worthy of moral consideration in themselves, just as humans are valued intrinsically and not just for their instrumental contribution to family or society.[15] On this view, pollution regulation is justified because we have a moral duty to prevent harm to all living organisms. However, like human and animal welfare approaches, biocentric theories are ultimately individualistic in scope, and it has been the place of ecocentric theories to stress the moral considerability of collective groups such as species and ecosytems, rather than just individual plants or animals within those groups. With ecocentric ethics, one might justify pollution control on the basis that we have a moral duty to protect ecosystems which may be harmed by pollution, or a species (say a rare lichen) which may be made extinct as a result of it.[16] As with anthropocentric theories, all of the above "extensionist" ethics are capable of being applied into the future. An animal welfare interpretation of sustainable development might, for example, stress the rights of future animals to a clean environment, or may stress the maximisation of the welfare of all sentient beings across all generations. A biocentric interpretation, on the other hand, would suggest that nature should be sustained for its own sake.[17]

[13] Impossible in the case of utilitarian theories (since only sentient creatures can experience pleasure and pain), and difficult in the case of deontological theories (*cf.* P. W. Taylor, *Respect for Nature: A Theory of Environmental Ethics* (Princeton, NJ, Princeton University Press, 1986) who, while stressing the moral duties of humans towards all living organisms, does not argue that they have corresponding rights, and C. D. Stone, "Should Trees Have Standing? Towards Legal Rights for Natural Objects" (1972) 45 *Southern California Law Review* 450, who argues that *legal* rights ought to be conferred on nature).

[14] While the various theories here are presented as *alternatives*, Stone has argued for a moral *pluralist* approach, whereby different moral theories may apply in different contexts (*e.g.* utilitarianism for animals, and intrinsic value for plants). This is in contrast to moral *monism*, where it is seen as important to have a grand, unifying moral theory (*e.g.* utilitarianism) which is capable of addressing all of our problems: C. D. Stone, "Moral Pluralism and the Course of Environmental Ethics" (1988) 10 *Environmental Ethics* 139.

[15] J. Baird Callicott, 'Intrinsic Value in Nature: A Metaethical Analysis' (1995) 3 *The Electronic Journal of Analytical Philosophy* (http://phil.indiana.edu/ejap/1995.spring/callicott.1995.spring.html), para. 4.

[16] Two of the best known proponents of this "holism", are Aldo Leopold with his "Land Ethic" and Holmes Rolston III: see A. Leopold, *A Sand County Almanac* (1949) (Oxford, OUP, 1968); and H. Rolston, "Value in Nature and the Nature of Value" in R. Attfield and A. Belsey (eds.), *Philosophy and the Natural Environment* (Cambridge, CUP, 1994), p. 13, and *Environmental Ethics: Duties to and Values in The Natural World* (Philadelphia, Penn., Temple University Press, 1988), pp. 141–9).

[17] A. Voinov and C. Smith, "Dimensions of Sustainability"(http://kabir.cbl.cees.edu/AV/PUBS/DS/Sust_Dim.html), pp. 4–5.

The problem with most of the above accounts, even the anthropocentric ones, is that they operate at a high level of generality. They tell us at an abstract level why we should be controlling pollution, but they do not tell us exactly what level of pollution—and thus what trade-off with non-environmental human welfare—is acceptable. Does my human right to a clean environment mean that I have a right that everyone in the UK gives up his or her car so I can breathe clean air? And while in general one can say that a cleaner environment will improve human welfare, a very clean, zero-pollution approach may mean that non-environmental human welfare will be decreased because we will have to go without products that we have come to depend upon. Similarly, does a biocentric moral duty towards all living organisms mean that we can never allow pollution to harm any plant, or even a virus? That would involve shutting down most factories and much more besides. Looking into the future is no easier: we may, for example, owe a duty to future generations of humans to protect the environment that they will inherit from pollution, but do they have a right to an environment in no worse state than we enjoy today? If so, that would mean respecting the assimilative capacity of the environment in relation to degradable wastes and laying down zero-emissions standards for toxic wastes that are bio-accumulative or persistent. And what about global warming? Since scientists are now reasonably certain that human interference is contributing to the greenhouse effect, does this mean that we have to curb our energy-intensive lifestyles drastically in order to pass on an atmosphere unwarmed by human input?

Of course most theorists working within environmental ethics, whatever their persuasion, acknowledge that trade-offs with non-environmental human welfare are necessary,[18] and that morality does not provide easy answers to every practical problem. Indeed Deep Ecologists and ecofeminists suggest that the whole enterprise of an extensionist ethics is misguided. Though there are key differences between the two schools of thought,[19] they are united in arguing for a concrete, personal approach rather than the abstract concerns of traditional ethics. What is needed to solve the environmental crisis is not extended *ethics*, but rather metaphysics which emphasise the rootedness of the human self and identity in nature (Deep Ecology),[20] or virtue-based ethics of caring and concern for the environment (ecofeminism).[21]

[18] Most do so by creating a hierarchy of valued entities to provide some guidance in cases of conflict—see A. Dobson, *Green Political Thought*, 2nd edn. (London, Routledge, 1995), pp. 54–5.

[19] See *e.g.* R. Sessions, "Deep Ecology Versus Ecofeminism: Healthy Differences or Incompatible Philosophies" in K. Warren (edn.), *Ecological Feminist Philosophies* (Bloomington, Indiana University Press, 1996), p. 137; M. E. Zimmerman, "Feminism, Deep Ecology, and Environmental Ethics" in A. Drengson and Y. Inoue (eds.), *The Deep Ecology Movement: An Introductory Anthology* (Berkeley, CA, North Atlantic Books, 1995), p. 169.

[20] As Fox notes, "deep ecology obviously refers to a psychologically based approach to the question of our relationship with nature as opposed to an axiologically based (i.e., a value theory based) approach" (W. Fox, *Toward a Transpersonal Ecology: Developing New Foundations for Environmentalism* (New York, State University of New York Press, 1995), p. 197. Dobson has labelled this a "state of being" as opposed to a "code of conduct" approach (*supra* n.18, pp. 49–61).

[21] V. Plumwood, *Feminism and the Mastery of Nature* (London, Routledge, 1993), pp. 172–3; Zimmerman, *supra* n.19, at 183; *cf.* R. J. H. King, "Caring About Nature: Feminist Ethics and the

Welfare economics

The abstraction, and hence practical weakness, of traditional environmental ethics, and the lack of concrete public policy application offered by metaphysical or value-ethics approaches,[22] have led to the near hegemonic status of welfare economics and their justification for pollution control. As *Blueprint 2* states, "[as] yet, no operational rules for decision-makers have emerged from the 'value in things' literature".[23] Welfare economics—an applied version of preference utilitarianism—have sought to provide such rules. As normative economics they are not describing, for example, how markets operate, but are arguing that social policy ought to be aimed at the maximisation of human welfare.[24] In ideal circumstances, markets are said to produce allocative efficiency, whereby resources are allocated to their most efficient use and welfare is maximised. Perhaps the best known model of allocative efficiency is that established by Pareto. An outcome is said to be Pareto efficient when nobody can be made better off without someone else being made worse off. In practice this will be very difficult to satisfy, because the veto of just one individual could prevent an otherwise efficient solution.[25] Because of this, many economists prefer Kaldor-Hicks efficiency, where total benefits exceed total costs so that the winners can *in theory* compensate the losers.[26] Allocative efficiency is threatened by the existence of market failure, sources of which include "spillovers" or "negative externalities" such as pollution. The idea is that polluting firms impose external costs on society, which are not taken into account by firms or consumers in their manufacturing or consumption decisions. This leads to an inefficient allocation of resources because more of the goods are produced than would otherwise have been the case. Regulation is therefore justified on public interest grounds in order to internalise these external costs, thus ensuring that firms and consumers face the true social costs of production and restoring the efficiency of the market.

At present, most external costs are internalised via techniques familiar to lawyers. They are internalised either through the common law (with a polluter paying damages or being restrained by an injunction), or, more commonly, through command-and-control regulation (where firms are required to pay for the costs of abating pollution to keep within specified levels). The "Pigouvian"[27]

Environment" in Warren *supra* n.19, p. 82, and D. K. Johnson and K. R. Johnson, "The Limits of Partiality: Ecofeminism, Animal Rights and Environmental Concern" in K. Warren (ed.), *Ecological Feminism* (London, Routledge, 1994), p. 106.

[22] Which see the environmental crisis as essentially personal rather than political (though of course, as in feminism, the argument is that the personal is political).

[23] D. Pearce (ed.), *Blueprint 2: Greening the World Economy* (London, Earthscan, 1991), p. 4.

[24] Welfare being measured via human preferences, expressed either through consumption decisions in real markets, or through, e.g., willingness to pay (WTP) surveys in hypothetical markets.

[25] Ogus, *supra* n.3, p. 24.

[26] *Ibid.*

[27] A. Pigou, *The Economics of Welfare* (London, Macmillan, 1920).

approach to internalisation favoured by many economists is to impose a pollution tax on firms which reflects the social costs of production. However, the Coase Theorem[28] suggests that a Pigouvian tax is not necessary to achieve the economist's ideal of efficiency—all that is required is a bargained solution between polluter and polluted.[29] Pigou would have government intervene in the market to correct market failure—albeit that such regulation would be modelled on market principles (the price mechanism of a tax); Coase, in contrast, is a true free marketeer, who believes that an efficient solution can be found without the need for government intervention of any kind. Coase's insight was that the matter of costs is reciprocal: the polluter can be viewed as imposing external costs on the victim; on the other hand, should the polluter have to reduce emissions, the victim can be regarded as imposing costs on the polluter. Thus, it makes no difference from the point of view of efficiency whether the victim bargains with the polluter to make cutbacks, or whether the polluter compensates the victim.[30]

The outcome of the Coaseian bargain will be Pareto efficient and welfare maximising because contracts are, by their nature, efficient: if it were possible for either party to be made better off without making the other worse off, the bargain would have been struck differently. However, with the other internalisation mechanisms examined above, we need to know when damages or an injunction, command-and-control standards or taxes will be efficient, so as to correct the market failure. The answer is that, with all three, this is determined by cost-benefit analysis (CBA). To achieve an optimally efficient level of pollution under a command-and-control system, standards should be set at a level where the total benefits exceed the total costs by the greatest amount (and where marginal costs and benefits are equalised).[31] Under a tax system, the tax set should be equal to the marginal damage caused to others by the firms' emissions,[32] in which case total benefits will exceed total costs. With tort law, assuming the local population has an absolute entitlement[33] to be free from pollution, there are two ways in which a court could protect this entitlement in a civil

[28] See R. Coase, "The Problem of Social Cost" (1960) 3 *The Journal of Law & Economics* 1.

[29] However, it has long been pointed out that the theorem falls down where large numbers are involved and where bargaining cannot therefore take place without considerable transaction costs: see e.g. D. Helm and D. Pearce, "Assessment: Economic Policy Towards the Environment" (1990) 6 *Oxford Review of Economic Policy* 1, pp. 6–7. Most modern pollution problems do of course involve large numbers, which means that the Coaseian approach is of limited utility.

[30] Although, as we shall see, it does make a difference to equity and the polluter pays principle. In the eyes of neo-classical economists, the Pigouvian approach commits the error of confusing distributional issues with efficiency.

[31] Ogus, *supra* n.3, pp. 153, 160.

[32] *Ibid.*, p. 246.

[33] For the sake of simplicity, I am assuming here that their entitlement is an "absolute" one—i.e. a right to be completely free from pollution. In reality, a court may also grant an "intermediate" entitlement—i.e. a right to be free of pollution above a given level. This intermediate entitlement could similarly be protected by way of a property rule (injunction) or a liability rule (damages). On this, see further A. M. Polinsky, *An Introduction to Law and Economics*, (2nd edn. Boston, Mass., Little Brown & Co, 1989), p. 19.

action. First, a court could impose a "property rule"—granting local residents an injunction to protect their entitlement to be free from pollution. This will be efficient only if the total benefits to the local community of being free from pollution are greater than the cost to the firm of not polluting. On the other hand, a court may proceed by way of a "liability rule" rather than a property rule.[34] In other words, rather than protecting the local residents' entitlement by way of an injunction, the court may require the firm to pay damages. For the law to achieve efficiency, these damages would have to be awarded at a level which reflected the social cost of the pollution to the local population. The important point to note is that, with all of the above mechanisms, to achieve an efficient solution, the relevant costs and benefits would have to be determined via CBA.[35] Though CBA will be criticised in Chapter 5, that does not mean that the language of external cost does not have a beneficial rhetorical role to play: it remains useful to conceive of a polluter imposing unpaid costs on society even if one remains doubtful whether such costs can adequately be measured through CBA.

How then does the above approach compare with that taken by environmental ethics? The answer is that—not surprisingly given the earlier observation about the utilitarian roots of welfare economics—it most closely resembles the anthropocentric utilitarian version. Except here, generality is avoided and specific levels of environmental quality are indicated as a guide to policy makers—those levels being efficient ones where benefits exceed costs as determined by CBA, thus improving human welfare.

Welfare economics and sustainability

The above account of welfare economics considers only the present. What of sustainable development and the future? David Pearce and his colleagues are perhaps the best-known advocates of what has become known as the "weak" version of sustainability.[36] Under this version, humans have a moral duty to *sustain the overall capital stock* for future generations, with man-made capital[37] acting as a possible substitute for depleted natural capital.[38] However, as Beckerman has noted, it is not clear how this version of sustainability is any different from the ordinary moral imperative of welfare economics which, as we

[34] The terms "property rules" and "liability rules" derive from G. Calabresi and A. Melamed, "Property Rules, Liability Rules, and Inalienability: One View of the Cathedral" (1972) 85 *Harv LR* 1089.

[35] Damages to natural resources under the US Oil Pollution Act 1990 (introduced in the wake of the *Exxon Valdez* Alaskan oil spill) are calculated on the basis of CBA.

[36] See e.g. D. Pearce (ed.), *Blueprint 3: Measuring Sustainable Development* (London, Earthscan, 1993).

[37] Roads, machinery, knowledge etc.

[38] In the context of pollution, natural capital is clean air, water etc.

have seen, is welfare maximisation.[39] What weak sustainability advocates are essentially arguing is that the welfare of future generations can be maximised by giving them more man-made capital (such as factories), to make up for low levels of natural capital (for example, high levels of pollution). In other words, weak sustainability is really about *sustaining human welfare* at the highest level over time, but since this is what welfare economics are all about anyway, then sustainability as a separate objective of regulatory policy is redundant. However, as Jacobs has noted,[40] this redundancy argument crucially depends on acceptance of one the key premises of the weak sustainability thesis—the substitutability of natural and man-made capital.

If natural and man-made capital are substitutes, then welfare economics do indeed maximise the welfare of future generations. Costs and benefits within CBA are subjected to "discounting", so that costs and benefits accruing in the future are reduced by a given percentage. At first sight, one might think that this is the very opposite of maximising the interests of future generations, and that the only way to ensure this would be to abandon the discount rate altogether. However, according to Beckerman, this is not so. Take the example of a dam which will produce benefits of £1 million in 100 years' time. With a discount rate of 10 per cent, that £1 million becomes just £73 today.[41] There are two key justifications for discounting in this way. The first is an alternative investment argument: working forwards, if I invest my £1 million today with interest at 10 per cent, in 100 years' time, I will have the £1 million and much more besides;[42] thus, working backwards, that £1 million should be discounted at the same rate. While future generations will appreciate the dam's £1 million benefits, they would presumably appreciate a much larger sum even more. The welfare of future generations is not being discounted here; indeed, by discounting the future benefits, one ensures that the welfare of future generations is maximised because they will only inherit projects that yield higher overall returns than alternative investment.[43] The second argument in favour of discounting is one based on the diminishing marginal utility of consumption. An extra pound for a poor person may increase his welfare considerably, but an extra pound given to a rich person will make little difference to his welfare. Assuming that future generations are generally better off than us, the argument is therefore that discounting does not detract from their welfare because pounds in the future will be worth less in welfare terms to them than they are to us in the present.

[39] W. Beckerman, " 'Sustainable Development': Is It a Useful Concept?" (1994) 3 *Environmental Values* 191, p. 195.

[40] M. Jacobs, "Sustainable Development, Capital Substitution and Economic Humility: A Response to Beckerman" (1995) 4 *Environmental Values* 57, p. 59.

[41] The figures are taken from an example provided by M. Jacobs, *The Green Economy: Environment, Sustainable Development and the Politics of the Future* (London, Pluto Press, 1991), p. 69.

[42] And as Beckerman adds (*supra* n.39, p. 198), even without the interest, due to productivity increases (and allowing for inflation), my £1 million will go much further.

[43] *Ibid.*, p. 199.

However, natural and man made capital are not substitutes[44]—extra factories cannot replace clean rivers. This means that welfare economics, which rely on CBA and discounting, do indeed discount the welfare of future generations. As Jacobs points out, if substitutability does not apply, returns on environmental investments simply cannot be equated with those on financial investments.[45] It may be appropriate to discount the future *economic* benefits of man-made capital such as a dam, because these can be compared with the *economic* benefits which alternative financial investment would have produced. However, it simply does not make sense to discount the future benefits of, say, pollution control in the same way. Alternative financial investment would have produced *economic* benefits, but these are not the same as *environmental* benefits. To discount these environmental benefits is to discount the welfare of future generations. The diminishing marginal utility thesis is similarly flawed because, while future generations may be better off economically and may thus not be too bothered about receiving additional economic benefits, the same is not true of environmental benefits. Indeed, at current rates of environmental exploitation, they are likely to be poorer in environmental terms and may thus receive more welfare than us from additional environmental benefits.[46]

Private interest theories

While normative theories tell us why we ought to regulate to prevent pollution, descriptive or positive theories tell us why we do regulate. The normative theories above are based on the idea that regulation should be based on morality or on an economic vision of the public interest (efficiency). In contrast, a common thread linking many descriptive theories is private interest: the argument is that, in practice, regulation will not necessarily be in accordance with morality or the public interest; instead, it is the result of competing private interests.[47] This, in essence, is the view of both political science theories such as pluralism, and economic theories such as public choice.

Pluralism sees regulation as the result of a competition by interest groups for the triumph of their private interest.[48] Public choice[49] is essentially economics applied to politics: in the political economy, interests demand regulation and

[44] See further H. Daly, "On Wilfred Beckerman's Critique of Sustainable Development" (1995) 4 *Environmental Values* 49, p. 51.

[45] Jacobs, *supra* n.40, p. 59.

[46] Jacobs, *supra* n.41, p. 200.

[47] Ogus, *supra* n.3, p. 75.

[48] R. Baldwin and M. Cave, *Understanding Regulation: Theory, Strategy, and Practice* (Oxford, OUP, 1999), p. 21.

[49] See further Ogus, *supra* n.3, pp. 55–75; P. Göran Hägg, "Theories on the Economics of Regulation: A Survey of the Literature from a European Perspective" (1997) 4 *European Journal of Law and Economics* 337; B. Yandle, "Public Choice at the Intersection of Environmental Law and Economics" (1999) 8 *European Journal of Law and Economics* 5; P. McAuslan, "Public Law and Public Choice" (1988) 51 *MLR* 681.

politicians supply it.[50] Early public choice theories asserted the dominance of producer interests.[51] The view was that the logic of collective action meant that only concentrated interests such as producers would organise themselves to lobby for regulation. Diffuse interests such as consumers and the environment would fail to produce collective action because free rider problems would be too great.[52] While it may seem counter-intuitive for producer interests to be seeking costly regulation, such lobbying can be explained on "rent-seeking" grounds. The regulatory costs imposed on the industry may be outweighed by the increased "rents" or benefits they will achieve by decreasing competition in the market, squeezing out small firms unable to meet the new standards. As payment for supplying this regulation, producer interests supposedly provide votes, campaign finance and related benefits.[53] In the UK, the duty of care in relation to waste might be analysed in such terms: powerful sections of the waste industry were in favour of this regulation because it would rid them of competition from "cowboy" operators who could undercut their prices by cutting corners on environmental safety. As for return payment, this would require investigation of whether, for example, any political contributions were made by the industry.

One of the problems with these early public choice theories was that, in asserting the primacy of producer interests, they downplayed the influence of ordinary voters in elections and failed to account for the growing strength of consumer and environmental interest groups.[54] Later theories addressed this problem by recasting the process as one involving competition between *all* of these interests.[55] Without this shift in position, it would be hard to explain how certain items of environmental legislation have come into being at all. In the case of the duty of care example above, producers, voters and environmental interest groups would all have been supportive—no doubt increasing the attractiveness of the measure for politicians.[56] However, this will not always be so. Not all regulation is of competitive benefit to, and hence supported by, powerful producers. Indeed some regulatory measures—like recent UK vehicle fuel duties and the proposed UK energy tax—are quite the reverse. Since industry has lobbied hard against such measures, it would be difficult to explain their appearance without bringing the voting public and environmental interest groups into the equation.[57]

[50] Göran Hägg, *supra* n.49, p. 352.

[51] *Ibid.*, pp. 343, 347, citing as examples M. Olson, *The Logic of Collective Action: Public Goods and the Theory of Groups* (Cambridge, Mass., Harvard UP, 1965); and G. Stigler, "The Theory of Economic Regulation" (1971) 2 *Bell J of Econ* 3.

[52] Göran Hägg, *supra* n.49.

[53] *Ibid.*, p. 343.

[54] *Ibid.*, p. 344.

[55] *Ibid.*, pp. 344–6, citing S. Peltzman, "Towards a More General Theory of Regulation" (1976) 19 *J Law & Econ* 211; and G. Becker, "A Theory of Competition Among Pressure Groups for Political Influence" (1983) 98 *Quarterly J of Econ.* 371.

[56] In Yandle's terms (*supra*, n.49), a coalition of "bootleggers" and "baptists" is a winning one.

[57] The proposed energy tax, though opposed by much of industry, is supported by many environmental interest groups and probably by much of the public (since it will face the extra costs only

Besides being sceptical about the reasons for introducing primary legislation, public choice theorists would also stress the danger of being over-optimistic about the implementation of this legislation. One reason is that regulatory agencies may be "captured" by the industry or firms that they are regulating. The public choice version of capture theory sees regulators as wealth maximisers, who may thus be bribed by a firm, or who may have an economic eye on future employment in the industry and thus be tempted to dilute public interest goals.

The assumption shared by public choice theories in general—that regulators are rational wealth maximisers—is one of its main weaknesses.[58] Many critics have pointed out that regulators are often motivated by factors other than self-interest, such as ideology.[59] Others have observed that institutional constraints and social processes are just as important as, if not more important than, wealth maximisation in explaining behaviour.[60] That is not to say, however, that critics in the latter camp would disagree with the idea that regulatory capture takes place, with the consequent derailing of the public interest in favour of the private interest of the firm. On the one hand, they might view such capture as the inevitable result of social processes.[61] An individual moving from industry to work for a regulator, for example, is likely to maintain a degree of social affinity with his ex-colleagues. On the other hand, critics may regard capture as the inevitable result of the institutional structure of regulation.[62] In many cases, for example, there is likely to be an imbalance or "asymmetry" of expertise or information as between the firm and the regulator, whereby the regulator effectively bows to the firm's judgement.[63] In the UK, there are information asymmetries at both the delegated legislation and at the agency rule-making and application stages. With delegated legislation on special waste or the landfill tax for example, the DoE, the Environment Agency and Customs and Excise were clearly reliant on information from the waste industry to ensure that the system being introduced was workable. While environmental interest groups and the voting public may be important at the framework legislation stage, their interests arguably count for less than those of producers when it comes down to detail because the regulator does not "need" them to the same extent.

WHO REGULATES?

Although legislatures are typically responsible for setting the broad framework of a regulatory system, they seldom if ever take on responsibility for the

indirectly). Increased vehicle excise duties on the other hand are supported by environmental groups but opposed by much of industry and the public, since both face the costs directly.

[58] Ogus, *supra* n.3, p. 73; Baldwin and Cave, *supra* n.48, pp. 24–7.

[59] *Ibid.*

[60] Baldwin and Cave, *supra* n.48, p. 27.

[61] *Ibid.*, p. 29.

[62] *Ibid.*, p. 27.

[63] Göran Hägg, *supra* n.49, p. 352.

detailed, day-to-day operation of that system.[64] Among other reasons, they lack the time and the expertise. While government departments have more time and a degree of expertise (although the UK civil service has historically been based on the principle of "generalism", which means that individuals may build up expertise only to move on), there is always the danger of political interference.[65] Delegation to an agency, on the other hand, provides not only time and specialist expertise, but also a degree of independence from government. This lends the area policy credibility and continuity: both the public and the regulated know that, come an economic downturn, the government will not easily be able to relax pollution controls in favour of, say, employment.[66] However, delegation creates a Catch 22 situation: too great a reliance on independent experts creates problems of accountability; but too much accountability undermines the key reasons for delegating to an agency in the first place.

Of course, the above presupposes that pollution control should be under the supervision of a public regulator. However, there are those who, in answer to the question "Who should regulate?" would answer "Firms". Nevertheless, few would advocate self-regulation as a complete *replacement* for regulation in the context of pollution control: in a competitive environment, firms will simply not adopt expensive control measures voluntarily; regulation is needed to ensure a more level playing field.[67] Instead, most see self-regulation as a valuable *supplement* to public regulatory programmes.

[64] Baldwin and Cave, *supra* n.48, pp. 66–7.

[65] *Ibid.*, pp. 68–9.

[66] G. Majone, "Theories of Regulation" in G. Majone (ed.), *Regulating Europe* (London, Routledge, 1996), p. 28 at 41–2. As Majone observes (*ibid.*, p. 40), the issue of policy credibility just as much explains delegation by national politicians to the independent Community regulator as it does delegation by them to independent national agencies.

[67] This issue is explored in greater detail in Ch. 6.

2

Privatisation, Liberalisation and Deregulation

All too often in the past, the environmental consequences of privatisation, liberalisation and deregulation have been ignored by the relevant policy-makers, who have focused instead on the effects on consumers and industry.[1] Nevertheless—given the recent emphasis on integrating environmental considerations into other policy areas[2]—there are signs that this is beginning to change.[3] Before discussing the impact that these policies have had on pollution, it is necessary to define the terms being used. Privatisation involves the transfer of ownership of a particular industry from the state to the private sector, and is the reverse of nationalisation.[4] The term deregulation is generally reserved below for social rather than economic deregulation. In other words, it is being used to refer to the lifting of the burdens of social regulation from industry—not the lifting of economic regulations (such as quotas) restricting entry to the market. The latter will, instead, generally be referred to as liberalisation. Liberalisation is thus being used here in a narrow sense to refer to the process of opening up of a particular market to competition from a previous position of monopoly.[5] It should however be noted that the term is sometimes used in a more general sense to describe the freeing up of state control in favour of the market; used in this broad sense, liberalisation encompasses both privatisation

[1] See e.g. *Privatising Electricity: The Government's Proposal for the Privatisation of the Electricity Supply Industry in England and Wales* (Cm 322, London, HMSO, 1988). *Cf.* water privatisation, where environmental factors were (eventually) considered at some length: *Privatisation of the Water Authorities in England and Wales* (Cmnd. 9734, London, HMSO, 1986).

[2] See the UK Government's Greening Government Initiative (HC Environmental Audit Committee, *The Greening Government Initiative*, Second Report, 1997/98, HC 517; *The Greening Government Initiative 1999*, Sixth Report, 1998/99, HC 426; http://www.environment.detr.gov.uk/greening/index.htm) and Art. 6 EC.

[3] See e.g. the *Commission Communication on the Single Market and the Environment*, COM(99)263, which considers the environmental implications of, in particular, energy and transport liberalisation.

[4] What Bennett terms "divestment" privatisation. Other types would encompass activities such as the private finance initiative (PFI) and contracting out—see further A. Bennett, "The Measurement of Privatization and Related Issues" in A. Bennett (ed.), *How Does Privatization Work? Essays on Privatization in Honour of Professor V.V. Ramanadham* (London, Routledge, 1997), p. 3 at 4.

[5] It should however be noted that the distinction between social deregulation and liberalisation is far from watertight. Insofar as economic regulations have social aims, deregulation will produce social consequences (*i.e.* liberalisation may amount to social deregulation). And explicitly social regulation may act as a trade barrier, in which case deregulation will have the effect of opening up the market to competition from foreign goods (*i.e.* social deregulation may amount to liberalisation).

and economic and social deregulation. In addition, it is worth observing that while privatisation, liberalisation and deregulation often go together, they can operate separately. It is for example possible to have a state-owned industry (such as an airline) that is subjected to competition in a liberalised market.[6]

Liberalisation in a broad sense forms an important part of EU policy,[7] and is now widely practised in individual Member States by governments across the political spectrum. However, its European origins arguably lie in the UK, where it formed a key plank of the Thatcher Government's neo-liberal or New Right policy during the 1980s. The driving forces behind the policy were part ideological and part economic. Liberalisation's ideological roots lay in the New Right's general hostility to state intervention because of the threat it was seen as posing to personal freedom.[8] In contrast, the market was favoured because of the perceived benefits it offered in terms of freedom and choice. In economic terms, it was thought that liberalised and deregulated markets would promote competition, and thus efficiency. And privatisation was seen as a way of improving the efficiency of state-owned organisations, and also as a means of reducing state borrowing.[9] The latter was particularly important in the context of privatisation of the water industry in England and Wales, where very expensive environmental improvements were needed in order to fulfil the UK's obligations under various EC water directives. Without privatisation, the government would have been forced to pay for these improvements by a combination of sizeable public borrowing and increasing water bills[10]—both politically unacceptable. Under privatisation, the improvements would be funded via private borrowing and increases in customer bills—the latter being politically palatable because the increases would be associated with private companies rather than directly with ministers.[11]

PRIVATISATION

What are the implications of state as against private ownership for pollution control? Collier states, quite rightly, that in the absence of regulation privately owned companies are likely to externalise environmental costs on society.[12] Indeed, this is true whether such companies are monopolies or if they are

[6] Although this is often a precursor to privatisation.

[7] With the exception of privatisation, on which it is supposedly policy-neutral.

[8] F. A. Hayek, *The Road to Serfdom* (London, Routledge, 1979).

[9] See M. Bishop, J. Kay and C. Mayer, "Introduction: Privatization in Performance" in M. Bishop, J. Kay and C. Mayer (eds.), *Privatization and Economic Performance* (Oxford, OUP, 1994), p. 1 at 3–6.

[10] D. Kinnersley, *Coming Clean: The Politics of Water and the Environment* (London, Penguin, 1994), pp. 60–1.

[11] *Ibid.*

[12] U. Collier, "Liberalisation in the Energy Sector: Environmental Threat or Opportunity?" in U. Collier (ed.), *Deregulation in the European Union: Environmental Perspectives* (London, Routledge, 1998), p. 93 at 98.

operating in a liberalised, competitive market. The latter will force them to externalise, because their competitors will be doing likewise. And profit maximisation will also provide an incentive to externalise in the monopoly situation: why be environmentally virtuous if it will cost you profits? What then of state ownership? Although predominantly a means of *economic* regulation as a response to monopoly market failure,[13] it has in the past also been used incidentally as a means of *social* policy or regulation, for example in relation to employment creation[14] and consumer protection.[15] There is thus no reason why the same could not be true of the environment. As Collier points out, state owned companies could, in theory, "be used as a vehicle for realising policy objectives, including the internalisation of environmental costs".[16] However, in practice, as she notes, most state companies have been controlled by industry or economic ministries, which have typically prioritised economic factors and ignored environmental ones.[17] She cites the Central Electricity Generating Board (CEGB) as a good example of a UK state company which—particularly in relation to its foot-dragging over acid rain—was hardly a model of environmental performance.[18] Given this reality, privatisation can hardly be considered to be harmful to the environment. Indeed, given that inefficiencies in production processes are closely associated with poor environmental performance and that state industries have a history of such inefficiencies, it could be argued that privatisation is likely to result in an improvement in pollution.

While the above is concerned with the *inherent* effect of ownership on pollution, certain UK privatisations have also had more *incidental* effects on pollution.[19] The privatisation of the water industry in England and Wales had two beneficial environmental effects. First, it led, in time, to the overcoming of the pre-existing poacher/gamekeeper problem that lay behind a significant amount of water pollution: prior to privatisation, the water authorities were pollution regulators who also operated sewage works, which were among the worst water polluters. This, it has been argued, led them to take a soft line in the setting[20] and policing not only of their own consents, but also those of others, since they

[13] G. Majone, "Regulation and its Modes" in G. Majone (ed.), *Regulating Europe* (London, Routledge, 1996) p. 9 at 9–11.

[14] U. Collier, "The Environmental Dimensions of Deregulation: An Introduction" in Collier, *supra* n.11, p. 3 at 7.

[15] See Majone, *supra* n.13, p. 13.

[16] Collier, *supra* n.12, p. 98. This again presumably applies whether the state company is a monopoly, or whether it operates in a liberalised, competitive market. Even in the latter case, government subsidy could in theory shield it from any negative competitive effects arising from voluntary cost internalisation.

[17] *Ibid.*, and see also Collier, *supra* n.14, p. 7.

[18] *Ibid.* See further S. Boehmer-Christiansen and J. Skea, *Acid Politics: Environmental and Energy Policies in Britain and Germany* (London, Belhaven, 1991).

[19] For details of the legal duties in relation to the environment associated with the various privatisations, see J. F. McEldowney and S. McEldowney, *Environment and the Law: An Introduction for Environmental Scientists and Lawyers* (Harlow, Longman, 1996), pp. 69–77.

[20] Although some control was in theory provided by their consent applications being decided by the Secretary of State.

could hardly come down hard on others when their own house was in such disarray. With the privatisation of the water industry by the Water Act 1989, this problem was solved, as the regulatory function was given to a public agency—the National Rivers Authority (NRA)[21]—and the operational functions to the new private water and sewerage companies. Secondly, as Cowan states, water privatisation also benefited the environment, in that the capital investment necessary to deliver the many EC-inspired quality improvements was undertaken more quickly than it would have been if the industry had remained in public ownership.[22]

LIBERALISATION

Energy

Single market-based Community policy liberalising the energy market is a relatively recent phenomenon.[23] In the UK, the Gas Act 1986 privatised British Gas and the Electricity Act 1989 privatised a major part of the UK electricity industry.[24] However, the process of liberalisation in the gas and electricity industries has been an ongoing affair, and it is this process, rather than privatisation, that has arguably produced the most significant environmental effects. On the positive side, liberalisation of the electricity *generation* industry following privatisation opened up the market to cleaner fuels. In particular, it heralded a "dash for gas", with electricity generators switching from expensive coal-fired stations to new and cheaper gas-fired plant.[25] This led to considerable reductions in carbon dioxide and sulphur dioxide emissions, with associated benefits in terms of global warming and acid rain. Liberalisation of the electricity generation industry also provided opportunities for renewables to enter the market.[26] However, the cost of renewables compared with cheaper generation options such as gas meant that they would not have been viable without government support. This was provided in the form of the Non-Fossil Fuel Obligation (NFFO) under the 1989 Act, which obliged suppliers to contract for the generation of a certain amount of non-fossil fuel electricity, with a levy raised on consumers to meet the

[21] Water pollution in England and Wales is now the responsibility of the Environment Agency.

[22] S. Cowan, "Market and Regulatory Failure in the Water Sector" in Collier, *supra* n.12, p. 131 at 140.

[23] See the Internal Market for Electricity Dir. 96/92 [1997] OJ L27/20, and the Internal Market for Gas Dir. 98/30 [1998] OJ L204/1.

[24] The exception being nuclear power, which was not privatised until 1996—and then only the modern plants.

[25] Collier, *supra* n.12, p. 101; see further U. Collier, *Electricity Privatisation and Environmental Policy in the UK: Some Lessons for the Rest of Europe*, EUI Working Paper RSC No. 95/2 (Florence, EUI, 1995), and M. Parker, *The UK "Coal Crisis": Origins and Resolution* (London, Royal Institute of International Affairs, 1993).

[26] See the Commission's White Paper on Renewables, COM(97)599 final, p. 6.

extra costs involved.[27] More recent moves in the late 1990s involving liberalisation of electricity *supply* may also aid renewables by enabling consumers to pay a premium "green tariff" and choose "green electricity" from a renewable supplier.[28]

In contrast, liberalisation has not been kind to nuclear power. Like coal, high-cost nuclear power could not compete in a liberalised market. The reduction and eventual withdrawal of the NFFO subsidy for nuclear power after the industry's privatisation in 1996 was simply the final nail in the coffin. Whether this decline brought about by liberalisation is positive or negative in environmental terms is difficult to judge. In terms of global warming and acid rain, the decline is negative; however, in terms of reducing the risk of environmental accidents and long-term waste problems, it is undoubtedly positive.[29]

Besides affecting fuel choices, liberalisation also has an impact on energy efficiency. On the positive side, it has been argued that competitive pressure brought about by the liberalisation of energy markets may improve the efficiency of energy *production*.[30] On the negative side, competition in the gas and electricity industries forces prices down, which does not help the cause of energy efficiency on the customer side of the meter.[31] However, until recently, the government was arguing that supply liberalisation would make "demand side management" measures on that side of the meter more likely.[32] The claim was—that as rational consumers saw the benefits of energy efficiency—so energy supply companies would become energy *service* companies, competing to provide consumers with both energy supply and energy efficiency measures.[33] In practice, this has not so far happened and competition exists only in relation to the price of energy supply. The demand-side management that has taken place has been thanks to regulation. With both gas and electricity, the economic regulator[34] is under a (secondary) statutory duty to promote energy efficiency.[35] In the case of electricity, this duty has been fulfilled by the exercise of a statutory power to set energy efficiency standards of performance (EESOPs) for certain

[27] Ss. 32–33 of the Electricity Act 1989. UK Renewables policy is currently undergoing reform—see further DTI, *New and Renewable Energy: Prospects for the 21st Century* (London, DTI, 1999).

[28] *Ibid.*, p. 5. See further R. Fouquet, "The United Kingdom Demand for Renewable Electricity in a Liberalised Market" (1998) 26 *Energy Policy* 281. However, industrial consumers may not wish to threaten their competitiveness by paying premium prices, and experience with green consumerism in relation to conventional products suggests that neither will many domestic consumers want to pay a premium.

[29] Collier, *supra* n.12, p. 104.

[30] See the Commission Communication on Energy Efficiency COM(98)246 final, p. 4.

[31] Though *cf.* N. Eyre, "A Golden Age or a False Dawn? Energy Efficiency in UK Competitive Energy Markets" (1998) 26 *Energy Policy* 963, p. 964, who argues that while consumers will only invest in energy efficiency if prices are increased significantly due to relative price inelasticity, lowering them will not decrease energy *efficiency*, though it may increase *demand*.

[32] *Ibid.*, p. 966; G. Owen, "Who Controls Energy Efficiency Policy? A Case Study of The Energy Saving Trust" (1997) 25 *Energy Policy* 959, pp. 959, 963.

[33] Eyre, *supra* n.31, p. 966.

[34] The Directors General for electricity and gas supply and their offices (Ofgas and Offer) merged in 1999 (the office becoming Ofgem).

[35] The principal primary one being to promote (or in the case of Gas to secure) competition.

electricity suppliers, allowing them to raise £1 *per* customer *per annum* for spending on approved energy efficiency schemes.[36]

Transport

Liberalisation in the air transport sector has also lowered prices.[37] Again, this is good for consumers in economic terms, but bad for the environment, because of the pollution associated with ever increasing air traffic.[38] Although other environmentally critical sectors of the UK transport industry have seen liberalisation, it is not as easy to draw direct links between these and pollution. Road haulage, for example, was liberalised in the UK as early as the 1960s.[39] While this might have been expected to lower prices and to increase pollution by drawing freight away from rail, prices did not drop significantly until the 1980s because other factors such as governmental price controls prevented this.[40] However, single market, Community liberalisation of road haulage[41]—a more recent phenomenon—does appear to have lowered prices in other Member States, making road transport more attractive than rail.[42] Nevertheless, one should not be too quick to lay environmental responsibility on liberalisation and consequent low prices. As Teutsch points out, the pre-existing quantity regulation of road haulage with its associated *high* prices, had itself "failed completely to meet the envisaged target of protecting the railways and to impede the growth of road transport".[43] Factors other than price, such as flexibility and changes in production and distribution techniques,[44] are arguably more important in explaining the trend towards road transport.[45]

[36] Although a similar power existed for gas, the relevant Director General was unhappy about the conflict with her duty to protect customer interests on price and thus none were set: see Ofgem, *Energy Efficiency: A Consultation Paper* (Birminghan, Ofgem, 1999), para. 2.10.

[37] On liberalisation in the UK, see K. Button (ed.), *Airline Deregulation: International Experiences* (London, David Fulton Publishers, 1991), pp. 85–6, 96–7; on liberalisation in the Community, see K. Button, K. Haynes and R. Stough, *Flying into The Future: Air Transport Policy in the European Union* (Cheltenham, Edward Elgar, 1998), pp. 30-53.

[38] See e.g. 291 ENDS Report (1999) 8.

[39] See the Transport Act 1968.

[40] M. E. Beesley, "UK Experience With Freight and Passenger Regulation" in M E Beesley (ed.), *Privatization, Regulation and Deregulation* (London, Routledge/IEA, 1992), p. 188.

[41] On which see further J. F. L. Ross, *Linking Europe: Transport Policies and Politics in the European Union* (London, Praeger, 1998), pp. 104–5.

[42] See e.g. U. von Weizacker, "Regulatory Reform and the Environment: The Cause for Environmental Taxes" in G. Majone (ed.), *Deregulation or Re-Regulation? Regulatory Reform in Europe and the United States* (London, Pinter, 1990), p. 198 at 201; M. Teutsch, "Liberalisation or Deregulation? The EU's Transport Policy and the Environment" in Collier, *supra* n.11, p. 114 at 118–9.

[43] *Ibid.*, p. 118.

[44] Including just-in-time delivery.

[45] *Ibid.*, pp. 125–6. See further C. Gerondeau, *Transport in Europe* (London, Artech House, 1997), pp. 51–6.

Direct links between liberalisation and pollution are, again, difficult to draw with the liberalisation of local bus services that took place in Great Britain in the mid-1980s.[46] From what we have seen above, one might have expected competition to produce a lowering in fares, providing an incentive for people to switch from cars to less polluting "public" transport.[47] However, liberalisation was accompanied by a decrease in subsidy, which actually led to an increase in fares.[48] Liberalisation also gave rise to route instability and reliability problems in many areas.[49] What is clear is that, after liberalisation, fewer people used the buses. What is less clear is the extent to which this decrease in passenger levels can be attributed to liberalisation. Fare increases and a lack of consumer confidence cannot have helped patronage. However, the former was arguably due to an external policy factor in the form of subsidy decreases and cannot be attributed to liberalisation *per se*. And other external factors such as the decreasing costs and relative comfort of motoring are arguably just as, if not more, important.[50]

Redressing the problems of liberalisation

Generally, what the above analysis reveals is the need for social environmental regulation to redress the environmental imbalance introduced by economic deregulation or liberalisation. In the case of airlines, energy and road haulage, liberalisation has made polluting behaviour more rather than less financially attractive by reducing prices. In the case of local buses, prices have not decreased despite liberalisation, and yet the price of the polluting alternative (the car) has decreased. What is needed in all of these cases to boost prices is not a return to the inefficiencies of quantity regulation, but rather taxes to ensure that the environmental costs of the polluting activity are internalised.[51] In the EC, problems with reaching agreement on taxation measures have hampered any significant moves in this direction. In the UK, some efforts have been made. With energy, for example, VAT was introduced for domestic fuel,[52] and there are current proposals to introduce an energy tax on industry.[53] With UK road haulage, the fuel duty escalator of recent years and increases in vehicle excise duty have

[46] See the Transport Act 1985.

[47] Though other factors, such as the relative comfort and privacy of cars, and bus service provision, frequency and reliability, are also important.

[48] P. Mackie and J. Preston, *The Local Bus Market: A Case Study of Regulatory Change* (Aldershot, Avebury, 1996), pp. 197–200.

[49] *Ibid.*

[50] *Ibid.*, pp. 199–200.

[51] See the references at n.42 *supra*.

[52] The Government announced the introduction of an 8% rate in the March 1993 Budget, which was due to rise to 17.5% in a second stage. However, the latter proposal was dropped after concerns were raised over "fuel poverty", and the incoming Labour Government subsequently reduced the rate from 8% to its current 5%.

[53] See Ch. 6.

similarly made some attempt to redress the balance.[54] However, just as we have seen that price decreases do not tell the whole story in terms of trends to more polluting transport methods, so one should not jump to the conclusion that price increases through taxation will reverse such trends. Though taxation is undoubtedly necessary, it is not sufficient.[55] Getting people out of their cars and onto public transport, and getting freight off the road and onto rail or inland waterways is not likely to take place through price signals alone. Additional steps, tackling the other factors that led to the switch to road transport, will also be needed.[56]

DEREGULATION

There are two elements to EC social deregulation. First, the single market rules on the free movement of goods have in many cases required the deregulation of *Member State* social regulations forming a barrier to entry of foreign, Community goods. And, secondly, the doctrine of subsidiarity has led to partial deregulation of *Community* social regulation.

The single market

Under the landmark *Cassis de Dijon* case,[57] the Court of Justice ruled that indirectly discriminatory national regulations were caught by Article 30 (now Article 28) EC,[58] and that they could remain in place only if they were justified under the "mandatory requirements" doctrine. Otherwise, the principle of "mutual recognition" would apply, whereby if a product were lawfully marketed in one Member State, it would have to be allowed access to the market of any other Member State. Regulations in the Member State of origin are, in other words, assumed to be equivalent to those in the destination state,[59] unless the destination state can make a case otherwise to justify its access-impeding rules under mandatory requirements.

[54] See e.g. 290 ENDS Report (1999) 3; 291 ENDS Report (1999) 37.

[55] Teutsch, *supra* n.42, p. 126.

[56] *Ibid.* E.g. service provision, reliability and comfort in the case of buses, and flexibility in the case of alternatives to road haulage such as railways and inland waterways.

[57] Case 120/78 *Rewe-Zentrale AG* v. *Bundesmonopolverwaltung für Branntwein* [1979] ECR 649, [1979] 3 CMLR 494.

[58] Prior to *Cassis*, it was assumed that only directly discriminatory measures fell within Art. 30 EC. Direct discrimination involves the law discriminating directly on its face between home products and Community imports. Indirect discrimination occurs where a measure is indistinctly applicable on its face as between home products and imports, but which is nevertheless discriminatory in effect against imports. Many social regulations (such as the German consumer protection measure in *Cassis* itself) are indirectly discriminatory and thus caught by Art. 28.

[59] Hence the idea of mutual recognition.

While *Cassis* has led to deregulation of a significant amount of national social regulation regarded as unjustified by the Court, environmental regulation has escaped relatively lightly. First, environmental process standards are currently immune from challenge under the free movement provisions. This is because, as Chalmers and Szyszczak note, whilst *Cassis* placed restraints "on Member States' freedom to regulate imports, it left them free to regulate the conditions of production of domestic products".[60] Process standards do not threaten imports—they threaten only exports and domestically produced goods on the home market. With exports, since such process standards will typically be non-discriminatory as between goods destined for the home market and those destined for export, they will not be caught by Article 29 EC.[61] And although process standards will discriminate against domestic goods on the home market—placing them at a potential competitive disadvantage as against imports not subject to such controls—reverse discrimination of this kind does not fall within Article 28.[62]

Secondly, product-based[63] standards or controls have often been seen as justified by the Court. In the *Walloon Waste* case,[64] a ban on the import of waste for disposal was regarded as justified under the doctrine of mandatory requirements and allowed to stand. And in the *Danish Bottles* case,[65] Danish regulations on the recovery of bottles were left largely intact. More recently, in *Aher-Waggon*,[66] the Court ruled that, although they impeded trade, strict German standards on aircraft noise emissions were justified on grounds of public health and environmental protection. And in the *Danish Bees* case,[67] the Court regarded a restriction on bee imports as justified under Article 36 (now Article 30).

Only the recent *Dusseldorp*[68] ruling has seen the wholesale deregulation of a national environmental provision. In that case, the Court ruled, *inter alia*, that Dutch restrictions on the export of waste oil filters for recovery were not justified on environmental or human health grounds. The Dutch processor which burned these oil filters as fuel could always resort to an alternative fuel with a similar environmental impact (albeit that this would be more costly). And there was no evidence that transport to, or emissions from, the German

[60] D. Chalmers and E. Szyszczak, *European Union Law, Volume II: Towards a European Polity* (Aldershot, Dartmouth, 1998), p. 287.

[61] Case 15/79 *Groenveld* v. *Produktschap voor Vee en Vlees* [1979] ECR 3409, [1981] 1 CMLR 207; and see further C. Hilson, "Discrimination in Community Free Movement Law" (1999) 24 *ELRev* 445, p. 458.

[62] Case 98/86 *Ministère Public* v. *Mathot* [1987] ECR 809, [1988] 1 CMLR 411; and see further Hilson, *supra* n.61, pp. 459–460.

[63] Including waste, which is regarded as a product within EC free movement law on goods.

[64] Case C–2/90 *Commission* v. *Belgium* [1992] ECR I-4431, [1993] 1 CMLR 365.

[65] Case 302/86 *Commission* v. *Denmark* [1988] ECR 4607, [1989] 1 CMLR 619.

[66] Case C–389/96 *Aher-Waggon GmbH* v. *Germany* [1998] ECR I–4473, [1999] 2 CMLR 589.

[67] Case C–67/97 *Ditlev Bluhme* [1999] 1 CMLR 612.

[68] Case C–203/96 *Chemische Afvalstoffen Dusseldorp BV and Others* v. *Minister van Volkshuisvesting, Ruimtelijke Ordening en Milieubeheer* [1998] ECR I–4075, [1998] 3 CMLR 873, (1999) 11 JEL 121.

processor to which Dusseldorp wished to export posed any greater threat to the environment or human health than the Dutch operation. Thus one should not assume that all national environmental regulations significantly protect the environment: *Dusseldorp* appears to be a good example of a case where deregulation in the cause of free trade will not produce any significant harm to the environment. In contrast, had the national measures in the other cases mentioned above been completely deregulated, significant harm would arguably have resulted.

Thus, with both process and product standards, the balance between free trade and the environment has often come down on the side of the environment. Nevertheless, more broadly, the law of the single market has had negative environmental effects. Trade barriers caused by Member State economic and social regulations *have* been significantly dismantled—through negative harmonisation relying on Article 28 where possible or, alternatively, through positive harmonisation. This single market liberalisation has not only produced the environmental effects in the specific sectors described in the previous section (through lowering energy and transport prices); more generally, it has also produced an increase in both economic growth and in trade-related transport movements, with harmful consequences in terms of pollution.[69]

Subsidiarity

There are arguably three separate deregulatory elements to subsidiarity. First, in so far as subsidiarity involves the allocation of power[70] between Member States and the Community, it was seen by some as a mechanism for deregulation of Community power, with control left instead to the Member States.[71] However, as Golub points out, it is *in theory* a "Janus-faced" concept which can as easily justify EC regulation as it can Community deregulation in favour of Member State control.[72] As the Amsterdam Protocol on the application of the principles of subsidiarity and proportionality puts it, "[i]t allows Community action within the limits of its powers to be expanded where circumstances so require, and conversely, to be restricted or discontinued where it is no longer justified". Nevertheless, after the introduction of the principle in the Maastricht Treaty, the Commission withdrew a number of *existing* environmental propos-

[69] Not surprisingly, the Court in *ibid.* did not tackle the general issue of whether restrictions on exports could be justified on the environmental ground that trade increases transport distances and pollution (as opposed to the specific issue of whether waste poses a transport hazard). Had it done so, it might have ended up calling the whole single market project into question.

[70] In a secondary sense—see Ch. 3, n.1. Ch. 3 explores this federal aspect of subsidiarity in much more detail.

[71] See e.g. the UK government's "hit-list", recommending Community legislation (including environmental legislation) for repeal (The *Financial Times*, 8 Dec. 1992, p. 2).

[72] J. Golub, "Sovereignty and Subsidiarity in EU Environmental Policy" (1996) 44 *Political Studies* 686, pp. 686–7.

als,[73] and there was a significant decrease in the number of *new* environmental proposals it put forward.[74] In addition, it has been argued that the key legislation that has come through has left significant discretion in the hands of Member States. For example, the Integrated Pollution Prevention and Control Directive[75] and the proposed Water Framework Directive[76] have signalled a shift from uniform Community emission standards—which gave Member States little discretion—to an approach which allows them to tailor controls to local circumstances.[77] Whatever the theory, this evidence suggests that subsidiarity has, *in practice*, had deregulatory effects—though perhaps not to the extent feared in some quarters.

Secondly, subsidiarity has given rise to deregulation in the sense of legislative simplification or consolidation.[78] Ironically, Community regulation can be viewed as deregulatory in this sense, since the complexity of numerous different *Member State* measures is reduced via Community harmonisation.[79] However, the more common context is probably the simplification and consolidation of the numerous *Community* measures. The proposed Water Framework Directive,[80] which would replace and thus see the repeal of a number of existing water directives,[81] is perhaps the best example of such a streamlining or consolidation measure.

Finally, subsidiarity has given rise to deregulation in the sense that non-regulatory instruments have been used in place of traditional command-and-control regulatory techniques. However, at present, the only real example of this is the July 1998 voluntary agreement between the European Commission

[73] See 233 ENDS Report (1993) 35.

[74] Golub, *supra* n. 72, pp. 699–700. The extent to which this latter decrease was caused by subsidiarity is debatable. (It may be that the drop-off was the result of the major work on the environment having been completed.)

[75] Dir. 96/61 [1996] OJ L257/26

[76] COM(97)49 final, COM(97)614 final, COM(98)76 final and COM(99)271 final.

[77] A. J. Jordan, "Editorial Introduction: The Construction of a Multilevel Environmental Governance System" (1999) 17 *Environment and Planning* C 1, p. 15; L. Krämer, *E.C. Treaty and Environmental Law*, (3rd edn., London, Sweet & Maxwell, 1998), pp. 8, 191–2. While this is undoubtedly deregulatory in that Member States have more power than before (to set standards according to local conditions), it is arguably not deregulatory in a *negative* sense since, in theory, both Dirs. should offer the environment more protection than with a uniform standards approach, not less. They are simply regulating at a different level. However, Krämer's concern is that, in practice, Member State discretion will be abused and that the environment will be less well protected.

[78] Indeed, in recent years, the Commission's reports on subsidiarity have been entitled "Better Lawmaking" (compare the earlier reports on subsidiarity COM(93)545 final; COM(94)533 final with the later reports on better lawmaking CSE(95)580; CSE(96)7; COM(97)626 final; COM(1998)715 final; COM(1999)562 final). See further C. M. Radaelli, "Governing European Regulation: The Challenges Ahead", RSC Policy Paper No 98/3 (Florence, EUI, 1998); A. J. Jordan, "The Politics of Multi-Level Environmental Governance: Subsidiarity and European Union Environmental Policy", *Environment and Planning A*, forthcoming.

[79] Although, if the Community measure is a dir., national implementation will re-establish an element of diversity.

[80] *Supra*, n.76.

[81] Including the Abstraction of Surface Water for Drinking Dir. 75/440 [1975] OJ L194/26, the Freshwater Fish Dir. 78/659 [1978] OJ L222/1, the Shellfish Water Dir. 79/923 [1979] OJ L281/47 and the Groundwater Dir. 80/68 [1980] OJ L20/43.

and the European Automobile Manufacturers Association (ACEA) to reduce CO_2 from new passenger cars by 25% by the year 2008.[82] While it may be tempting to point to other voluntary instruments such as the Eco-Labelling and EMAS Regulations as evidence of deregulation, these have not been used as substitutes to traditional command-and-control techniques, but rather as compliments and thus cannot be considered deregulatory as such.

Deregulation in the UK

The Deregulation and Contracting Out Act 1994 was introduced as a key plank of the previous Conservative Government's deregulation drive.[83] Sections 1–4 of this Act famously contain a power to introduce deregulation orders, enabling primary legislation to be amended by secondary legislation. This so-called "Henry VIII" power can be used to remove or reduce a burden on business, on condition that no necessary protection provided by the measure is removed. A further safeguard is provided by the close scrutiny of proposals by two parliamentary committees. Indeed, it has been claimed that deregulation orders attract greater parliamentary scrutiny than some primary legislation. In practice, however, no environmental legislation has been subject to this procedure. One reason for this is no doubt the difficulty of demonstrating that the protection offered by most environmental legislation is not necessary. Section 5 of the Act has been more important as far as the environment is concerned. This provides ministers with the power to introduce an order to improve enforcement procedures by adopting one or more of the safeguards for business set out in Schedule 1.[84] While the principles in Schedule 1 to the Act were not introduced in legislative form in this way (i.e. by order) in relation to environmental enforcement,[85] the previous Government did informally "order" the Environment Agency to incorporate them into its non-statutory enforcement code.[86]

[82] COM(1998)495 final; http://europa.eu.int/comm/dg11/co2/co2_agre.htm.

[83] For how the deregulation provisions of this Act now apply to Scotland, Wales and Northern Ireland, see Cabinet Office, *Proposals to Improve the Quality of Enforcement Services: A Consultative Document on Section 5 of the Deregulation and Contracting Out Act 1994* (London, Cabinet Office, 1999), paras. 28–31.

[84] Sched. 1 contains rules on the procedure to be followed before taking enforcement action including the following: an explanation must be provided for any remedial action that is being demanded; an explanation must be given of the reasons for enforcement action being taken; and a person must be informed of their right to make representations and of the existence of any right of appeal.

[85] Indeed, there is only one example where an order has been introduced. The Deregulation (Improvement of Enforcement Procedures) (Food Safety Act 1990) Order 1996 (SI 1996 No. 1683) requires a food safety enforcement officer to provide an explanation of reasons for intended enforcement action and to inform the person of their ability to make representations before an improvement notice is served on them.

[86] See 278 ENDS Report (1998) 39.

The present Labour Government broadly supports sections 1–4 of the 1994 Act. Although it intends to amend these sections,[87] the proposed amendments are mostly designed to broaden rather than narrow the Act's scope. One proposal, which could well be used in relation to the environment, is to extend the order-making power to allow statutory burdens to be lifted not just from the regulated, but also from the regulators such as the Environment Agency. Not surprisingly therefore, the new Government is not keen on section 5 of the 1994 Act: this section may relieve the burden on business, but it places burdens on regulators that the Government regards as "inflexible and bureaucratic".[88] Towards the end of 1999, it thus issued a proposal to replace section 5 with a discretionary power for ministers to introduce a code of good enforcement via secondary legislation.[89] This code would be along the lines of the existing, voluntary Enforcement Concordat.[90] The Government has stated that it intends to use this power only if voluntary take-up of the existing Concordat is insufficiently widespread.

As with subsidiarity, just because no environmental measures have been "axed" under the formal procedures in the 1994 Act, that does not mean that deregulation has not taken place or been influential. First, some have pointed to deregulatory pruning under "ordinary" amending legislation. Bell, for example, cites various changes made by the Environment Act 1995 to the Water Resources Act 1991, including a reduction in public involvement in the setting of discharge consents, and an extension to the minimum period within which consents cannot be varied.[91] While these lift burdens from the regulated, he also cites the Act's abolition of the requirement for tripartite sampling as an example of deregulation that lifts the burden off the regulator.[92] Secondly, the ENDS Report points out that "while the Government's deregulation initiative has had limited effect on pollution control legislation to date, the DoE has ample scope to reduce burdens on business by non-statutory means", citing relaxation of controls in Local Authority air pollution control guidance notes as an example.[93]

However, deregulation has arguably had the greatest influence *ex ante* rather than *ex post*—the idea being that it is better to adopt deregulatory procedures to prevent unnecessarily burdensome legislation from getting onto the statute books in the first place, rather than deregulating such material once it is already there. The ENDS Report cites one example of a proposal on environmental assessment that left out certain classes of project that were originally included

[87] Cabinet Office, *Proposed Amendments to the Deregulation and Contracting Out Act 1994: A Consultation Paper* (London, Cabinet Office, 1999).

[88] Cabinet Office, *supra* n.83, p. 1 and para. 14. S. Bell, *Ball & Bell on Environmental Law*. (4th edn., (London, Blackstone Press, 1997), p. 116.

[89] *Ibid.*

[90] Cabinet Office, *Enforcement Concordat*, (London, Cabinet Office, 1998).

[91] Bell, *supra* n.88, p. 117.

[92] *Ibid.*

[93] 229 ENDS Report (1994) 30; see also 233 ENDS Report (1994) 30.

because of deregulatory concerns.[94] However, there are, no doubt, numerous other examples where the plug has been pulled on environmental proposals because of concerns about regulatory burdens. Indeed, that was the whole point of the compliance cost assessment (CCA) and regulatory appraisal procedures introduced by the previous Conservative Government.[95] Although the present Labour Government has now replaced CCA with a system of regulatory impact assessment,[96] the basic idea remains much the same. And that is that legislative proposals should be checked for the costs they impose on business; and those which are excessive in this respect when compared with the benefits they bring should be dropped.

[94] 230 ENDS Report (1994) 34.

[95] See Cabinet Office, Deregulation Unit, *Checking the Cost of Regulation: A Guide to Compliance Cost Assessment* (London, Cabinet Office, 1996), and *Regulation in the Balance: A Guide to Regulatory Appraisal Incorporating Risk Assessment* (London, Cabinet Office, 1996).

[96] See Cabinet Office, Better Regulation Unit, *The Better Regulation Guide* (London, Cabinet Office, 1998); and *Modernising Government* (Cm 4310, London, TSO, 1999).

3

Choosing the Level: Regulation and Federalism

THE THEORETICAL CASE FOR FEDERAL REGULATION

In any federal or multi-level governance structure, one is faced with the difficult question of deciding which level should regulate. In recent years, arguments have raged in the USA between those who favour federal environmental regulation and those who believe that regulatory control should be devolved to the states. Similar debates have arisen in the EU in the context of subsidiarity, which involves the allocation of regulatory competence between Member States and the Community.[1] Though such arguments have been conspicuous by their absence in relation to devolution within the UK, they are in principle relevant there too.

Arguments for and against federal or Community-level action can be divided broadly into three separate camps: arguments involving economic theory, arguments from democracy and those involving rights and morality.

Physical spillovers

Within economic theory, most commentators support federal action in the case of physical pollution externalities or spillovers. Just as firms are likely to externalise pollution costs onto society, justifying regulation to internalise these costs, so states are likely to ignore transboundary pollution costs which they impose on other states. In theory of course—just as with pollution by firms—one could leave it to the market and allow states to bargain between themselves to reach a solution. However, here—as there—significant transaction costs are likely to make this an unrealistic prospect. The more effective solution is thus to adopt federal regulatory control, where all of the appropriate costs and benefits will be fully considered by a central body before adopting an efficient federal standard.

[1] Subsidiarity involves the allocation of competence in a secondary sense. There can be no question that the Community enjoys competence on the environment in a primary sense (which it shares with the Member States). However, subsidiarity concerns whether the Community should exercise that competence in relation to a particular environmental issue (such as packaging waste). If the answer is that there is no justification for Community regulation on that issue, then the Community can be said to lack secondary competence on it, that competence remaining with the Member States.

Economic spillovers or preventing a "race to the bottom"

Much more contentious is the race to the bottom rationale for federal regulation of pollution. The argument is that, if left to their own devices, states will compete for industrial location by offering lax environmental process standards. This will lead to a sub-optimal result, because states will be forced into a downward race, ending up with environmental standards lower than they would have chosen in the absence of such competition. This too can be analysed in externality terms. There is no inter-state, transboundary pollution in this context, and thus no physical externality.[2] Rather, there is an economic spillover or externality[3] in that low standard states do not take into account the external economic effects which their regulatory choices have on other states: either those other states also, sub-optimally, lower their environmental standards, or they suffer the negative effects of industrial flight on their economies. Again, high transaction costs rule out bargaining between states to solve this source of market failure, and federal regulation is thus seen as justified in order to ensure an optimal, welfare-maximising outcome.

This race to the bottom justification for federal level regulation has been called into question in recent years. It has, for example, been criticised as empirically inaccurate. The theory rests on two key assumptions. The first is that, in the absence of federal regulation, states will race to the bottom in order to attract firms or to prevent them from relocating. The second assumption is that firms will relocate to "pollution havens". The way to test these assumptions is to examine empirical data on how states and firms actually behave in the absence of federal pollution regulation. However, such an examination is far from straightforward. As will be seen below, most firms do not relocate on a *single* regulatory issue such as pollution—they are likely to weigh up *all* of the regulations that affect them, together with the other costs of doing business in one state as opposed to another. Even if it *is* possible to separate out pollution regulation from all of these other factors, there is a remaining problem in seeking empirical data on how states and firms behave *in the absence of federal pollution regulation.* And that is that, in the EU, most pollution regulation *is* Community-based. Race to the bottom theorists are essentially arguing that if you remove this, there will be a welfare-reducing race, if not exactly to the bottom, then certainly towards it.[4] There are three places one might look to seek empirical support for this hypothesis. The first is to go back to before the Community regulated to see how states and firms behaved. However, that is likely to be of limited use: pollution was not as significant an issue in the past, and standards and control costs were generally lower relative to those of today,

[2] D. C. Esty, "Revitalizing Environmental Federalism" (1996) 95 *Mich. L Rev.* 570, p. 593.

[3] R. B. Stewart, "Pyramids of Sacrifice? Problems of Federalism in Mandating State Implementation of National Environmental Policy" (1977) 86 *Yale LJ* 1196, p. 1215.

[4] D. C. Esty and D. Geradin, "Market Access, Competitiveness, and Harmonization: Environmental Protection in Regional Trade Agreements" (1997) 21 *Harv. Envtl. L. Rev.* 265, p. 272.

providing little incentive for firms to relocate and little incentive for governments to lower standards. The second is to look at the situation where states are allowed to set stricter environmental standards than in Community harmonisation measures. However, this would only provide evidence of whether *firms* relocate in response to strict environmental standards—it could not confirm whether *states* race to the bottom, since the harmonising measure acts as a floor, preventing them from doing so. In any event, in practice few states seem to have made use of their ability to adopt higher standards, which means that even firm relocation data are likely to be sparse. The final place to look for empirical support is in the few environmental areas currently untouched by Community harmonisation.[5] One such area is environmental taxation. Recent UK experience with high fuel and vehicle excise duties appears to indicate that neither of the race to the bottom theory's two key assumptions is applicable in practice: the UK government did not back down and lower fuel taxes or the high licence fees for lorries; and neither do many, if any, road haulage companies appear to have relocated or "flagged out" to other Member States.[6]

However, it is dangerous to read too much into one example. Just because Member State governments do not currently appear to race to the bottom in the few environmental areas remaining within their control[7] does not mean that they would not be tempted to do so if all environmental Community process legislation were cleared away. But would industry relocate if such a regulatory clearout took place and some states lowered their environmental standards? Firms are only likely to relocate only if the financial benefit of lower environmental standards outweighs the various costs of relocation. Esty and Geradin suggest that the *benefits* of relocation are unlikely to be as great in the EU as the USA because environmental standards are generally lower in the EU. This means that environmental costs will form a lower percentage of overall production costs, leading to less of an incentive to relocate.[8] They also suggest that the *costs* of relocating are likely to be greater. These costs may take various forms. They may consist of other regulatory or fiscal costs. For example, one of the main reasons UK haulage firms did not relocate was probably that, while vehicle and fuel taxes were lower in other Member States, other taxes were higher, leading to no net advantage in relocating.[9] Other costs might include expensive redundancy payments following plant shutdowns, the additional transport costs firms would face from more remote states, and the costs of working in a

[5] Their small number may thus make their representitiveness questionable.

[6] See further 291 ENDS Report (1999) 37.

[7] See also J. Golub, "Global Competition and EU Environmental Policy: Introduction and Overview" in J. Golub (ed.), *Global Competition and EU Environmental Policy* (London, Routledge, 1998), p.1 at 12, who states that "EU governments do not strategically repeal existing environmental legislation in order to attract investment or maintain market share for their domestic industries".

[8] Esty and Geradin, *supra* n.4, pp. 321–2.

[9] See 290 ENDS Report (1999) 3.

different language and in a different legal and administrative system.[10] Esty and Geradin claim that the less advantageous overall balance of costs and benefits in the EU means that environmental relocation is likely to be less common than in the USA, and they suggest that this may explain why race to the bottom theories have been less influential here.[11]

Race to the bottom justifications for federal regulation have also been criticised on theoretical grounds, in particular by Richard Revesz.[12] Revesz makes two key arguments against race to the bottom theories. First, he implicitly contests the connotations of undesirability associated with the word "bottom". He does not disagree that regulatory competition may exert a downward pressure on standards. There may, in other words, be a race to laxity.[13] However, he contests the view that such a result will be undesirable.[14] Instead he argues that—just as competition in normal product markets can be expected to produce an efficient allocation of resources—so too can regulatory competition between states for industrial location. States may lower their environmental standards, but this is unlikely to be sub-optimal because they will only do so where the benefits of, for example, increased jobs outweigh the costs of lower environmental quality. Revesz's second argument is that, even if state regulation of pollution does give rise to a welfare-reducing race to the bottom, imposing federal control will not solve the problem of welfare reduction. This is because, he claims, states will simply indulge in welfare-reducing races to the bottom in other fields such as health and safety or taxation. The logic of race to the bottom theories therefore leads to a profoundly centralised system where *all* regulatory and fiscal decisions are taken at federal level.

Revesz's first argument will be examined in the next section. In response to his second argument, one could argue that it assumes that the race is just beginning. If, in contrast, one starts with the assumption that the race is near its end and that states are already near the bottom in many areas, then the case for federal intervention in even one of these areas becomes compelling. After all, to tackle just one area such as pollution will surely bring some welfare benefits; it may not provide the optimal solution, but it is surely still efficient in economic terms.

Psychic spillovers

In simple terms, Revesz's first argument above can be characterised as a plea for preferences in individual states to be respected: if a particular state wishes to

[10] Esty and Geradin, *supra* n.4, pp. 322–3. Although some of these factors must surely also apply in the USA.

[11] *Ibid.*, pp. 321–3.

[12] R. L. Revesz, "Rehabilitating Interstate Competition: Rethinking the 'Race-to-the-bottom' Rationale For Federal Environmental Regulation" (1992) 67 *NYUL Rev* 1210.

[13] P. Swire, "The Race to Laxity and the Race to Undesirability: Explaining Failures in Competition Among Jurisdictions in Environmental Law" (1996) 14 *Yale J on Reg.* 67.

[14] *Ibid.*

make a trade-off between the environment and jobs, then it should be allowed to do so; higher environmental standards which do not accord with preferences in that state would be inefficient. Critics of Revesz's approach from within the economic paradigm have pointed out that this ignores the "psychic" spillovers or external costs which a low standard state imposes on citizens of other states.[15] If one asks only citizens in state A how much they are willing to pay for an unpolluted environment, then one may end up with a low but efficient standard as a result of cost-benefit analysis. Yet, if one takes into account the existence values[16] which citizens of other states place on the environment in state A, then a much higher standard will be efficient. There are two possible responses to this. First, one might claim that it is none of their business and that the preferences of citizens should only count in relation to their own state. However, this is to conceive of citizenship in a very restricted manner, and it can be argued in the EU context for example that, as EU citizens, we have an interest in the environment throughout the Union.[17] Secondly, one might claim, as Revesz does, that existence or non-use values are only appropriately taken into account in relation to exceptional natural resources such as national parks. However, while there must come a point at which non-use values are inappropriate (Wils cites the example of lawnmower noise[18]), it is far from clear why citizens should not be concerned with, for example, pollution of non-exceptional rivers and lakes in other states.[19]

Competitive spillovers

Within the EC, much more influential than race to the bottom theories has been the argument that Community regulation is justified on single market competition or "level playing field" grounds.[20] The aim is to prevent firms in states with low *process* standards from enjoying an unfair competitive advantage over firms in high-standard states, causing the latter to lose market share. This can be described as a low-standard state imposing a *competitive* spillover or externality on firms from high-standard states, justifying Community harmonisation to

[15] Esty, *supra* n.2, pp. 594–5 and 638–47; see also Stewart, *supra* n.3, p. 1215; W. Wils, "Subsidiarity and EC Environmental Policy: Taking People's Concerns Seriously" (1994) 6 *JEL* 85.

[16] See further Ch. 5, n.29.

[17] For citizenship arguments in a US context see Esty, *supra* n.2, pp. 638–47.

[18] *Supra* n.15, p. 90. It is, in other words, overstepping the boundaries of concern to suggest that people in state B have a legitimate concern for those suffering lawnmower noise in state A. However, Community regulation of lawnmower noise can be justified on a product spillover ground considered further below in the text (at n.43).

[19] One might seek to draw a distinction between protection of nature and of humans: the latter can look after themselves (e.g. with lawnmowers), whereas the former is defenceless and may need allies from neighbouring states.

[20] See e.g. G. Close, "Harmonisation of Laws: Use or Abuse of the Powers Under the EEC Treaty?" (1978) 3 *ELRev*. 461, pp. 466–71.

address this market failure.[21] However, such arguments presuppose that the increased pollution control costs associated with higher standards do affect competitiveness[22]—a point much contested in the literature.[23] One might expect those industries where pollution control costs form a reasonably high percentage of overall production costs to be hit the hardest in competitiveness terms. In the titanium dioxide industry for example, pollution control costs have in the past accounted for between 10 and 20 per cent of the final product price.[24] However, empirical evidence suggests that not all industries with high pollution control costs have lost competitiveness.[25] This is because other factors besides cost will have a bearing on competitiveness, including profit margins and concentration in the industry: firms or industries with high profit margins may be able to absorb higher pollution control costs, and it may be easier for firms in highly concentrated industries to pass on these costs to consumers.[26] Conversely, even a small, 3 per cent increase in production costs may affect competitiveness in an industry where profit margins are tight[27] or where there are low levels of concentration.

Even where pollution control costs do affect competitiveness, this may be thought capable of justifying only *vertical* Community harmonisation for that particular industry, as with the Titanium Dioxide Directive.[28] Most pollution directives are, however, *horizontal* measures. The Waste Framework Directive is a good example. While this Directive may be justifiable on competitiveness grounds for *some* industries (those with significant waste disposal costs), there are likely to be many industries covered by it where such a justification does not apply.[29] There are two possible saving arguments. The first is to say that it would be inefficient to have a series of individual vertical measures for the industries whose competitiveness is affected, but to acknowledge that a horizontal measure, though more efficient, will necessarily be over-inclusive.[30] The

[21] It thus differs from the race to the bottom *economic* externality in that it focuses on the competitive loss suffered by *firms* and not the economic effects suffered by *states*.

[22] Similarly presupposed by race to the bottom theories.

[23] See further T. Barker and J. Köhler (eds.), *International Competitiveness and Environmental Policies* (Cheltenham, Edward Elgar, 1998); OECD, *Environmental Policies and Industrial Competitiveness* (Paris, OECD, 1993); EC Commission, *Communication on Industrial Competitiveness and Protection of the Environment*, SEC(92)1986; R. Jenkins, "Environmental Regulation and International Competitiveness: A Review of Literature and Some European Evidence" INTECH Discussion Paper 9801 (Maastricht, UNU/INTECH, 1998), http://www.intech. unu.edu .

[24] See Tesauro AG in the *Titanium Dioxide* case, Case C–300/89 *Commission* v. *Council* [1991] ECR I–2867.

[25] Jenkins, *supra* n.23.

[26] *Ibid.*

[27] Golub, *supra* n.7, p. 7.

[28] An appropriate case for the single market Art. 100a EC (now Art. 95) as a legal base therefore—see Case C–300/89, *supra* n.24.

[29] It is thus not surprising that the ECJ ruled that this Dir. was only ancillary to the single market and thus appropriately based on Art. 130s (now Art. 175) rather than Art. 100a (Case C–155/91 *Commission* v. *Council* [1993] ECR I-939).

[30] There is some support for such an approach within EC trade law: in its jurisprudence on the free movement of goods, the ECJ seems to assume that all "dual burden" regulations fall within Art. 28 EC, without inquiring whether such a dual burden really threatens the competitiveness of foreign, Community goods.

second possibility is to argue that, for industries whose competitiveness is not affected, *fairness* or equality before the law nevertheless dictates that they should face a harmonised level playing field, even if competition *per se* does not require it.[31] However, this would be a novel argument at Community level.[32] In addition, it would have implications for the form which harmonisation takes. If competitiveness is the key, then only *minimum* harmonisation is required. There, the Community measure itself provides the floor but not the ceiling.[33] This prevents unfair competition by low-standards states (which cannot go below the floor), and it is up to individual states whether they wish to risk competitiveness by adopting higher standards (the only ceiling being compatibility of the national measure with the Treaty rules such as Articles 28–30[34]). If, however, the aim is to secure fairness, then it becomes necessary to close rather than just narrow the gap, which means that *total* harmonisation would be required.

Another argument is that—in much the same way as race to the bottom theories—the logic of the competitiveness rationale for Community environmental regulation requires the federalisation of virtually all government decision-making that imposes costs on business.[35] There are a number of points that might be made in response to this argument. First, one might argue that that is indeed the logic of a single market, as posited by classic "spillover" theories of integration.[36] Many of those arguing against the single currency in the EU, for example, were concerned that, as price transparency threw its spotlight on the remaining bumps in the level playing field, there would be increasing pressure for more and more state powers to be harmonised at Community level. However, the second possibility is to refute this "necessity" logic and to claim that, just because you level up the playing field in one area, it does not necessarily mean that you must do so in all. The fact that other factors also impinge on competitiveness does not stop pollution control from having an impact on the single market. And while industry might like harmonisation across all of these relevant factors, it presumably will settle for harmonisation of just one or two such as pollution rather than none at all.

Finally it is worth noting that support for federal regulation on competitiveness grounds does not necessarily mean support for *uniform* federal

31 N. Bernard, "The Future of Economic Law in the Light of the Principle of Subsidiarity" (1996) 33 *CML Rev*. 633, p. 643.

32 Bernard (*ibid*.) dismisses it on the basis that, within EC competition law, the Commission and the Court have only ever bothered with *effective* competition, not fairness. However, such an argument perhaps confuses competition law, which involves actions by firms, with trade law, which involves actions by states/supranational institutions. Within a polity (whether national or EU), commercial actors expect political institutions to be fair in terms of ensuring equality before the law.

33 See S. Weatherill, "Beyond Preemption? Shared Competence and Constitutional Change in the European Community" in D. O'Keefe and P. Twomey (eds.), *Legal Issues of the Maastricht Treaty* (London, Wiley Chancery, 1994), p. 13 at 25.

34 *Ibid*.

35 R. B. Stewart, "Environmental Regulation and International Competitiveness" (1993) 102 *Yale LJ* 2039, p. 2097.

36 Not to be confused with economic spillovers. Spillover here implies that limited economic integration will inevitably spill over into other areas.

regulation.[37] Where normal emissions are concerned, there will need to be uniform ambient quality standards. However, emission standards needed to meet these ambient standards should be allowed to differ according to the assimilative capacity of the local environment. While this would confer a competitive advantage on firms in states with a high assimilative capacity, this cannot be regarded as an unfair competitive advantage. It is simply a matter of benefiting from comparative advantage, which lies at the heart of theories supporting international trade. As the British official quoted by Vogel put it: "Italy economically benefits from the amount of sunshine it receives each year. Why should not our industry be able to take similar advantage of our long coastline, high winds and rapidly flowing rivers?"[38] However, for dangerous substances—which cannot be assimilated by the environment—there is a need for uniform emission standards as well as uniform ambient quality standards. If firms in a particular Member State are benefiting from low emission standards in relation to dangerous substances, then this is conferring an unfair competitive advantage: comparative advantage is a matter of using local environmental conditions to your advantage, not abusing them.[39]

A race to the top, or competitive advantage?

In recent years, many have claimed that leaving environmental regulation to the states is just as likely to give rise to a race to the top as a race to the bottom, and that high environmental standards confer a competitive advantage on firms. Vogel, for example, speaks of the "California effect", based on the example of California's strict auto emission standards, which led to a ratcheting upward of standards in other states. Vogel argues that producer and environmental interests in the lead state will be united in support of strict standards where domestic producers are already well placed to meet them compared with external competitors. Where the lead state is a large market, export-oriented producers from other states will be forced to adapt to the strict standards if they wish to maintain their lucrative exports there. Once they are meeting them, foreign producers will in turn have an incentive to pressure their own state governments to adopt the same strict standards in order to provide them with a competitive advantage in their domestic market. And so the process of ratcheting up continues.

While Vogel concedes that such an effect is likely to be limited to product standards, others have suggested that process standards too may give rise to a race to the top, or may advance rather than impede competitiveness.[40] With the

[37] See Close, *supra* n.20, p. 471.

[38] D. Vogel, *National Styles of Regulation: Environmental Policy in Great Britain and the United States* (Ithaca, NY, Cornell University Press, 1986), p. 103.

[39] This also explains why ambient standards must be uniform in the case of normal emissions.

[40] This is one of the key elements of theories of "ecological modernisation", on which see e.g. A. Weale, *The New Politics of Pollution* (Manchester, Manchester UP, 1992) and M. Hajer, *The Politics of Environmental Discourse: Ecological Modernization and the Policy Process* (Oxford, Clarendon, 1995).

race to the top argument, just as with the race to the bottom, it is important to distinguish between government perception of an advantage in racing to the top and the continuing location of industries in strict standard states. One perceived advantage may be that firms facing strict pollution production standards will make cost savings on waste disposal and resource inputs. Whether firms share this perception is another matter. While, for reasons outlined earlier, the EU may not experience relocation to low-standard states, strict process standards are likely to threaten the competitiveness of at least some industries. Some cost savings can undoubtedly arise through pollution control, but most pollution regulation remains a significant cost burden. Were it otherwise, that would be a justification not only for getting rid of federal regulation, but for getting rid of regulation altogether, with the incentives provided by the market left to control pollution. Another perceived advantage for governments racing to the top with process standards is that it will produce a domestic environmental technology industry with significant export potential. However, though these benefits may be considerable, such an industry is likely to be relatively small and the benefits need to be weighed carefully against the costs of diminished competitiveness that are likely to fall on a much greater number of firms as a result of strict production standards.

The Commission has talked up the competitiveness advantages of high environmental standards in recent years.[41] While one can understand why—after all, it has an interest in persuading low-standard states that they have nothing to fear in adopting higher standards—such arguments are rather contradictory. They undermine one of its typical justifications for Community intervention, which is that low-standard states threaten the competitiveness of industries in high-standard states.[42] However, it may just be that the Commission would now turn this on its head and argue that harmonisation is still justified on single market, competitiveness grounds, but that it is now a matter of ensuring that firms from low-standard states are not disadvantaged by their own states' low standards.

Product spillovers

Vogel's California effect leads us on to what Lenaerts terms a "product" spillover justification for Community harmonisation.[43] Although the *Cassis de Dijon* case introduced the principle of mutual recognition—meaning that a product lawfully manufactured and marketed in a low standard Member State must be allowed onto the market of higher standard Member States—it is only

[41] Golub, *supra* n.7, p. 16.

[42] *Ibid.*

[43] K. Lenaerts, "The Principle of Subsidiarity and the Environment in the European Union: Keeping the Balance of Federalism" (1994) 17 *Fordham Int'l LJ* 846. This might also be called a market access justification: Esty and Geradin, *supra* n.4, or a trade barrier justification.

a presumption. It can be overridden if a high standard Member State can point to a justification[44] for its strict regulation and can establish that the measure is proportionate to the aim under consideration. However, if a Member State's regulatory measure survives this justification process (and is not subjected to "negative" harmonisation through the Court ruling it in breach of Article 28), it will continue to be a barrier to trade. Most such Member State measures will consist not of bans, but rather of stringent technical standards (such as requiring the returnability of bottles, or emission standards for car exhausts). These constitute trade barriers because they impede lower-standard foreign producers from selling there. Such producers are subject to a "dual burden" of their own state rules and then another set of destination state rules. If they want to sell in the high-standard market, they will have to run an expensive, dedicated production line. This prevents them from realising the economies of scale which would come from having one production line for the whole EU market, and effectively shelters the high-standard state's industry from price-competition on its home market. The high-standard state, in other words, imposes a product spillover or external cost on producers in other Member States.

Now of course, to the extent that Vogel's California effect operates in practice, "positive" harmonisation[45] by the Community is unnecessary to correct this spillover, because the trade barrier can be expected to free itself as everyone moves upwards to the same common standard. However, this effect is likely to operate only where the high standard market is a large and important one. Where, as in the case of the Danish drinks market,[46] the market is relatively small, the trade barriers will remain in place. Here, positive harmonisation by the Community will be justified in order to remove the trade barrier. And, in these circumstances, one can argue that harmonisation should be total, with the Community harmonising measure providing both the floor and, more importantly in trade terms, the ceiling. Member States should, in other words, be pre-empted from acting. If the rationale for introducing Community legislation was the elimination of trade barriers, it seems rather strange to allow these very same barriers to be maintained or subsequently introduced in the form of stricter national measures.[47]

[44] Art. 30 EC provides a limited number of very specific environmental justifications, while the *Danish Bottles* case (Case 302/86 *Commission* v. *Denmark* [1988] ECR 4607, [1989] 1 CMLR 619) allowed for a much broader range of environmental justifications under the doctrine of "mandatory requirements".

[45] I.e. legislation as opposed to the case-by-case approach of the Court with negative harmonisation.

[46] See the *Danish Bottles* case, *supra* n.44.

[47] Art. 95 EC allows Member States to maintain or introduce more stringent national measures post-harmonisation, as long as the Commission is satisfied that these do not constitute a means of arbitrary discrimination, a disguised restriction on trade or an obstacle to the functioning of the single market. This presumably means that Member States can keep or introduce some standards, but not the ones forming trade barriers that led to the harmonisation in the first place. *Cf.* Art. 175—a minimum harmonisation Art. where no such limitations apply (see Art. 176).

It is also worth noting why the product spillover justification for Community harmonisation does not work in relation to process standards. After all, if a Member State with strict product standards can successfully erect trade barriers to protect those standards, why can a strict process standard state not do the same? Such barriers could consist of a ban on products from states with low process standards, a tax on foreign products reflecting the difference in pollution control costs between the Member States, or a subsidy paid to the high standard state's own industry to compensate for its relative lack of competitiveness.[48] The answer appears to be that Member States are allowed to maintain certain trade barriers in relation to products because the negative environmental effects would be felt on their own territory. However it seems that Community law—in line with all the other major trade regimes—does not allow Member States to use trade barriers in relation to process standards, which can be seen as trying to protect the environment of another state. Were such extra-territorial action allowed, then the California effect could operate with process standards too, and in smaller markets, there would again be a product spillover justification for Community harmonisation.

Economies of scale versus experimental workshops

Another argument for federal regulation is that it brings administrative economies of scale and prevents wasteful duplication of regulatory effort by numerous states. However this is obviously true only of certain stages of the regulatory process.[49] The results of risk assessments of chemicals, for example, ought to be the same wherever they are carried out, and it thus does not make economic sense to duplicate such assessments.[50] However, there are likely to be no real economies of scale in a federal regulator tailoring standards for individual plants and enforcing these.

In contrast, those arguing for state regulation argue that it is beneficial to have numerous states trying their own regulatory experiments.[51] Just as competition between car-makers can be expected to lead to improvements in car quality, so competition between state regulators should lead to the best form of regulation. However, where federal regulation is taking over state regulation, then the federal regulator *can* choose from the best, existing state "laboratory". Where regulation is truly new, a federal regulator may well choose a regulatory "turkey". Nevertheless, this is unlikely, since states will have an opportunity to comment on proposals and, in any case, a failure can at least be amended. However, if

[48] Esty and Geradin, *supra* n.4, pp. 277–9; Stewart, *supra* n.35, pp. 2044–51; G. Cross, "Subsidiarity and the Environment" (1995) 15 *YEL* 107. Only the subsidy will protect exporters from the high-standard state as well as producers selling on the domestic market.

[49] Esty, *supra* n.2, pp. 613–17.

[50] *Ibid.*, pp. 613–14.

[51] See further *ibid.*, pp. 615–18.

states are regulating, then—in the absence of a California effect for products—there is little reason to expect poor laboratory states to follow the best practice of good laboratory states.

Public choice

So far, we have considered only normative economic justifications for federal action on pollution, consisting mainly of various kinds of spillover—physical, economic, psychic, competitive and product. In the USA, positive economic, public choice explanations for federal action on pollution have also been provided.[52] The principal claim is that environmental groups enjoy greater influence at federal level than at state level, and that one can therefore expect a greater supply of regulation at that level. Nevertheless, this appears to have been translated into a *normative* justification for federal regulation—that environmental groups are under-represented at state level and that federal regulation is justified because such groups are better represented at that level. However, this is an argument without foundation, because one might equally respond that environmental groups have an *appropriate* influence at state level and are over-represented at federal level. It all depends, in other words, on one's view of the correct standard of environmental quality. What is required is not a discussion of the *outputs* produced by decision-making at state and federal levels, but rather one concerning the respective merits of the democratic decision-making *process* itself at these levels.

Democracy

In the context of the subsidiarity debate in the EU, one of the key arguments made for *state* control of pollution is that of democracy.[53] The argument tends to be, on the one hand, that the states are closer to the citizens than the Community; and on the other, that, *in the absence of externalities*, states' democratic choices on the environment ought to be respected. Drinking water quality is a good example: this does not generally involve any externalities,[55] and it

[52] See e.g. *ibid.*, pp. 648–52; Swire, *supra* n.13, pp. 100–3; *cf.* R. L. Revesz, "The Race to the Bottom and Federal Environmental Regulation: A Response to Critics" (1997) 82 *Minn. L Rev.* 535, pp. 558–61.

[53] J. Golub, "Sovereignty and Subsidiarity in EU Environmental Policy" (1996) 44 *Political Studies* 686, pp. 696–9.

[54] Of *any* of the kinds discussed earlier.

[55] See Centre for Economic Policy Research, *Making Sense of Subsidiarity: How Much Centralization for Europe?* (London, CEPR, 1993), pp. 139–41.

has been argued that states ought to be free to choose low quality if this reflects the preferences of their citizens.[56]

The emphasis on the absence of externalities is important—and this includes economic externalities. Take the example of a low process standard state, whose citizens prefer that low standard, which *is* imposing an economic externality on higher standard states, forcing them to race to the bottom against the preferences of their citizens. Assuming the high-standard states are in the majority, it can be argued that the preferences of their citizens for a high standard ought to override those of the citizens in the low standard state.[57] The argument here is much the same as the concept of psychic spillovers discussed earlier—not surprisingly given that welfare economics and democracy are both based on preference satisfaction.

However, there are still a number of possible justifications for Community regulation that remain. The first is that Community decision-making is more in line with a preferable, civic republican model of democracy.[58] The argument here could take two different forms—intra-institutional or inter-institutional. Intra-institutionally, one could claim that while, for example, low drinking water quality reflects the preferences of citizens in a particular state, the forum which represents such preferences (national parliament) is less truly deliberative or discursive than the various EC institutions involved in the Community legislative process. However, it is submitted that such an argument would be difficult to substantiate.[59] Alternatively, one could claim that the inter-institutional arrangements at Community level better reflect Madisonian designs for the separation of powers, and are thus less likely to produce a tyranny of the majority.[60] On this view, the fact that many of the Community institutions are insulated from direct electoral control[61] is something to be celebrated, not criticised in the language of a "democratic deficit". The EC may be less democratic than Member States in terms of majoritarian models of democracy, but it is more democratic in civic republican inter-institutional terms.[62] Majoritarian democracy may deliver what we want, but civic republicanism may protect us from ourselves and deliver what is truly in the public interest.

[56] *Cf.* bathing water. While physical, economic or competitive externalities are similarly unlikely to exist, there may be psychic ones: I may not have a legitimate concern which justifies interfering with human preferences for dirty bathing water, but I do have a legitimate concern in-so-far as bathing water standards also protect defenceless marine life. With drinking water, there are no such psychic externalities: if humans in other states wish to drink dirty water, then that is up to them.

[57] See generally J. D. Sarnoff, "The Continuing Imperative (But Only from a National Perspective) For Federal Environmental Protection" (1997) 7 *Duke Environmental Law and Policy Forum* 225.

[58] See further P. Craig, "The Nature of the Community: Integration, Democracy, and Legitimacy" in P. Craig and G. de Búrca (eds.), *The Evolution of EU Law* (Oxford, OUP, 1999) p. 1.

[59] See Ch. 5.

[60] G. Majone, "Regulatory Legitimacy" in G. Majone (ed.), *Regulating Europe* (London, Routledge, 1996), p. 284 at 286; Craig, *supra* n.58.

[61] In the same way as, e.g., independent central banks.

[62] Majone, *supra* n.60; Craig, *supra* n.58.

Environmental ethics and Community law

Other possible justifications for federal or Community-level regulation are centred on environmental ethics on the one hand and the Treaty and Community rights on the other.[63] An environmental ethics rationale for federal regulation could be based on a limited, human right to a clean environment, or could be broader and more ecocentric in orientation. With drinking water for example, one might argue that federal regulation is necessary because humans have a right to clean drinking water, which should trump the democratic preferences of a majority in a particular state for low standards. And with ecological regulation, it could be argued that federal regulation is justified because its typically higher standards better reflect our moral duties towards the environment.[64] Of course, a claim that there is a moral duty to reach a given level of environmental quality is just as applicable to state regulators as it is to those regulating at federal level. What is really being claimed, therefore, is that federal-level regulation is justified because its institutional design makes it more likely that this moral vision will be realised. The problem with this approach lies in the absence of any consensus by Member States on environmental ethics.[65] Member States may claim that their low standards reflect an appropriate moral duty to the environment and may disagree with the stricter moral vision laid down by the Community.

Legal, Treaty-based justifications appear to offer a firmer ground for Community regulation, because these are the result of some degree of consensus. Community regulation could, for example, be justified on the basis that it reflects the sustainable development duty in Article 2 of the EC Treaty. Alternatively, it could be justified by reference to EU citizenship and Community free movement rights.[66] The claim here would be that the right of EU citizens to move freely throughout the EU will be effectively impeded unless there is a harmonised level of environmental quality. If, for example, I know that Member State X has low drinking water standards or poor air quality, I may be put off moving or travelling there. This is a thin version of EU environmental citizenship. It does not amount to a (human) right to a clean environment as such—only to a harmonised level of environmental quality, which could be far from clean: in free movement terms, I will not be impeded from going to a dirty Member State if mine is equally dirty. A thicker conception of EU environmental citizenship would arguably require a right to a clean environment (in the sense of a minimum standard of environmental quality) to be included within the EC Treaty. However, even those justifications already within the Treaty would be far from controversial. There may have been con-

[63] Golub, *supra* n.53, pp. 696–8.

[64] Stewart, *supra* n.3, pp. 1264–5. See further Chs. 1 and 5.

[65] In a US context, see H. N. Butler and J. R. Macey, *Using Federalism to Improve Environmental Policy* (Washington, DC, AEI Press, 1996), p. 31.

[66] Golub, *supra* n.53, p. 696.

sensus on the adoption of the relevant principles of sustainable development and citizenship, but there is little consensus on what each might entail. Justification of Community-level regulation by reference to such principles may be theoretically sound, but it is unlikely to be well received by a number of Member States as a matter of practical politics.

PRACTICE IN THE EU AND UK

Subsidiarity

Article 5 EC states:

> The Community shall act within the limits of the powers conferred upon it by this Treaty and of the objectives assigned to it therein.
>
> In areas which do not fall within its exclusive competence, the Community shall take action, in accordance with the principle of subsidiarity, only if and insofar as the objectives of the proposed action cannot be sufficiently achieved by the Member States and can therefore, by reason of the scale or effects of the proposed action, be better achieved by the Community.
>
> Any action by the Community shall not go beyond what is necessary to achieve the objectives of this Treaty.

Although this is often described as the subsidiarity Article, only the second paragraph really concerns subsidiarity as such, with the first paragraph involving competence and the final paragraph proportionality. The paragraphs have been rephrased by some to form the following questions regarding Community power: "can it act?" (competence), "should it act?" (subsidiarity), and "how intensely can it act?" (proportionality).

Subsidiarity's scope

It is clear from the wording of Article 5b that the subsidiarity principle applies only in areas which do not fall within the exclusive competence of the Community. Early views on when Community competence was exclusive, rather than shared with Member States, differed markedly. Toth stated that all of the powers granted to the EEC under the original Treaty of Rome were exclusive, whether or not these had been exercised.[67] Steiner, in contrast, claimed that Community competence became exclusive only once the Community had legislated on a particular topic.[68] The Commission expressed the view that Community competence was exclusive in areas where it was under an obligation to act. One key duty is that of creating a common market, leading the

[67] A. Toth, "The Principle of Subsidiarity in the Maastricht Treaty" (1992) 29 *CML Rev* 1079.

[68] J. Steiner, "Subsidiarity Under the Maastricht Treaty" in O'Keefe and Twomey, *supra* n.33, p. 49.

Commission to see the following as exclusive powers: the free movement of goods, persons, services and capital; the common commercial policy, competition law; the common agricultural policy, fisheries conservation; and the essential elements of transport policy.[69]

However, all of the above views are now rather dated. More recent commentators have drawn a distinction between *a priori* exclusive competence and exclusive competence by pre-emption.[70] *A priori* exclusive competence means that Member States cannot act, irrespective of whether the Community has acted.[71] The common commercial policy under Article 133 EC provides a good example of this: Member State action and the idea of a common commercial policy are flatly contradictory at *any* stage. In most areas however, Member States have always been free to act until the Community acts. In the past, when any such Community legislation was actually introduced, it would often be said to have "occupied the field", pre-empting Member States from acting on that topic thereafter.[72] Because Member States could not act, it thus became an area of exclusive Community competence by pre-emption. However, in recent times, the existence of Treaty Articles such as Article 95(4)–(5) EC and minimum harmonisation Articles such as Articles 153(5) and 176, means that old-style pre-emption is now the exception rather than the rule: within limits, Member States are now often free to act even after Community legislation has been introduced. This is certainly true of Community environmental legislation: whether it is introduced under Article 95 or 175, Member States can still act, and hence competence remains shared rather than becoming exclusive to the Community.[73]

Content of the principle

The core of the subsidiarity Article talks of the Community taking action only where the objectives of the proposed action cannot be sufficiently achieved by the Member States, and can, therefore, by reason of the scale or effects of the proposed action, be better achieved by the Community. Guidance in the protocol on the application of the principles of subsidiarity and proportionality attached to the Amsterdam Treaty states that, for Community action to be justified, both aspects of the subsidiarity principle must be met: the objectives of the proposed action must be insufficiently achievable by Member States' action, and better achievable by Community action.

[69] Commission Communication to the Council and the European Parliament SEC(92)1990 final, 27 Oct. 1992, cited in D. Chalmers, *European Union Law, Volume I: Law and EU Government* (Aldershot, Dartmouth, 1998), p. 222.

[70] Bernard, *supra* n.31, pp. 654–64. See also Weatherill, *supra* n.33, whose analysis is similar, although the terms he uses differ from Bernard's.

[71] *Ibid.*

[72] See the *Dim-dip Headlights* case, Case 60/86 *Commission* v. *United Kingdom* [1988] ECR 3921.

[73] *Cf.* Golub, *supra* n.53, p. 695, who implies that Art. 100a (now Art. 95) confers exclusive competence, thus taking legislation introduced under it outside the scope of subsidiarity; see also Toth, *supra* n.67.

The protocol suggests that this is likely to be the case in the following circumstances: where there are transnational aspects; where there is a need to prevent distortions of competition, disguised restrictions on trade, or to strengthen economic and social cohesion; and where action at Community level would produce clear benefits by reason of its scale or effects compared with action at the level of the Member States. The protocol, in other words, closely mirrors some of the theoretical justifications for federal action discussed earlier in this chapter.[74] "Transnational aspects" could be equated with physical and psychic spillovers, "distortion of competition" with the competitive spillover justification, "disguised restriction on trade" with product spillover and "scale or effects" with the economies of scale justification.[75] While these are all economic justifications for Community action, the reference to the need "to strengthen economic and social cohesion" could be seen as supporting Community action on environmental citizenship grounds. However the economic justifications no doubt dominate because, in this context, economics can be seen as providing a relatively neutral, expert view of the Community's appropriate role. While, as we have seen, some of these economic justifications have been called into question, political, moral and legal justifications centred around democracy, environmental ethics, and sustainable development and citizenship respectively, are much more likely to be contested by Member States.

Practical application and justiciability

The subsidiarity principle thus tells us that the Community should take action only where action at Community level can be justified. There are then questions about who is responsible for applying the subsidiarity test, which Community law it applies to (old or just new), and the extent to which the principle is justiciable. On the first of these, the Amsterdam protocol states that each institution is responsible for ensuring that the principle of subsidiarity is complied with when exercising its powers. It also states that subsidiarity and proportionality justifications must be given for all Community legislative proposals, and that these must be substantiated by qualitative or, wherever possible, quantitative indicators. In practice the main responsibility in this regard will fall on the Commission, which must provide details of its subsidiarity justification in the explanatory memorandum accompanying a proposal. The European Parliament and the Council are then required—as an integral part of their overall examination of the Commission proposal—to consider its consistency with subsidiarity. Any amendments that they intend making must also be tested against the principle.

[74] Lenaerts, *supra* n.43, pp. 880–2.

[75] *Ibid.* However, Lenaerts equates his pollution (physical) spillover with both transboundary and scale/effects, and does not link scale/effects to economies of scale. He also limits his preservation (psychic) spillovers to *special* natural resources.

In relation to the question of which Community law subsidiarity applies to, mention of "proposals" in the protocol suggests that it applies *in law* only to new Community legislation and this is confirmed by a statement that subsidiarity is not meant to call into question the existing body of Community law (the *acquis communautaire*).[76] As for justiciability, what approach is the ECJ likely to take if a Member State, under Article 230 seeks the annulment of a Community pollution directive on subsidiarity grounds? In principle, the intensity of review could vary.[77] First, the Court could adopt substantive review, becoming involved itself with the highly political question of whether Community action was justified.[78] Secondly, it could adopt a less intensive style of substantive review, interfering with institutional judgement only where it felt a manifest error had been made.[79] Finally, it could adopt simply procedural review—intervening only where the subsidiarity question had not been asked. In practice, the Court appears to adopt only a weak version of procedural review. The *Working Time Directive* case[80] suggests that it is not prepared to countenance substantive review at all, since in that case the Court effectively stated that if the Council had concluded that Community action was justified, then it was. *Germany* v. *European Parliament and Council*[81] reveals the weak nature of the procedural review adopted, the Court effectively ruling that subsidiarity need not be mentioned *in form* in the recitals to Community legislation, as long it is clear from them that the test has been applied *in substance*.[82] However, one should not conclude from the above that subsidiarity will remain loosely justiciable for all time. The ECJ has examined substantive elements of subsidiarity in the context of Member State law and its own jurisprudence on the single market.[83] And there is likely to be pressure for it to adopt substantive review of the law of the EU political institutions. If the Court chooses to build on the former to adopt the latter, then the analysis in this chapter will move squarely into the legal arena.

[76] Although, as a matter of practical politics, the Commission did scrutinise many existing items of legislation after the general principle was first introduced at Maastricht. In addition of course, when legislation is being altered or consolidated for other reasons (e.g. the new Community Water Policy), old can become new and subsidiarity justification will have to be considered afresh.

[77] P. Craig and G. de Búrca, *EU Law: Text, Cases and Materials* (2nd edn., Oxford, OUP, 1998), pp. 128–9.

[78] *Ibid*, p. 129.

[79] *Ibid.*

[80] Case C–84/94 *United Kingdom* v. *Council* [1996] ECR I–5755, [1996] 3 CMLR 671.

[81] Case C–233/94 [1997] ECR I–2405, [1997] 3 CMLR 1379.

[82] While this is in line with the general attitude of the Court, which is in the habit of looking to substance rather than form, it is regrettable here because transparency arguably requires a clear reference to the actual term subsidiarity.

[83] See Case C–415/93 *Union Royale Belge des Sociétés de Football Association* v. *Jean-Marc Bosman* [1995] ECR I–4921, [1996] 1 CMLR 645.

Devolution in the UK

Full legislative power in relation to the environment has been devolved to the Scottish Parliament, and to the new Northern Ireland Assembly.[84] With Wales, the UK Parliament at Westminster will continue to pass primary legislation for England and Wales on all matters including the environment, but competence over secondary legislation has been devolved to the new Welsh Assembly. Since much UK environmental legislation is of a framework nature, with the detail left to secondary legislation, the Welsh position will not differ too significantly from that in Scotland or Northern Ireland.

The new UK constitutional arrangements thus take it close to being a federal state.[85] One might thus have expected subsidiarity-type issues to be discussed in the context of devolution. And indeed some have been; but the discussion has been very one-sided, with the consultation papers on devolution mentioning only democracy justifications for devolution to the "states". Justifications for maintaining some power in relation to the environment at the centre appear to have been overlooked. Where there are physical, pollution externalities for example, does this not justify pollution regulation by the UK Parliament? And what of competitive externalities? Does a worry that Scotland, Wales or Northern Ireland might choose lower environmental process standards not justify UK level pollution regulation to prevent their firms from enjoying an unfair competitive advantage over their English counterparts? However as things stand, at least in relation to Scotland and Northern Ireland, competence over the environment is now the exclusive preserve of the states. The UK Parliament does not appear to have maintained any power to legislate on the environment for the UK as a whole.

The probable reason for this—and one that may make the above situation slightly less of a concern—is that where there is a justification for a federal approach, this will be tackled at Community level. In other words, the federal environmental debate at UK national level has been by-passed because the Community already addresses the relevant concerns at supranational level. Whether this is true across the board remains to be seen; gaps may yet emerge.

Of course, subsidiarity-type issues arose in the UK long before devolution, in the choice between local and national control of pollution. One reason for allowing local authorities to keep hold of air pollution control (APC) under Part I of the Environmental Protection Act 1990 in England and Wales is that of democratic accountability. Of course the same could have been said of waste regulation, which was taken out of democratic, local authority control and placed with the national Environment Agency. However, in that case the risk of

[84] At the time of going to press, the Northern Ireland Assembly was suspended (under the Northern Ireland Act 2000).

[85] For a distinction between devolution and federalism see B. Burrows and G. Denton, *Devolution or Federalism? Options for a United Kingdom* (London, Macmillan, 1980).

local authorities adopting NIMBY (not in my back yard) standards that are too high—externalising their waste problems on other parts of the country[86]—could be said to have justified national control by the Environment Agency. Alternatively, economies of scale in a highly technical area such as waste may have justified such control.

[86] I.e. an undesirable race to the top—see further Swire, *supra* n.13, pp. 105–7.

4

The Institutional Legitimacy of Pollution Regulation

One of the key themes of this book is the legitimacy of pollution regulation. This chapter is concerned with the legitimacy of those bodies taking regulatory decisions on pollution. While the legitimacy of the decision-making tools and regulatory instruments they use plays an important part in the overall legitimacy of regulatory bodies, these will be left for discussion in other chapters.[1] The focus here will, instead, be on institutional legitimacy.

A key element of legitimacy is the acceptance of power. Legitimacy may be normative and process based: in Western polities, the procedure of democracy is often regarded as the key legitimating factor.[2] Or it may be popular and outcome-based: even undemocratic power that produces effective substantive outcomes may be seen as legitimate.[3] With both, the support or consent of at least a majority of the governed is an essential component. However, in many Western *liberal* democracies, there is an extra normative component to legitimacy: fundamental rights. Without these, majority support can override the interests of minorities. Nevertheless, the focus in this chapter will be on the democratic element of legitimacy. While one can argue that there should be a fundamental right to a clean environment, no such right yet exists in the UK or the EU. With the environment, institutional legitimacy is instead very much about trying to secure democracy.

LEGITIMACY OF THE INSTITUTIONAL ARRANGEMENTS FOR POLLUTION REGULATION IN THE UK

The UK Parliament has primary legislative power in relation to pollution in England and Wales. In Scotland, this power is exercised by the Scottish Parliament, and in Northern Ireland by the new Northern Ireland Assembly. These institutions set the broad *framework* of pollution regulation in the United Kingdom and, as directly elected democratic institutions, their legitimacy has

[1] On the legitimacy of decision-making tools, see Ch. 5, and on the legitimacy of regulatory instruments, see Ch. 6.

[2] G. de Búrca, "The Quest for Legitimacy in the European Union" (1996) 59 *MLR* 349.

[3] J. Scott, "Law, Legitimacy and EC Governance: Prospects for Partnership" (1998) 36 *JCMS* 175, p. 176; J. Weiler, "Does Europe Need a Constitution? Reflections on Demos, Telos and the German Maastricht Decision" (1995) 1 *ELJ* 219, p. 232.

passed largely unquestioned in much of the literature on regulation.[4] Regulatory *detail* is typically delegated to the executive. Significant detail will typically be contained in delegated legislation issued by central government departments or the Welsh Assembly in the form of statutory instruments.[5] The legitimacy of delegated legislation stems partly from the fact that the executives and the Welsh Assembly are elected, and partly from endorsement of such legislation by the respective parliaments. However, the stamp of legitimacy conferred by the latter has historically been relatively weak, as statutory instruments have received limited parliamentary scrutiny. Nevertheless, this may now change in the devolved administrations—particularly in the case of Wales, where secondary legislation is the only form that the Welsh Assembly can scrutinise.

In order to implement this primary and secondary legislation, further regulatory detail is again filled in by central government departments or the Welsh Assembly, and also by regulatory agencies[6] in the form of codes of practice, guidance notes, licensing decisions and so on. While departments can again claim legitimacy from their direct control by ministers of an elected government, and the Welsh Assembly is directly elected, the legitimacy of independent or semi-independent agencies has long been regarded as problematic in the literature on administrative law.[7] The problem of agency legitimacy is often conceptualised in terms of a principal–agent model. The questions that tend to be asked are: "what justifies the delegation of power from a legitimate principal to an agent?" or, alternatively, "how can the exercise of power by that agent be made legitimate?"[8]

Expertise

One possible justification for the delegation of power to an agency is that of expertise.[9] Parliament does not have the time or expertise, so it delegates to

[4] For a critical discussion of the limits of voting in securing legitimacy and the strengths of deliberation in parliaments and other policy fora, see E. O. Eriksen, "The Question of Deliberative Supranationalism in the EU", *ARENA Working Papers* WP 99/4 (Oslo, Arena, 1999).

[5] Under direct rule in Northern Ireland, not only secondary legislation took this form, but also much of what equates to primary legislation (as Northern Ireland Orders in Council issued by the UK government and endorsed by the UK Parliament).

[6] Although the principal focus here will be on public *agencies* such as the Environment Agency in England and Wales and SEPA in Scotland, many of the arguments are equally applicable to the other public and private bodies which have limited pollution regulation functions (e.g. in England and Wales: local authorities in relation to air pollution and water companies in relation to discharges to sewer).

[7] J. O. Freedman, *Crisis and Legitimacy: The Administrative Process and American Government* (Cambridge, CUP, 1978); R. Baldwin and C. McCrudden, *Regulation and Public Law* (London, Weidenfeld and Nicolson, 1987); T. Jones, "Administrative Law, Regulation and Legitimacy" (1989) 16 *Jo. of Law & Soc.* 410.

[8] To similar effect, see Note, "Civic Republican Administrative Theory: Bureaucrats as Deliberative Democrats" (1994) 107 *Harv. L Rev.* 1401, pp. 1414–5.

[9] Baldwin and McCrudden, *supra* n.7, p. 48; Jones, *supra* n.7, p. 420.

those who have. Under this New Deal inspired model, decision-making is seen as a technical rather than a political task, with the legitimacy of agency decisions resting, not on democracy, but upon the legitimacy of science or professional technique. Legitimacy here is, in other words, outcome- rather than process-based. While outcomes are satisfactory, the legitimacy of the agency is unlikely to be called into question. However, where a crisis occurs, an agency legitimation crisis is likely to follow, with calls for greater process-based accountability and control.[10] If a series of crises occur, as has happened in recent decades with scientific risk-control agencies in the UK,[11] then the fiction that technical decision-making is free from politics is revealed as just that, and the expertise foundations of legitimacy begin to look rather insecure.

The transmission belt

If the New Deal model lies at one end of the spectrum—full of confidence in the ability of agencies to deliver what is in the public interest—then at the other end lies the "transmission belt" model of administration.[12] Under this model, the democratic legislature is seen as the fount of all legitimacy, and delegation to an unelected agency is viewed with considerable suspicion. While reality dictates that such delegation must take place, the agency is kept on a tight leash by a closely circumscribed legislative mandate. The mechanisms involved in defining this mandate may be described as *ex ante* accountability of the agent to the principal. Under this model, since the agency lacks discretion and simply does exactly what it is told, the democratic legitimacy of the legislature is passed down the transmission belt to the agency along with its policy instructions.

Ex post accountability

Of course, in reality, no legislature can foresee every eventuality that might arise. And that means that agencies require a degree of flexibility in their mandates, leaving them with discretion as to how they best achieve the broad public interest goals set for them. This leads on to the *ex post* accountability model of agency legitimacy. Like the transmission belt model, the *ex post* accountability model regards the democratic legitimacy of Parliament as the ideal and the source from which agency legitimacy is derived. However the accountability model recognises that the policy transmission belt is far from perfect, and hence the need for discretion. It is, nevertheless, conscious of the danger of agencies misusing this discretion by engaging in activities that go against the public

[10] E.g. an economic crisis in relation to independent central banks.

[11] E.g. with BSE, genetically modified food and crops, and rail safety.

[12] R. B. Stewart, "The Reformation of American Administrative Law" (1975) 88 *Harv. L Rev.* 1669, p. 1675.

interest goals set for them. A close eye thus has to be kept on them to try to ensure that this does not happen. Making agencies accountable to the regulated, to the public and to Parliament through a variety of *ex post* accountability mechanisms (such as judicial review, reports, select committees and so on) is meant to provide this oversight. A key purpose of these mechanisms is to prevent agencies from straying too far from their broad democratic mandates, and hence to keep the holes in the legitimacy transmission belt to a minimum.

Participation

Finally, there is the participatory model.[13] Here, legitimacy is secured not by maintaining a connection between the agency and the democratic legislature, but by encouraging the participation of individuals and interest groups in agency rule making. If a cross-section of society participates in making agency decisions, legitimacy is no longer derived solely from the representative democracy of Parliament, but also from the bottom up via participatory democracy. The idea is that if those who will be affected by a regulatory decision have participated in its design, they are more likely to accept the final outcome as legitimate. Naturally, this pre-supposes that the quality of participation is "thick": all too often in the past, public participation has been a "thin", paper exercise, which many have accused of lending an *unwarranted* air of legitimacy to flawed projects. At the thickest end of the spectrum—and arguably most legitimate within the participatory model—come civic republican, discursive fora, with decisions reached after rational discussion amongst all interested parties.[14] At the other end of the spectrum lie pluralistic consultation exercises, which simply aggregate preferences in a sequential manner without subjecting them to debate.

In practice, agency legitimacy is conferred by a mix of all of the above models. However, fashions change, and while expertise may once have provided a significant part of the legitimacy budget, its contribution has shrunk in recent decades. With delegation to UK agencies, its place was taken by *ex post* accountability and participation, which have been dominant for much of the 1990s.[15] And within participation, civic republican modes are very much in vogue at present.[16]

It is also worth noting that the models are not watertight. First, they may overlap in places. So, for example, while judicial review is predominantly a form

[13] In the literature, participation is often also referred to as *ex ante* accountability. However, participation will be reserved here for *public* input, while *ex ante* accountability is used to refer to the prior shaping of agent mandates by *political* principals (as in the paragraph in the text above on the transmission belt model).

[14] Civic republicanism is thus being used here to refer to fora that combine participation by interest groups *and* deliberation. If one privileges simply deliberation, then there is a danger of idealising existing bureaucratic arrangements (see Note, *supra*, n.8).

[15] With delegation by the UK to the EC, as will be seen later in the ch., the focus still tends to be on *ex ante* accountability and the (rather forlorn) hope of a transmission belt.

[16] See further Ch. 5.

of *ex post* accountability, it may be used to enforce participation rights;[17] and more generally, the proceedings themselves can be seen as a forum for participation in regulatory decision-making. Secondly, an increase in the use of one model may have knock-on effects on the others and on non-process-based aspects of legitimacy. For example, an increase in civic republican-style participation may dilute expertise. And an increase in participation or accountability is likely to slow the regulatory system down, impeding effectiveness by delaying public interest outcomes. The regulatory system in the USA is often cited as an example of one that has traded regulatory effectiveness for its commitment to strong accountability.[18] A careful balance between process-based legitimacy and effectiveness or outcome legitimacy is thus needed.

LEGITIMACY OF THE INSTITUTIONAL ARRANGEMENTS FOR POLLUTION REGULATION IN THE EC

Community decision-making on pollution can also be analysed in terms of agency theory. Here, directly elected Member State parliaments are the principals that have delegated power to the Community to act as an agent in certain fields such as environmental policy.[19] As with delegation from national parliaments to national agencies, the question again is what legitimates the exercise of power by that agent?

Prior to the Single European Act (SEA), the Community in general was regarded by many as a technocratic, economic project, and its legitimacy could thus be based on the expertise model.[20] As far as environmental policy in particular is concerned, the lack of a specific legal base in the Treaty at the time renders some of the non-single market related environmental measures introduced before the SEA of dubious legal legitimacy: the EC had clearly stepped outside the legal mandate provided by its principals in the shape of the Treaty. Nevertheless, this lack of legal legitimacy was arguably made up for by popular legitimacy:[21] in many Member States, there was popular support for environmental protection measures.

With the expansion of competence into more overtly political areas after the SEA, and more so after Maastricht, the Community could no longer base its claim to legitimacy on expertise. The problems that a number of Member States

[17] Particularly in US administrative law with its "notice and comment" rule-making requirements.

[18] F. E. Bignami, "The Democratic Deficit in European Community Rulemaking: A Call for Notice and Comment in Comitology" (1999) 40 *Harvard ILJ* 451, p. 503.

[19] For a detailed, agency theory-based analysis of this level of delegation, see e.g. M. A. Pollack, "Delegation, Agency and Agenda Setting in the Treaty of Amsterdam" (1999) 3(6) *European Integration online Papers* http://eiop.or.at/eiop/texte/1999-006a.htm.

[20] de Búrca, *supra* n.2, p. 350; see also P. Craig, "The Nature of the Community: Integration, Democracy, and Legitimacy" in P. Craig and G. de Búrca (eds.), *The Evolution of EU Law* (Oxford, OUP, 1999) p. 1 at 6–7.

[21] M. Everson, "Administering Europe?" (1998) 36 *JCMS* 195, p. 197.

faced in securing the ratification of the Maastricht Treaty were symptomatic of a crisis in popular legitimacy or support for the EU. One of the causes of this crisis was alleged to be a lack of normative legitimacy—typically discussed in the language of a "democratic deficit".[22] Space precludes a full discussion of what is now a vast literature.[23] However, in straightforward terms, the so-called democratic deficit arose because the legislative power delegated by democratically elected national parliaments was exercised principally by the indirectly democratic Council of Ministers rather than the directly elected European Parliament: democracy was lost in the transfer of power.

Amsterdam has undoubtedly made inroads into this deficit by enhancing the parliamentary model of democracy in the EU.[24] In most areas now, including the environment, the co-decision procedure has become the norm, providing a much greater role for the directly elected European Parliament in the law-making process. However, in agency terms one cannot conclude that the delegation of law-making power by the Member State principals to the EU is now fully legitimate because their agent is now more democratically legitimate. After all the UK national Parliament delegates certain pollution regulation functions to local authorities,[25] but the fact that they are directly elected does not fully address the legitimacy issue. What is missing from the equation is the idea of maintaining accountability to the principal.

There is, in other words, a tension between a view of the Community as an independent polity and a view of it as an agent. To understand this, it is instructive to compare national parliamentary delegation to national agencies, with delegation by national parliaments to the supranational agency of the EC. With the former type of delegation, it is taken for granted that the agency is undemocratic in the sense of a parliamentary model of democracy. Its legitimacy must therefore come from a mix of the models described earlier, such as accountability and participation. With the latter however, parliamentary democracy tends to have been expected—as evidenced by the widely held arguments about the presence of a democratic deficit. But such arguments presuppose a view of the Community as a polity. Agency-type legitimating factors have been underplayed.[26] For example, *accountability*[27] to Member State principals is not often focused on in agency terms,[28] although it is implicit in the following: notification of national parliaments by the Commission of draft legislative pro-

[22] Although opposition to deeper political integration was perhaps a more likely cause of the ratification troubles. On this and other possible causes, see de Búrca, *supra* n.2.

[23] See e.g. J.-C. Piris, "After Maastricht, are the Community Institutions More Efficacious, More Democratic and More Transparent?" (1994) 19 *ELRev.* 449; J. Lodge, "Transparency and Democratic Legitimacy" (1994) 32 *JCMS* 343; Craig, *supra* n.20; D. Chalmers, *European Union Law Volume I: Law and EU Government* (Aldershot, Dartmouth, 1998), p. 182.

[24] R. Dehousse, "European Institutional Architecture After Amsterdam: Parliamentary System or Regulatory Structure?" (1998) 35 *CML Rev* 595.

[25] See *supra* n.6.

[26] With the exception of G. Majone (see e.g. *Regulating Europe* (London, Routledge, 1996)).

[27] Both *ex ante* (see *supra* n.13) and *ex post.*

[28] Though cf. Pollack, *supra* n.19.

posals[29]; the Council's key role in the law-making process; the ability of Member States to seek judicial review under Article 230 EC to ensure that Community action remains within the legal confines of its Treaty mandate[30]; and periodic IGC Treaty negotiations to redefine that mandate. Similarly, only relatively recently has mainstream literature suggested the possibility of conferring legitimacy via agency-style bottom-up *participation* as an alternative to the parliamentary, top-down model of democracy.[31]

Having examined the delegation of *law-making* power by the Member States *to* the Community, we will now consider the delegation of detailed, regulatory *rule-making* and implementation power *from* the EC legislators.[32] Delegation from the EC legislators occurs to two separate agents.[33] On the one hand, and extensively,[34] the detailed implementation of directives is delegated back to the Member States. In this respect, the EC model of regulation differs from that in the USA, where implementation of environmental regulation is often delegated to the Environmental Protection Agency. The EC is not a direct regulator in this sense.[35] On the other hand, and less extensively, detailed rule-making power is delegated to committees. This, in Euro-speak, is the problem of comitology. Although little attention has been given to the issue until recently, delegation to committees on environmental matters is now a common occurrence.[36] For example, both the Waste Framework Directive[37] and the Hazardous Waste Directive[38] delegate to a regulatory committee the task of drawing up a waste list[39] and a hazardous waste list[40] respectively.[41]

[29] See the protocol on the role of national parliaments in the EU in the Amsterdam Treaty.

[30] See e.g. the *Working Time Directive* case (Case C–84/94 *United Kingdom* v. *Council* [1996] ECR I–5755, [1996] 3 CMLR 671.

[31] Craig, *supra* n.20; Dehousse, *supra* n.24; D. Curtin, *Postnational Democracy: The European Union in Search of a Political Philosophy* (Dordrecht, Kluwer, 1997).

[32] Ironically, the situation at Community level is thus the mirror image of the position at Member State level: while regulatory literature on the latter has tended to focus on the legitimacy of the delagatee—ignoring the legitimacy of the delegator—the focus of the literature on the former has, until recently, been the other way around.

[33] On agency theory at this level, see F. Franchino, "The Determinants of Control of Commission's Executive Functions" (1999) 3 *European Integration online Papers*, http://eiop.or.at/eiop/texte/1999-002a.htm; and *ibid*., "Institutionalism and Commission's Executive Discretion: an Empirical Analysis" (1998) 2 *EIoP* http://eiop.or.at/eiop/texte/1998-006.htm .

[34] Bignami, *supra* n.18, p. 487.

[35] The European Environment Agency has a predominantly information gathering role as opposed to that of a direct regulator.

[36] According to Franchino, the environment is one of four areas where more than 50% of new legislation has comitology arrangements ("The Determinants of Control of Commission's Executive Functions", *supra* n.33, p. 8). See further T. Gehring, "Bargaining, Arguing and Functional Differentiation of Decision-making: The Role of Committees in European Environmental Process Regulation" in C. Joerges and E. Vos (eds.), *EU Committees: Social Regulation, Law and Politics* (Oxford, Hart Publishing, 1999), p. 195.

[37] Dir. 91/156 [1991] OJ L78/32.

[38] Dir. 91/689 [1991] OJ L377/20.

[39] Arts. 1(a) and 18. This list, known as the European Waste Catalogue, was adopted by Commission Decision 94/3 [1994] OJ L5/15.

[40] Art. 1(4). This list was adopted by Council Decision 94/904 [1994] OJ L356/14.

[41] See also the IPPC Dir. 96/61 [1996] OJ L257/26 (Arts. 15(3) and 19), and the amended proposal for a Water Framework Dir., COM(99)271 final (Arts. 24 and 25).

The question arises yet again of what legitimates the exercise of delegated power by the Member States and by these committees? With Member States, the powers are delegated back to democratically elected Member State parliaments, which, having formally implemented the relevant directive in legislation, are then themselves likely to delegate to an independent environment agency for practical implementation.

With the initial delegation to Member State parliaments, one should again not conclude that the democratic nature of the Member State parliaments is sufficient to legitimise the delegation of power. Accountability is also called for to ensure that Member States remain within the mandate given to them—particularly given the trend in recent years to move from detailed, prescriptive directives to broader and more flexible mandates. The accountability provided is essentially legal. First, there is accountability to the Commission and other Member States,[42] through the enforcement procedure under Articles 226–228 EC. Reporting requirements imposed on Member States assist in this process. And, secondly, there is accountability to individual citizens or groups through actions in their national courts.

With subsequent delegation by national parliaments to environmental agencies, we effectively return to where we started at the beginning of the chapter, in that it is then a matter of ensuring the legitimacy of these agencies through accountability or participation. There is one key difference however, in that here, since the delegation to the agency is of *Community* power, the Community has an interest in ensuring that this accountability or participation takes place. The IPPC Directive is instructive in this respect, establishing, as it does, participation rights for individuals in agency permit decisions.[43] Whether this participation is pluralistic or civic republican will be up to the Member States.[44]

With committees, most of the focus so far has been on the accountability model of agency legitimacy: the aim has been to provide greater legal and political accountability of the agent to the legislative delegator that currently lacks power in the process—the European Parliament.[45] However, commentators have recently begun to stress the possibility of improving legitimacy through a more bottom-up, participatory process.[46]

[42] Rather than to the bicameral legislature of the Council and the European Parliament.

[43] *Supra* n.41, Art. 15 (cited by Scott, *supra* n.3, p. 192).

[44] As a local decision, it may be thought to offer the same opportunity for civic republican decision-making as Scott (*ibid.*) suggests that the structural funds present, with the presence there of local governance in a multi-level implementation partnership.

[45] Bignami, *supra* n.18, pp. 4626.

[46] See e.g. Bignami, *supra* n.18, Everson, *supra* n.21; and R. Dehousse, "Citizens Rights and the Reform of Comitology Procedures: The Case for a Pluralist Approach", RSC Policy Paper 98/4 (Florence, EUI, 1998). All three appear to recommend pluralist rather than civic republican participation. Cf. C. Joerges and J. Neyer, "From Intergovernmental Bargaining to Deliberative Political Processes: The Constitutionalisation of Comitology" (1997) 3 ELJ 273, who, in their theory of "deliberative supranationalism", suggest that the existing comitology system is deliberative. However, while deliberative, it lacks participation by outside interests and thus cannot be considered republican (see *supra* nn. 8, 14).

ACCOUNTABILITY

As was noted earlier, the expertise model of legitimacy in particular no longer holds much weight. Since Chapter 5 examines participation, the remainder of this chapter will thus explore in more detail the issue of *ex ante* and *ex post* accountability touched on in many of the preceding paragraphs.

Delegation of power from national parliaments to national agencies

In agency theory terms, the question we have been asking so far is how Parliament—the principal—ensures that its agent remains within its broad democratic mandate. In reality though, the situation is rather more complicated than this, because there are actually two levels of delegation involved in the implementation of pollution policy in the UK. In England and Wales, Parliament first delegates policy responsibility for pollution to the DETR,[47] to MAFF[48] and to the Welsh Assembly. And these bodies then delegate to the Environment Agency, which is an executive non-departmental public body (NDPB) or quango.[49] In Scotland, the Scottish Parliament similarly delegates to the Scottish Executive Rural Affairs Department (SERAD), which in turn delegates to the Scottish Environmental Protection Agency (SEPA)—again an NDPB. In Northern Ireland (NI), under direct rule, the UK Parliament delegated to the Secretary of State for NI who had direction and control of the NI Department of the Environment (DoE). With devolution, delegation is now from the NI Assembly to the NI DoE.[50] The NI DoE then delegates to the Environment and Heritage Service, which is a Next Steps executive agency within the Department rather than a NDPB. In all of the above cases, the agencies are thus accountable to two varieties of principal—on the one hand they are accountable to the minister responsible for the relevant government department or to the Welsh Assembly; and on the other hand, they are accountable to the relevant Parliament.

Not surprisingly therefore, there are two elements of *ex ante* accountability or mandate-setting involved. First, there is the legislative mandate set down by Parliament.[51] And secondly, there is a policy mandate and a budget set by the

[47] Department of Transport, the Environment and the Regions—previously the Department of the Environment (DoE).

[48] Ministry of Agriculture, Fisheries and Food. This has particular responsibility for marine and agricultural pollution policy.

[49] As opposed to a Next Steps executive agency. "A non-departmental public body (NDPB) is a body which has a role in the processes of national government, but is not a government department, or part of one, and which accordingly operates to a greater or lesser extent at arm's length from Ministers" (Cabinet Office, *Public Bodies 1998*, London, TSO, 1998). See also, *Executive Non-Departmental Public Bodies 1998 Report* (Cm 4157, London, TSO, 1998).

[50] At the time of going to press, the Assembly was suspended.

[51] This is stronger and much more explicit in the case of NDPBs, where the governing statute will typically set out the NDPBs functions; cf. executive agencies, where the statute may not mention the agency at all.

relevant minister or the Assembly.[52] In England and Wales, the institutional framework for the setting of these is described in the Environment Agency's Management Statement.[53] In relation to policy, the Statement spells out that the Agency should develop specific performance objectives and targets as part of its corporate planning process,[54] and that these should be approved by the relevant ministers (and now presumably the Welsh Assembly). Not only can the ministers (and the Assembly) set out any priorities, targets or specific action they require of the Agency as part of this periodic corporate planning process, but they are also able to issue specific guidance[55] and directions[56] to the Agency at any time.

There are, similarly, a number of directions for *ex post* accountability.[57] First, there is accountability of the agency to ministers and the Assembly. Secondly, there is accountability to Parliament. And thirdly, there is accountability to the public. An *ex post* accountability mechanism that is common to all three is reporting by the agency. The Environment Agency, for example, is obliged by law to provide a copy of its audited accounts, together with the auditor's report and an annual report of its activities, to the Assembly and to ministers.[58] In the latter case, the Secretary of State must then lay these before Parliament and must arrange for the annual report to be published.[59] Under the Agency's management statement, its annual report must include quantified output information on performance against targets set in the corporate plan.

[52] The power to appoint senior personnel is another form of *ex ante* accountability mechanism available to Ministers and the Assembly that helps to prevent the agencies diverting from desired goals. The power to dismiss is the corresponding *ex post* accountability mechanism.

[53] DoE, *The Environment Agency Management Statement* (London, DoE, 1996) (*i.e.* pre-devolution). This NDPB Management Statement has much in common with an executive agency "Framework Document".

[54] There are a number of levels to this. A long-term plan in contained in the Environmental Strategy (Environment Agency, *An Environmental Strategy for the Millenium and Beyond* (Bristol, Environment Agency, 1997). This is due for revision in 2000). Shorter term plans to implement this strategy are then contained in corporate plans (see e.g. in the case of England, Environment Agency, *Corporate Plan 2000/01* (Bristol, Environment Agency, 1999), and for Wales, Environment Agency, *Business Plan Wales* 1999/2000 (Cardiff, Environment Agency, 1998), and, at local level, in Local environment agency plans (LEAPS).

[55] See s.4 of the Environment Act 1995 and The National Assembly for Wales (Transfer of Functions) Order 1999 (SI 1999 No. 672). An example of guidance issued under s.4 before devolution is DoE, MAFF and the Welsh Office, *The Environment Agency and Sustainable Development* (London, DoE, 1996).

[56] See s.40 of the Environment Act 1995 and The National Assembly for Wales (Transfer of Functions) Order 1999 (SI 1999 No. 672).

[57] The Environment Agency's Management Statement (*supra* n.53) sets out a number of these. For a limited examination of the accountability of NDPBs in general, see further Cabinet Office, Central Secretariat, *Opening up Quangos: A Consultation Paper* (London, Cabinet Office, 1997); and the response, Cabinet Office, Central Secretariat, *Quangos: Opening the Doors* (London, Cabinet Office, 1998).

[58] Ss.46(3) and 52(1) of the Environment Act 1995; s.147(1)(b) of the Government of Wales Act 1998, and The National Assembly for Wales (Transfer of Functions) Order 1999 (SI 1999 No. 672).

[59] Ss.46(3) and 52(3) of the Environment Act 1995. There is no such duty on local authorities in relation to air pollution control. Sewerage undertakers, as private companies are required to issue annual reports as a matter of company law.

Reporting apart, the nature of *ex post* accountability to ministers and the Assembly, to Parliament and to the public is rather different. If ministers and the Assembly are dissatisfied with the Agency, they have the ability to revisit its policy instructions, its budget and can dismiss senior personnel. With Parliament and the public, McCubbins and Schwartz compare the "police patrol" oversight of the former with the "fire alarms" of the latter.[60] While the main focus below will be on English examples of these mechanisms, similar variants will invariably be present in other parts of the UK.[61]

Parliamentary debates, certain parliamentary questions,[62] parliamentary select committees, and audit all fall into the police patrol category: like police patrols, those involved with these activities cannot be everywhere at once and their oversight is therefore necessarily intermittent. Before considering their substance in more detail below, it is worth pausing to consider the respective roles in these mechanisms played by ministers and by agency chief executives (CEs).

First, it is customary to draw a distinction between accountability in the sense of providing an account, and accountability in the sense of responsibility, which connotes the acceptance of blame for deficiencies.[63] With both Next Steps agencies (the Northern Ireland Environment and Heritage Service) and NDPBs (the Environment Agency and SEPA), Ministers are conventionally accountable in the blame sense for policy decisions, and agency CEs for operational ones. Either may thus be expected to resign in appropriately serious circumstances. However, with regard to accountability in the sense of providing an account, the two types of agency differ. With Next Steps agencies, ministers reply to parliamentary questions (PQs) on policy matters and refer PQs on operational matters to agency CEs. Answers by CEs to these questions are published in Hansard in the same way as ministerial replies. However, if an MP is not satisfied with the answer given by the CE, she can always appeal to a minister and ask the minister to intervene.[64] And while Next Steps agency CEs can appear before select committees, they are civil servants and they thus give evidence on behalf of the minister and subject to that minister's instruction.[65] They are not, in other words, directly accountable to the committee—they are accountable through the minister.

With NDPBs, while ministers similarly reply to PQs on policy matters and refer PQs on operational matters to agency CEs, these replies are not published in Hansard. In addition, there is in theory nothing an MP can do if unsatisfied with the CE's reply. The position in relation to select committees also differs.

[60] M. D. McCubbins and T. Schwartz, "Congressional Oversight Overlooked: Police Patrols Versus Fire Alarms" (1984) 28 *American Journal of Political Science* 165.

[61] Where possible, these variants will be pointed out in footnotes below.

[62] Those not stemming from individual constituency cases.

[63] See HC Public Service Committee, Second Report, 1995/96, HC 313.

[64] *Ibid.*

[65] Cabinet Office, *Departmental Evidence and Response to Select Committees* (London, Cabinet Office, 1997) (known as the "Osmotherly Rules").

CEs may be required to appear before select committees, but since they are not civil servants, they can account directly to the Committee.

Of the various mechanisms, select committees and audit are arguably the strongest accountability mechanisms, because they adopt an in-depth inquisitorial approach, as opposed to the limited and adversarial nature of proceedings on the floor of Parliament. The body responsible for audit of the Environment Agency in England is the National Audit Office (NAO),[66] which in turn reports to the House of Commons Public Accounts Committee.[67] The NAO is entitled not only to inspect the Agency's accounts (financial audit), but may also conduct a value for money (VFM) audit in order to consider the economy, efficiency and effectiveness[68] with which the Agency has used its resources.[69] Although the merits of policy objectives cannot be called into question in these VFM examinations, consideration of policy effectiveness is a key concern. However, while the NAO issued VFM reports on the National Rivers Authority (NRA) and Her Majesty's Inspectorate of Pollution (HMIP),[70] it has yet to do so in relation to their successor, the Environment Agency.

As for other English parliamentary committees, although there are a number of these that touch on pollution issues, the most significant one is undoubtedly the House of Commons Environment, Transport and Regional Affairs Select Committee.[71] Under its terms of reference, this is responsible for examining not just policy effectiveness, but also administration and expenditure. Although in practice hardly any time is spent on the latter, it does illustrate that one cannot simply conclude that the NAO is responsible for financial accountability and the Environment Select Committee for policy accountability: the responsibilities overlap. In addition, although styled a *departmental* select committee, in common with other departmental select committees, the Environment Committee is responsible for oversight not just of the DETR but also of associated public bodies such as the Environment Agency.[72] Nevertheless, this means that the

[66] The relevant body for local authorities is the Audit Commission. In Northern Ireland, the Environment and Heritage Service is audited by the Northern Ireland Audit Office. In Wales, audit of the Environment Agency is now the responsibility of the Auditor General for Wales (s.147(1)(a) of the Government of Wales Act 1998 and The National Assembly for Wales (Transfer of Functions) Order 1999 (SI 1999 No. 672)). In Scotland, as from April 2000, SEPA will be subject to the Auditor General for Scotland (ss. 69–70, 120 of the Scotland Act 1998, and Scotland Act 1998 (Commencement) Order 1998 (SI 1998 No. 3178)).

[67] On the latter, see e.g. *Financial Management and Control in the National Rivers Authority*, Twenty Third Report, 1991/92, HC 216.

[68] The so-called "three Es".

[69] S.46(4) of the Environment Act 1995.

[70] *Control and Monitoring of Pollution: Review of the Pollution Inspectorate*, 1990/91, HC 637; *National Rivers Authority: River Pollution from Farms in England*, 1994/95, HC 235.

[71] Previously the Environment Committee. (And for the sake of brevity, the current Committee will be referred to as such below.) The equivalent committee of the Scottish Parliament is the Transport and Environment Committee; the equivalent in the Welsh Assembly is the Local Government and Environment Committee.

[72] As well as local authorities and water undertakers (the latter, in relation to regulation of discharges to sewers, appear to count as public bodies here). Recent reports that have considered the role of the Environment Agency, the DETR and these other bodies include: *Sustainable Waste*

Committee is not solely dedicated to the task of holding the Environment Agency to account. This has its advantages and disadvantages. On the positive side, it means that there is a "joined-up" approach to environmental policy scrutiny, since it will often be difficult to consider policy performance without examining the roles of both the DETR and the Agency. However, on the negative side, the Committee is also responsible for non-environmental matters that come within the DETR's remit (such as local government), which inevitably dilutes the amount of time that can be dedicated to the environment and the role of the Agency.[73]

Existing analysis reveals that the Environment Committee, particularly when under the Chairmanship of Sir Hugh Rossi, has been quite effective in holding the executive *as a whole* to account. One quantitative indicator of effectiveness is that the government, in its subsequent replies to the Committee reports, has accepted many of its recommendations.[74] Of course, to judge the Committee's effectiveness on this basis in holding the Environment Agency *in particular* to account, it would be necessary to analyse the number of recommendations relating specifically to the Agency that were subsequently accepted by the government. However, space precludes such an analysis at this juncture. In any event, as Hawes counsels, one should not read too much into quantitative measures of success.[75] The recommendations accepted by the government may be the minor ones[76]; and the effectiveness of committee reports is often a matter of "delayed drop" and influence rather than instant response.[77]

One of the significant disadvantages of "police patrol" mechanisms is that they are expensive: keeping a watchful eye costs public money. A "fire alarm", in contrast, is funded by a private party and alerts the authorities to a specific problem. Examples of fire alarm-type *ex post* accountability mechanisms include judicial review, the Ombudsmen, aspects of what used to be the Citizen's Charter, and complaints to MPs and associated parliamentary questions.

With judicial review, individuals bring proceedings, the aim of which is to ensure that the relevant public body has not acted *ultra vires*—in other words outside the powers delegated to it by Parliament. In practice however, this

Management, Sixth Report, 1997/98, HC 484; *Sewage Treatment and Disposal*, Second Report, 1997/98, HC 266; *The Environmental Impact of Cement Manufacture*, Third Report, 1996/97, HC 124. The last report in particular was highly critical of the Agency.

[73] This remains true despite the presence of a specialist sub-committee on the environment. A Cabinet Office consultation paper on quangos (*Opening up Quangos: A Consultation Paper*, *supra* n.57) recognised limited select committee scrutiny as a problem facing most NDPBs and, as a partial remedy, recommended, *inter alia*, that select committees scrutinised NDPB annual reports.

[74] See House of Commons Environment Committee, *Review of the Committee's Work 1983–1992*, Second Special Report, 1991/92, HC 340; D. Hawes, *Power on the Back Benches? The Growth of Select Committee Influence* (Bristol, School for Advanced Urban Studies, 1993), pp. 114–5.

[75] *Ibid.*, pp. 143–4.

[76] *Ibid.*, p. 104.

[77] *Ibid.*, pp. 114–5, 170.

mechanism has so far been little used in relation to agencies responsible for pollution regulation.[78] Indeed, in recent years there appear to have been only a handful of cases that have proceeded to the full hearing stage. Only two of these can be categorised as "public interest" challenges. In the *ex parte Greenpeace* line of cases, the environmental group challenged various decisions by HMIP and others relating to the authorisation of the THORP nuclear reprocessing plant.[79] And in *ex parte Gibson*,[80] local residents challenged a decision by HMIP to grant variations in IPC authorisations allowing the burning of substitute liquid fuels. In both, the substantive claims were unsuccessful. Industry challenges—though hardly greater in number—have fared rather better. For example, the claimants in *Meyer Parry Recycling*[81] and the applicants in *ex parte Dockgrange*[82] both succeeded in challenging the Environment Agency's interpretation of certain waste categories. Not all industry challenges have succeeded though: in *ex parte Petrus Oils Ltd*,[83] the court dismissed the company's challenge of a decision by the Environment Agency to issue it with a revocation notice.

It is relatively easy to pinpoint why companies do not use judicial review very frequently: they will typically have recourse to an alternative *ex post* accountability mechanism in the form of a statutory appeal.[84] Not only is this likely to be cheaper than judicial review, but also companies will invariably be required to exhaust this appeal route before seeking review.[85] Third parties, in contrast, cannot use these appeals procedures. Given that judicial review is their only option, it is difficult to establish an exact cause for the low number of public interest cases brought. It could be that there is simply little unlawful behaviour

[78] Most environmental judicial review cases involve challenges to *planning authority* decisions (see C. Reid, "Judicial Review and the Environment" in B. Hadfield (ed.), *Judicial Review: A Thematic Approach* (Dublin, Gill & Macmillan, 1995), p. 34, at 40–41; and, for a recent example, see R. v. *Bolton MBC, ex parte Kirkman* [1998] JPL 787). A number of other recent cases have involved statutory nuisance, which is not really regulatory in a continuing, anticipatory sense (see R. v. *Carrick DC, ex parte Shelley* [1996] JPL 857; R. v. *Falmouth and Truro Health Authority, ex parte South West Water Services Ltd* [1999] C.O.D. 35; R. v. *Bristol CC, ex parte Everett* [1999] 2 All ER 193).

[79] R. v. *Inspectorate of Pollution, ex parte Greenpeace Ltd.* [1994] 1 WLR 570; R. v. *Inspectorate of Pollution, ex parte Greenpeace Ltd (No. 2)* [1994] 4 All ER 329; R. v. *Secretary of State for the Environment and others, ex parte Greenpeace Ltd* [1994] 4 All ER 352.

[80] R. v. *Environment Agency and another, ex parte Gibson*, R. v. *Environment Agency and another, ex parte Leam*, R v. *Environment Agency, ex parte Sellers and another* [1998] All ER (D) 200.

[81] *Meyer Parry Recycling* v. *The Environment Agency* [1999] 1 CMLR 963, strictly speaking an originating summons rather than a judicial review case. However the difference is not of great significance here.

[82] *The Times*, 21 June 1997.

[83] R. v. *Environment Agency, ex parte Petrus Oils Ltd* [1999] JPL 839.

[84] See e.g. s.15 of the Environmental Protection Act 1990, which provides an appeal from the issue of a revocation notice under s.12.

[85] *Ex parte Petrus Oils Ltd*, *supra* n.83. See also the dismissal of Leigh Environmental's application for leave to apply for judicial review of conditions attached to its incineration authorisations: leave was refused on the ground that the Environmental Protection Act 1990 provided for appeals to be made to the Secretary of State (226 ENDS Report (1993) 44).

by pollution agencies, though this would make them rather unique in this respect. The low number can no longer be attributed to restrictive rules on standing for public interest challenges, as these have been liberalised in recent years.[86] However, cost no doubt remains a factor, which puts off interest groups and all but a few individuals who may receive legal aid. Cost involves not just the financial cost of bringing proceedings (including the possibility of having to pay the other side's costs if you lose)[87] but also the time-cost of keeping track of the technical minutiae of regulatory decision-making on pollution. Few individuals will have the expertise or inclination to check agency decisions, and the case law suggests that interest groups tend to concentrate their fire on macro-level policy or cause célèbre micro-level decisions such as nuclear reprocessing authorisations. Under-use of the pollution registers—information from which would form the likely basis for many micro-level judicial review claims—seems to confirm this picture.[88]

In addition, the substantive failure of most of the public interest, environmental judicial review cases that have been brought cannot have helped. While it is true that proceedings are often brought for delay or publicity purposes rather than in the realistic expectation of securing a public law remedy, the routine denial of remedies offers little hope for those applicants for whom delay or publicity are not important objectives. Alternatively, the failure rate may again be seen as simply confirming the low level of unlawful activity by environmental decision-makers. However, that would be to downplay the essentially political nature of judicial review. It is true that judicial review is meant to be a *review* of legality rather than an *appeal* on the merits,[89] but decisions in some

[86] An initial move towards liberalisation in *ex parte Greenpeace Ltd. (No. 2), supra* n.79 (on which see C. Hilson and I. Cram, "Judicial Review and Environmental Law—Is There a Coherent View of Standing" (1996) 16 *Legal Studies* 1) was furthered in *R.* v. *Somerset County Council and ARC Southern Ltd., ex parte Dixon* (1998) 75 P & CR 175, [1997] JPL 1030.

[87] *Cf. R.* v. *Secretary of State for the Environment and others, ex parte Greenpeace Ltd* [1994] 4 All ER 352, where Potts J exercised his discretion not to award costs against Greenpeace because of the public interest nature of the challenge (see M. Purdue, "A Harpoon for Greenpeace?: Judicial Review of the Regulation of Radioactive Substances" (1994) 6 *JEL* 337, pp. 341–2; see also Reid, *supra* n.78, pp. 47–9). More recent cases have awarded costs against applicants, but with a limited reduction to take into account "technical" illegality (see *Berkeley* v. *Secretary of State for the Environment (No. 2); Berkeley* v. *Fulham Football Club*, *The Times*, 7 Apr. 1998; and *ex parte Gibson* et al., *supra* n.80). The above cases involve the courts being generous on costs (in varying degrees) *after* the full hearing; only very rarely will the courts make a pre-emptive cost order *before* the full hearing in relation to public interest challenges (*R.* v. *Lord Chancellor, ex parte Child Poverty Action Group, R.* v. *DPP, ex parte Bull* [1998] 2 All ER 755).

[88] T. Burton, "Access to Environmental Information: The UK Experience of Water Registers" (1989) 1 *JEL* 192; J. Rowan-Robinson, A. Ross, W. Walton and J. Rothnie, "Public Access to Environmental Information: A Means to What End?" (1996) 8 *JEL* 18; T. Jewell, "Public Law and the Environment: The Prospects for Decision-Making" in T. Jewell and J. Steele (eds.), *Law in Environmental Decision-Making* (Oxford, Clarendon, 1998), p. 73. However things may improve with the recent introduction by the Environment Agency of the Pollution Inventory on the Internet. This enables the public to type in a postcode or click on a map to find out about emissions to the environment from industrial processes in any area.

[89] I.e. it is not sufficient that a reviewing court disagrees with the decision taken: it must be unlawful. Otherwise, unelected judges are effectively taking over the role entrusted to agencies by

fields and at some times are clearly more interventionist than those in others.[90] The environment is an area in which the judiciary has so far tended to adopt a conservative, hands-off stance rather than an interventionist one.

From the above, it is perhaps tempting to conclude that judicial review performs relatively poorly as an *ex post* accountability mechanism in relation to pollution control. However its utility cannot be judged solely by reference to the immediate success or otherwise of reported cases. A desire to avoid judicial review may promote good administrative practice within agencies, including a willingness to respond effectively to complaints made by individuals and interest groups.[91]

Cheaper and more accessible fire alarms come in the shape of non-court-based complaints mechanisms provided by the Ombudsmen and what used to be called the Citizen's Charter.[92] In relation to most of its functions, including pollution, the Environment Agency in England comes within the jurisdiction of the Parliamentary Commissioner for Administration (Parliamentary Ombudsman),[93] who in turn reports to a Commons select committee.[94] In England,[95] complaints to the Ombudsman must go through an MP.[96] And the Ombudsman has the power to deal only with complaints alleging maladministration. He will not investigate discretionary decisions taken without such maladministration that are simply unpopular. Neither is he likely to investigate complaints where an official appeal route is already provided, as is typically the case for the regulated (but not the public) with pollution regulation. Questions of legality which

Parliament. For similar statements along these lines in relation to the environment, see e.g. Mustill LJ in *Cutts* v. *Southern Water Authority* (1990) 4 LMELR 132 (full transcript on Lexis), and Potts J in *ex parte Greenpeace*, *supra* n.87.

90 Particularly given the flexibility of the *Wednesbury* ground of review.

91 For example, in 1991, Greenpeace successfully sought leave to challenge the National Rivers Authority's regulation of emissions from an Albright & Wilson chemical plant (see 201 ENDS Report (1991) 9). Greenpeace decided not to pursue the matter to a full hearing because, it claimed, the threat of proceedings had led to the improvements in emissions and in monitoring that they had been seeking (1992) 3(7) *Env. Law Brief* 61 (though *cf.* 206 ENDS Report (1992) 10). In other words, the background threat of judicial review may be as important as its actual use.

92 Now known as Service First—the new charter programme (see http://www.cabinet-office.gov.uk/servicefirst/).

93 In Northern Ireland, the Environment and Heritage Service is subject to the Parliamentary Ombudsman for Northern Ireland. In Scotland, SEPA is subject to the Scottish Parliamentary Commissioner for Administration—see the Scotland Act 1998 (Transitory and Transitional Provisions) (Complaints of Maladministration) Order 1999 (SI 1999 No. 1351). In Wales, the Welsh Administration Ombudsman again covers most of the Agency's functions (s.111 of the Government of Wales Act 1998 and Sched. 9, Pt. II). Local authorities in England and Wales are covered by the Local Commissioner for Administration (the Local Government Ombudsman), as is the Environment Agency in England and Wales in relation to its flood defence and land drainage functions. Sewerage undertakers in England and Wales are not subject to the jurisdiction of the Commissioners in relation to trade effluent consents. Complaints here go instead to the Customer Service Committees set up by the Director General of Water Services (OFWAT).

94 The Select Committee on Public Administration. However, whereas with the National Audit Office it is a police patrol of a police patrol, here it is a police patrol of fire alarms.

95 And in Scotland and Northern Ireland, but not in Wales.

96 The so-called "MP filter".

are better suited to judicial review are equally not within his remit, though a precise line between legality and maladministration may be difficult to draw. In 1998–9, the Parliamentary Ombudsman had a total of 21 complaints against the Environment Agency to deal with. Of these, one was held to be partly justified, four partly justified, two were carried forward to the next year, and the remaining 14 were rejected.[97] It is difficult to establish how many of these complaints related to the Agency's pollution functions. However, the only cases relating to the Agency that appear in the Ombudsman's recent "Selected Cases" reports involve fisheries and abstraction.[98]

The Citizen's Charter—Mr Major's "big idea"—was a ten-year government programme launched in 1991, the aim of which was to raise the standard of public services and to make them more responsive to their "consumers". The Labour Government has since re-launched the programme under a new name—Service First. But while there have been some changes in emphasis, many of the individual charters in existence still remain much the same. Broadly speaking, they all aim to set out the standards of service the public can expect and to provide effective complaints mechanisms and redress if these standards are not met. Various charter documents relating to the environment were issued in the period 1991–3. The DoE,[99] for example, in 1991 published a Citizen's Charter guide to the environment entitled *Green Rights and Responsibilities*.[100] In 1993, the DoE Central and Local Government Forum issued a model local environment charter,[101] and a charter guide to development control was published by the DoE's National Planning Forum.[102] However, this material did not receive anything like the kind of attention that charters in other areas received. One reason for this is probably that these initial environmental charter documents did little more than point the public to existing legislative entitlements. They did not, as the Patient's Charter did, set out standards unique to the charter and provide avenues of redress if these standards were not met.

Later charters issued by the NRA and HMIP did set out distinct standards of service and complaints procedures. However, pollution control is undoubtedly different from many other areas of public service. The relationship between citizens and pollution regulators is not the direct consumerist one that prevails in many other charter areas such as the Taxpayer's Charter or the Patient's Charter. The NRA and HMIP charters, and now the Environment Agency Customer Charter,[103] all acknowledge that pollution regulators have a range of

[97] PCA, *Annual Report 1998–99*, HC 572, Appendix A, Fig. 9.

[98] PCA, *Selected Cases and Summaries of Some Completed Investigations October 1998–March 1999*, HC 571, p. 184. Case Nos. C.1181/95 and C.400/96.

[99] Department of the Environment—now the DETR.

[100] DoE, *Green Rights and Responsibilities: A Citizen's Guide to the Environment* (London, DoE, 1991).

[101] DoE, *Your Council and the Environment: The Model Local Environment Charter* (London, DoE, 1993).

[102] DoE, *A Charter Guide: Development Control* (London, DoE, 1993).

[103] Environment Agency, *Customer Charter: A Guide to Our Services and Standards* (2nd edn, Bristol, Environment Agency, 1997).

"customers".[104] However, the main customers are arguably the regulated and the public. Both of these groups have an interest in "office-type" service standards such as response times for inquiries, complaints, permit applications and so on. But while the Agency's Customer Charter is strong on this type of standard, it is less strong on environmental protection standards, which are likely to be of greatest concern to the public. All that the Charter contains is a list of very general aims regarding the environment; there are no specific environmental targets that citizens are entitled to expect. To an extent this is understandable however. After all, the Charter is essentially a static document, whereas environmental targets are dynamic. The current practice of setting out these dynamic targets in corporate plans and publishing performance against them in annual reports is thus arguably more appropriate. The only weakness is that this offers no complaints procedure for the public when targets are not met—normally an integral part of the Charter machinery.

Delegation of power from national parliaments to the EC

Given the degree to which the UK has traditionally guarded its sovereignty, it is perhaps no surprise that there is a greater focus on *ex ante* accountability than on accountability of an *ex post* kind. The aim is very much that of shaping the mandate before the event—in terms both of Treaty revisions and specific items of legislation—in preference to trying to control it afterwards. Thus, with political accountability, one finds that the terms of reference of the two UK Parliamentary scrutiny select committees on Europe—the House of Commons Select Committee on European Scrutiny[105] and the House of Lords Select Committee on the European Communities[106]—focus on scrutiny of *proposed* Community legislation rather than on the efficacy of *existing* policy.[107] Although a well-known House of Lords' report on implementation considered existing policy,[108] even this was technically still a response to a Commission consultation document. This focus on proposals makes sense: while many have noted the respect which the House of Lords' reports command amongst the Community institutions,[109] *ex post* reports on existing policies would ulti-

[104] In the case of the Environment Agency Charter (*ibid.*), a customer is defined as anyone who contacts the Agency.

[105] It has been called this since Dec. 1998. It was previously known as the Select Committee on European Legislation. The Select Committee may recommend that proposals are considered further by one of the European Standing Committees or, exceptionally, on the floor of the House. In the case of environmental proposals, the relevant European Standing Committee is Committee A.

[106] Sub-committee C of which considers environment, consumer and public health proposals.

[107] In Scotland, the Transport and the Environment Committee of the Scottish Parliament examines, *inter alia*, EU environment proposals.

[108] *Report on the Implementation and Enforcement of Environmental Legislation*, Ninth Report, 1991/92, HL 53.

[109] C. Harlow, "Citizen Access to Political Power in the European Union", Working Paper RSC No. 99/2 (Florence, EUI, 1999), p. 11.

mately lack teeth. However, the focus on proposals arguably makes less sense than it did in the past: with the increasing use of qualified majority voting in the Council in recent years, *ex ante* control of secondary legislation by Member States has diminished. Not surprisingly therefore, Member States such as the UK have resorted instead to the *ex post* legal accountability mechanism of judicial review of Community action under Article 230 EC.[110]

What is striking at this level is the absence of a "fire alarm" role for citizens. Member States carry out a limited police patrol, but individuals and groups in environmental cases will invariably lack standing to challenge Community action before the ECJ under Article 230.[111] The most significant accountability mechanism available to them is the European Ombudsman. However, as with his domestic counterpart, this simply enables citizens to ensure that the Community is acting within a general mandate to observe good administrative practice. It does not—as judicial review would—enable them to ensure that the Community is not stepping outside its legal mandate.

Delegation by the EC to Member States and Committees

With delegation to Member States, there is a system of reporting by Member State agents which helps to alert the Community principal of any breaches of the mandate. We saw earlier that reporting tends to be supplemented by police patrols and fire alarms. However, here, there are simply too many Member State agents for the principal to patrol effectively. Although a skeleton patrol is provided, anything more would be beyond the Community's limited budget. There is thus a much greater reliance on the cheaper fire alarm method. Not only do individuals alert the Commission to Member State infringements under the Article 226 EC complaints procedure, but they also bring actions in their national courts to enforce their Community rights or interests.[112] In the UK, most environmental judicial review cases are now of this kind: their aim can be seen as one of keeping the UK within its Community mandate.[113] But judicial review is not the only type of action brought. In *Bowden* v. *South-West Services Ltd*,[114] for example, a shell-fisherman brought an ordinary civil action for

[110] E.g. the *Working Time Directive* case, *supra* n.30.

[111] See e.g. Case C321/95 P *Stichting Greenpeace Council (Greenpeace International)* v. *Commission* [1998] ECR I–1651, [1998] 3 CMLR 1 (on which see C. Hilson, (1999) 1 *Environmental Law Review* 52).

[112] On Community rights and interests, see C. Hilson and T. Downes, "Making Sense of Rights: Community Rights in E.C. Law" (1999) 24 *ELRev*. 121. Community rights are not the same as the fundamental rights mentioned at the start of this Ch. Whereas the latter trump democratic preferences, the former enable citizens to ensure that EU democratic preferences are upheld (albeit potentially trumping national preferences).

[113] See e.g. *R* v. *Secretary of State for the Environment, ex parte Friends of the Earth Ltd* [1996] 1 CMLR 117; Case C-293/97, *R*. v. *Secretary of State for the Environment, ex parte Standley* [1999] 2 CMLR 902.

[114] [1999] 3 CMLR 180.

damages against South West Water, again based on Community rights. Both types of action ensure that all organs of the state—from the DETR and MAFF through to the Environment Agency and water companies—are held accountable.

However, the previous attitude of the UK courts to EC-based environmental law actions meant that this accountability mechanism was in practice extremely weak. In the past, few, if any, such actions succeeded[115]—more often than not because of a questionable interpretation of EC law. Golub has suggested that the courts were unwilling to make Article 177 EC (now Article 234) references to seek guidance on interpretation because they saw themselves as gatekeepers to the traditional, pragmatic British approach to the environment and were unwilling to yield power to a more environmentalist European Court of Justice (ECJ).[116] There are, however, signs of a possible change of approach: in a notable recent case, the English High Court made its first reference to the ECJ in an environmental case.[117]

As for delegation to committees (comitology) by the bicameral Community legislature, there is strong *ex ante* political accountability to the Council, but little *ex ante* political accountability to the European Parliament. There is nevertheless *ex post* legal accountability to the Parliament, as illustrated by *Parliament* v. *Council*, where the Parliament successfully challenged committee legislation that took the Council outside its powers.[118] *Ex post* legal accountability stops there however, because there is invariably no standing for environmental interests before the ECJ:[119] here again, there are no fire alarms in relation to this form of delegated power.

[115] See C. Hilson, "Community Rights in Environmental Law: Rhetoric or Reality" in J. Holder (ed.), *The Impact of EC Environmental Law in the United Kingdom* (Chichester, John Wiley & Sons, 1997), p. 51.

[116] J. Golub, "Rethinking the Interaction Between National Courts and the European Court of Justice" (1996) 19 *West European Politics* 360.

[117] *Ex parte Standley*, *supra* n.113.

[118] Case C–303/94 [1996] ECR I–2943.

[119] See the *Greenpeace* case, *supra* n.111.

5

Deciding Regulatory Goals

How should regulatory goals or standards be set? Which tools ought to be used in the decision-making process? And how strict or weak should a standard or goal be? The answers to all of these questions are highly contested. The aim of this chapter is to discuss different models of decision-making and thus to explore this contested territory. The chapter will set out a number of ideal-typical methods for deciding appropriate pollution targets and will examine, in particular, the implications which each of these has for democracy and accountability.

MODELS OF DECISION-MAKING

The models or ideal types can be divided broadly into the approaches of nature, economics and politics.[1] The nature approach favours the setting of standards using a strong version of the precautionary principle, and strong sustainability[2] or critical loads, in order to achieve a pre-industrial state of nature. The economics approach favours the use of cost-benefit analysis (CBA) to set regulatory goals. And, finally, the politics approach has pollution goals decided discursively. As will be seen, while the results achieved by one of these approaches may in some circumstances be consistent with the results suggested by one of the other methods, more often than not those will conflict.

A brief caveat is necessary here. The three model approaches set out above are obviously not exactly replacements because they come from different points in the decision-making process: CBA is a tool used by decision-makers; a discursive approach is not necessarily concerned with tools, but rather with who participates in the decision and how that participation is structured; and the precautionary principle, sustainability and critical loads approaches represent actual outcomes of a decision rather than the process by which it is reached. Nevertheless, there is considerable value in considering them as alternatives,

[1] For similar approaches, see R. Ramchandani and D. Gourlay, "Alternative Approaches to Setting Effluent Quality Standards" (1992) 11 *IEM* 10; M. Jacobs, "Environmental Valuation, Deliberative Democracy and Public Decision-Making Institutions" in J. Foster (ed.), *Valuing Nature? Ethics, Economics and the Environment* (London, Routledge, 1997), p. 211; R. Kerry Turner, D. Pearce and I. Bateman, *Environmental Economics: An Elementary Introduction* (London, Harvester Wheatsheaf, 1994), pp. 190–201; T. O. McGarity, "Media-Quality, Technology, and Cost-Benefit Balancing Strategies For Health and Environmental Regulation" (1983) 46 *Law and Contemporary Problems* 159.

[2] As opposed to weak sustainability considered in Ch. 1.

because they can be seen as models of existing, real-world positions: the strong precautionary principle, along with critical loads and strong sustainability, is essentially a strong environmentalist approach; CBA represents the favoured approach of mainstream environmental economists, and discursive decision-making is the approach of civic republicans. Instead of "nature", "economics" and "politics", the three approaches could thus equally be labelled "ecologism", "economism" and "republicanism" respectively.

Ecologism

Strong sustainability and critical loads

Weak sustainability, which requires the overall capital stock to be sustained, was criticised in Chapter 1 because of its unrealistic view of the substitutability of man-made and natural capital. Strong sustainability, in contrast, rejects substitutability, although it has in common with welfare economics an attempt to make sustainability into an operational concept of use to regulatory policy-makers. Strong sustainability has been defined as requiring a constant stock of *natural* capital to be sustained.[3] And this constancy is typically expressed in physical rather than monetary terms. In other words, while it would, in theory, be possible to provide all natural capital assets with an economic valuation, and to say that it is the value of the total stock of these that must remain constant, this is not the route taken by most proponents of strong sustainability.[4] Instead, in the context of pollution, constancy is expressed in physical terms, as a rule that ecological quality should not deteriorate over time. With *degradable* wastes (such as sewage[5] or sulphur dioxide,[6] for example), this means that the assimilative capacity or critical load[7] of the receiving medium must be respected, because otherwise the wastes will build up in the environment causing harm, and ecological quality will decrease.[8] With dangerous substances, which are *non-degradable*, the situation is more difficult: these cannot be assimilated by

[3] See e.g. D. Pearce (ed.), *Blueprint 3: Measuring Sustainable Development* (London, Earthscan, 1993), pp. 16–27.

[4] Who are mostly suspicious of CBA, which would be necessary for such an approach.

[5] A key water pollutant.

[6] A gas that contributes to acid rain.

[7] As Ramchandani and Gourlay put it (*supra* n.1, p. 11), "[t]he environment can accept a certain level of effluent discharge without adverse biological effects. This is the assimilative capacity of the environment. The concentration at which damage begins to occur is the Critical Load concentration."

[8] M. Jacobs, *The Green Economy: Environment, Sustainable Development and the Politics of the Future* (London, Pluto Press, 1991), pp. 93–4. Nevertheless, there remains the question whether one might allow, for example, rivers in the South-East of England to decrease in quality, as long as this was matched by an increase in the quality of rivers in the North. In other words, does sustainability apply in respect of each watercourse, or does it apply only regionally or nationally, so that decreases in natural capital in some areas can be made up for by increases in another? On this, see e.g. Jacobs, *ibid.*, p. 97; Pearce, *supra* n.3, p. 73.

the environment at all, and it is very difficult to assess a critical load because we cannot pinpoint with certainty a level below which long-term damage will not occur.[9] This is where the precautionary principle comes into play—a principle that will be examined further in the section below.

The strongest approach to sustainability would be to have zero emissions of all substances. However, the strong version—based on a critical loads or assimilative capacity approach—allows for some human–environment interaction, but aims for no significant biological damage.[10] Nevertheless they share a vision of a pre-industrial state of nature. And a rapid implementation of this vision would come at considerable cost to society, even if the strong rather than the strongest version were used to achieve this. It is likely to be a much stricter approach than economism or republicanism would allow. With economism, cost benefit analysis (CBA) would weigh that high present cost against discounted future benefits and would invariably decide that such costs were not worthwhile in terms of human welfare. Republicans would say that paying that high cost should be a choice made within a discursive, democratic framework. It should not be imposed without democratic debate by authoritarian ecological mandarins.[11] They might add that, for those with a concern for the environment, there is a temptation to see a scientific "is" in the shape of critical loads, and to transpose this into a policy "ought". The apparent legitimacy of science and the natural can too easily become a replacement for democratic legitimacy.[12] A standard based on critical loads is a result; it should not be confused with the process of arriving at a result, which is where, republicans would argue, our attention ought to be focused. In reply, advocates of ecologism and strong sustainability would claim that it is not a matter of choice: we have an ethical *duty* to adopt a critical loads level. This ethical duty can be regarded as creating a corresponding right in nature, which acts as trump over our economic or democratic preferences.[13]

[9] See further M. MacGarvin, "Precaution, Science and the Sin of Hubris", and D. Bodansky, "The Precautionary Principle in US Environmental Law" in T. O'Riordan and J. Cameron, *Interpreting the Precautionary Principle* (London, Earthscan, 1994), p. 69 at 74–5, and p. 203 at 217 respectively.

[10] This approach recognises that any human activity is likely to have some impact on biological life, however small this impact may be. It also recognises that ecosystems are generally in flux, so that is not a matter of finding the natural level, but rather a level of ecosystem functioning judged by humans to be healthy—see Editorial (1993) 25 *IEM* 1.

[11] On ecological mandarins, see W. Ophuls, *Ecology and the Politics of Scarcity: A Prologue to a Political Theory of the Steady State* (San Francisco, Cal., W. H. Freeman, 1977).

[12] For a practical illustration, see D. Smith and P. Elliott, "Hazardous Waste and Technological Risk: The Limits of Science in Decision-Making" (1992) 2(1) *European Environment* 1. Greens might be accused of inconsistency in their approach to science: on the one hand they present scientific ecological limits as an uncontroversial basis for policy; on the other hand, they see modern science as the cause of our ills and wish to emphasise that science is not value-neutral, but rather has numerous moral and social implications: see M. Redclift, "Sustainable Development: Needs, Values, Rights" (1993) 2 *Environmental Values* 3 at pp. 3–4.

[13] Jacobs, *supra* n.1, p. 227.

Risk, uncertainty and the precautionary principle

A *hazard* can be defined as something which has a potential to cause harm. *Risk* is the *known* probability of a particular hazard giving rise to harm together with the seriousness of that harm. Thus, driving a car is a hazard. It is also a known risk because past accident statistics tell us that there is a reasonably high probability of being involved in a serious accident. In contrast, *uncertainty* exists where the risk is *unknown*—either because one cannot be sure that a potential hazard does give rise to harm, or where one is sure that it does, but one is unsure about the degree of harm which it may cause. With global warming for example, in the early days, there was uncertainty about whether increasing carbon dioxide levels were contributing to global warming. Much the same was true at the start in relation to the role of CFCs in ozone depletion and the role of sulphur dioxide and nitrous oxide in acid rain. However, with the ozone layer and acid rain, scientists are now reasonably certain that the above substances do cause harm, and they are also reasonably certain about the degree of harm that they cause. Uncertainty, in other words, has been wholly converted into known risk. With global warming, the conversion has been only partial: while scientists are now reasonably certain that greenhouse gases like carbon dioxide are contributing to global warming, there remains some uncertainty about the degree of damage that will be caused by such warming. Dangerous substances in surface and underground waters fall into this latter category: we know that these substances are harmful because of their toxicity, persistence or bio-accumulative nature, but there remains some uncertainty about the long-term effects of these substances on humans and flora and fauna, particularly at very low levels.

The essence of the precautionary principle is that, where there is a potential risk (or more precisely uncertainty), one should not wait for science to determine conclusively that the risk is real—one should take some precautionary action in the meantime. Thus, it was used to argue for early action on global warming, ozone depletion and acid rain, even when the scientific jury was still out on these issues. However, given that science has now established a link in such cases, the precautionary principle is arguably redundant in that context[14]; policy can now be governed by the strong sustainability/critical loads criteria considered in the previous section. Although not strictly relevant in relation to known risks therefore, the precautionary principle is nevertheless still relevant in remaining cases of total uncertainty (for example with genetically modified crops, radiation from mobile phones, and EMFs[15] from power lines) and in cases of partial uncertainty, such as global warming and dangerous substances.

The difficult question is how big does the potential risk have to be, and how much action should be taken? The strongest ecological version of the precau-

[14] N. Haigh, "The Introduction of the Precationary Principle into the UK", and J. Cameron, "The Status of the Precautionary Principle in International Law" in O'Riordan and Cameron, *supra* n.9, p. 229 at 241, and p. 262 at 275 respectively.

[15] Electro-magnetic fields.

tionary principle would require *effective* action to be taken against *all* potential risks, however small. A strong ecological version[16] would have *effective* precautionary action taken only to avoid a potential risk of *serious or irreversible harm*. Nevertheless, both are essentially hostile to "manufactured" environmental risks,[17] preferring a pre-industrial natural state where such risks were largely absent.

Applying even the strong precautionary principle to global warming would involve major, rapid reductions in greenhouse gas emissions. Applying it to dangerous substances could mean zero discharges and hence zero ambient concentrations above trace levels.[18] In other words, the strong approach is one that is cost-oblivious,[19] despite the fact that these costs are likely to be extremely high. If levels of dangerous substances, for example, were decided using CBA or discursively, it is by no means certain that a costly target standard of zero emissions would be chosen.[20] However, again, advocates of ecologism would point to the ethical imperative of a strong precautionary stance.[21]

Economism

Cost-benefit analysis (CBA)

CBA is being used here to refer to the highly specialised decision-making tool developed by economists, which provides a formal, systematic assessment of the costs and benefits of a proposed course of action. Where a non-specialist consideration of costs and benefits is being discussed, this will be referred to as cost-benefit balancing (CBB).[22] Under CBA, the aim is to achieve the optimal level of pollution control, where the total benefits of control outweigh the total costs by the greatest margin. In a "pure" model, this would be the level adopted.[23] However, in the real world, the level suggested by CBA would be just one input

16 The weak version will be considered below in the section on CBA.

17 As opposed to natural "external" risks—a distinction made by A. Giddens, "Risk and Responsibility" (1999) 62 *MLR* 1.

18 A strong approach can be found in D. Gee, D. McLaren and T. Crabtree, "Beyond Rhetoric: An Economic Framework for Environmental Policy Development in the 1990s", Friends of the Earth Discussion Paper No. 2 (London, Friends of the Earth, 1991). They state that the precautionary principle demands ambient standards of "no pollution" which can be translated into emission standards of zero emissions (p. 8).

19 A term used by W. H. Rodgers Jr, "Benefits, Costs, and Risks: Oversight of Health and Environmental Decisionmaking" (1980) 4 *Harv. Env. LR* 191 at pp. 201–2.

20 Bodansky notes that US environmental law has, for these very reasons, moved away from reliance on the (strong) precautionary principle towards CBA. He therefore finds it somewhat ironic that other actors seem to be moving towards use of the strong precautionary principle (*supra* n.9, p. 205).

21 See T. O'Riordan and A. Jordan, "The Precautionary Principle in Contemporary Environmental Politics" (1995) 4 *Environmental Values* 191, pp. 198–9.

22 Although rather confusingly, in much of the literature this is also often referred to as cost-benefit analysis.

23 Ramchandani and Gourlay, *supra* n.1.

into the decision-making process. In other words, the decision-maker is not bound to choose the CBA answer.

Costs are relatively easy to quantify and may include, for example, the cost of installing and operating pollution control technology, which has an actual market price, and the costs of administering a regulatory regime.[24] Benefits are the province of economic valuation which is concerned with the measurement of people's preferences.[25] Some preferences are uncontroversially revealed in actual market prices: a reduction in air pollution, for example, may lead to tangible savings in building maintenance. However, where there are no actual market prices, the task is to find some other way to measure people's preferences, and hence value. This is much more controversial. An indirect way of recording preferences is to rely on information from related markets.[26] Thus, "hedonic pricing" relies on differences in, for example, house prices[27] to reveal people's preferences for, and hence the value of, a particular environmental good (such as clean air). Similarly, under the "travel cost" method, expenditure on travel is used to value people's preferences for environmental amenities such as rivers or national parks. Alternatively, "contingent valuation methodology" (CVM)—a more direct way of measuring preferences—may be used. This generally measures people's preferences by asking them directly to express how much they would be willing to pay (WTP)[28] for, say, a reduction in pollution levels. The advantage claimed for CVM over the hedonic pricing and travel cost methods is that the latter can capture only use values, whereas the former can elicit both use and non-use values such as existence values.[29]

When CBA is criticised below, it should be borne in mind that criticism is being directed at the specialised version, which relies on controversial preference-based techniques for measuring the value of benefits, in particular, CVM. There is no doubt that some form of cost-benefit balancing (CBB)—which weighs the costs of environmental improvement with those benefits that are readily quantifiable, and with other benefits in a non-numerical form—is necessary in any sound regulatory decision-making process.

CBA has been criticised on ethical, political and methodological grounds.[30] As ethical objections—including, for example, CBA's anthropocentrism—were raised in Chapter 1, this section will focus on some of the methodological and political criticisms. One of the major methodological problems with CVM is

[24] Although the process is still far from straightforward: see McGarity, *supra* n. 1, pp. 181–3.

[25] See further D. Pearce, *Economic Values and the Natural World* (London, Earthscan, 1993).

[26] See DoE, *Policy Appraisal and the Environment: A Guide for Government Departments* (London, HMSO, 1991), p. 25 and Appendix C; Pearce, *supra* n.25, Appendix II. Both of these offer good introductory accounts of the techniques described below in the text.

[27] The price of a house depends on many other factors besides environmental amenity (e.g. shopping facilities, schools, transport etc.). By keeping these other factors constant, one can measure the environmental value component.

[28] Or, alternatively, how much they would be willing to accept (WTA) in compensation.

[29] E.g. how much you value the existence of a clean river that you may never use.

[30] S. C. Young, book review of *Valuing the Earth: Six Case Studies* (1992) 1 *Environmental Politics* 307.

people's unfamiliarity with the resource being valued and the practice of putting a price on it. People are used to paying for products like toothpaste and they know from experience how much they are willing to pay for it; the same cannot be said of clean rivers or clean air. Another problem is that while people are asked how much they would be WTP, they will not actually have to pay up. This means they are free to think up wild prices, unconstrained by their actual income and without thinking about how this extravagant expenditure may deprive them of other goods.[31]

There are various possible political objections to CBA. Before discussing these, it is necessary to bear in mind the models of administrative legitimacy outlined in Chapter 4.[32] Without this, the political objections to CBA are easily confused, with different discourses talking past each other. CBA poses problems under the accountability model of legitimacy. Although there is some truth in Helm's statement that CBA provides "a check on the exercise of regulatory discretion",[33] the question is whether the check itself raises greater accountability problems than the discretion. If environmental benefits are outlined in word form, the accountable decision-maker will be the one who weighs these benefits with the associated costs. If, on the other hand, environmental factors are included in numerical form, as economic values, the most important decisions are taken by the unaccountable analyst; after all, it is the analyst who decides on the appropriate methodology, and this determines the numbers that form the input into the decision that is eventually reached. Thus, while the ultimate decision is taken by somebody who is accountable, not by the analyst and while the CBA may be only one of a number of inputs into the decision-making process, CBA is presumably an important input; and the issue will to a certain extent have been pre-determined by the change in the form of the data from descriptive complexity to numerical simplicity. The discredited expertise model of legitimacy—the expert now being the analyst rather than the administrator—is in danger of replacing the accountability model.

In reply, one might state that these problems can be overcome by making the decision-maker fully aware of the assumptions and limitations of the methodology.[34] On this account, no information is hidden from the accountable decision-maker; no effective power to decide is transferred. However, this represents an extremely optimistic view. First, there is surely a danger that explanation will not occur. And secondly, one may question the extent to which an economist can fully explain the intricacies of supply and demand curves, differential calculus equations and specialist language to a generalist decision-maker

[31] See generally, Note, "'Ask a Silly Question . . .': Contingent Valuation of Natural Resource Damages" (1992) 105 *Harv. LR* 1981.

[32] These were: expertise, transmission belt, accountability and participation.

[33] D. Helm, "The Assessment: Reforming Environmental Regulation in the UK" (1993) 9 *Oxford Review of Economic Policy* 1, p. 8.

[34] See Rodgers, *supra* n.19, p. 198.

with limited time.[35] The numerical result of the CBA is likely to shine out as a beacon of light in the darkness of economic jargon.

If what has happened is in effect the further delegation of power to an unaccountable economic expert, the issue then becomes how one holds this economic expert to account.[36] To hold someone accountable, one must understand the basis for their decisions.[37] As we have seen, agencies are accountable on an *ex post* basis, *inter alia*, to the courts, Parliament and the public. Agency decisions based on CBA are not easily comprehensible by generalist courts, politicians or the public, and thus CBA threatens this form of accountability.[38] The task of explaining the assumptions and limitations of CBA to this wider audience may be even harder to overcome.

In reply to the above criticisms relating to accountability, one might then say that CBA is still democratic because it counts the "dollar" votes of consumers in real or simulated markets. (The advantage of this type of voting, it is claimed, is that, unlike traditional parliamentary voting, one can measure not just people's preferences but the *intensity* of those preferences.)[39] In other words, there is another kind of "surrogate political process" at work here,[40] with consumer sovereignty replacing parliamentary sovereignty. The problems mentioned earlier (of effective delegation of some power to the analyst, and the difficulty of the courts, the legislature and the public reviewing decisions the bases of which they do not understand), do not threaten accountability because the analyst is merely channelling more democracy from below in the form of citizen participation in, for example, contingent valuation questionnaires. In other words, as with the participation model of agency legitimacy, the accountability model is replaced by a bottom-up approach.

However, there are a number of problems with the above argument. First, the market is not democratic because some people are better off than others—it is not "one person, one vote".[41] Secondly, in relation to the point about the intensity of preferences, although it is true that normal voting will not reveal the intensity of people's preferences, this is generally not the context in which CBA might be used as an alternative. Rather than comparing CBA with normal voting, one should be comparing it with administrative decision-making, for it is at this level that CBA will often be used. If one does this, there *is* a model which is

[35] See B. Bennett, "Cost-Benefit Analysis, the Market, and Political Legitimacy" (1988) 23 *Univ. of San Fran. LR* 23, p. 63.

[36] See H. P. Green, "The Risk-Benefit Calculus In Safety Determinations" (1975) 43 *Geo. Wash. LR* 791, p. 806.

[37] *Ibid.*

[38] *Ibid.*

[39] See e.g. D. W. Pearce and C. A. Nash, *The Social Appraisal of Projects: A Text in Cost-Benefit Analysis* (London, Macmillan, 1981), p. 7; A. K. Dasgupta and D. W. Pearce, *Cost-Benefit Analysis: Theory and Practice* (London, Macmillan, 1972), pp. 43–4.

[40] To borrow the words of R. B. Stewart in "The Reformation of American Administrative Law" (1975) 88 *Harv. LR* 1669.

[41] Though one may nevertheless seek to defend this: see e.g. Dasgupta and Pearce, *supra* n.39, p. 38.

capable of revealing the intensity of people's preferences—a discursive, republican version of the participatory model.[42] Finally, with CBA, though the accountability model is replaced by bottom-up participation, this is far from the bottom-up participation of the discursive model. Participation in the latter involves having a voice to state and argue your case, whereas participation in the former means having a voice only to name your price.

Related to the final point above, a common criticism of CBA is that it merely aggregates unquestioned, existing preferences, whereas politics should be about reaching a conclusion based on debate amongst the citizenry.[43] However, it should be noted that this criticism is premised on the discursive, republican model and is perhaps therefore a little unfair. After all, until recently, our traditional regulatory arrangements for participation have tended to consist of sequential consultation of third party interests rather than a round-table debate involving all concerned citizens. Such arrangments are, in other words, no more discursive in design than CBA.

Having examined a number of criticisms of CBA, it is appropriate to look at two of the key defences that have been made in its favour. First, proponents of CBA argue that it can only be better for the environment than what has gone before.[44] Would the road through Twyford Down, for example, have gone ahead if a full CBA had been carried out? In other words, using economic valuation is better than leaving the environment unpriced. However, there is the issue of what in fact went before: it may be true to say that conventional CBA is better than a report which does not consider environmental benefits at all, or which lists them totally separately; but, that is not to say that it is better than a report which fully integrates non-numeric environmental benefits.

Furthermore, as Jacobs suggests, the results of CBA may be favourable to the environmentalists' cause, but on the other hand, they may not. One cannot be sure that it will only produce better results than those so far:

> Critics of monetary valuation tell environmentalists to beware. These methods may generate some useful results . . . but they can equally easily "undervalue" what conservationists regard as important environmental assets. Thus, for example, survey respondents may not realise a particular habitat's ecological significance, and so place a low monetary value on it . . . In these cases environmentalists might wish to override the results of the CBA. But if they have accepted the results of similar exercises elsewhere when it suited them, critics warn, they will find themselves (as it were) without a leg to stand on.[45]

One may add that it is not just results which concern environmentalists, but also the procedure used in reaching them. The medium is the message: prices do not

[42] Pearce implicitly recognises this: see Pearce and Nash, *supra* n.39, p. 17.

[43] R. B. Reich, "Public Administration and Public Deliberation: An Interpretive Essay" (1985) 94 *Yale LJ* 1617, p. 1637; M. Sagoff, *The Economy of The Earth* (Cambridge, CUP, 1988), pp. 10–11; C. Sunstein, "Interest Groups In American Public Law" (1985) 38 *Stanf. LR* 29, p. 32.

[44] See e.g. D. Pearce, "Toward the Sustainable Economy: Environment and Economics" (1991) 172 *The Royal Bank of Scotland Review* 3, p. 6.

[45] Jacobs, *supra* n.8, pp. 206–7.

elicit reverence and the environment becomes just another thing that can be bought and sold. Approaching the environment in money terms may thus encourage the very attitudes which caused its destruction in the first place. Tribe puts it thus:

> What the environmentalist may not perceive is that, by couching his claim in terms of human self-interest—by articulating environmental goals wholly in terms of human needs and preferences—he may be helping to legitimate a system of discourse which so structures human thought and feeling as to erode, over the long run, the very sense of obligation which provided the initial impetus for his own protective efforts.[46]

On the other hand, it has also beeen claimed that putting a price on the environment may help by horrifying us into action.[47] Being asked to quote a price for some aspect of the environment may cause some people to become aware of the environment for the first time, and discomfort at naming a price may spur them into action on its behalf.

Secondly, and related to the above, proponents argue that with CBA the environment will not be overlooked. Here, one might accuse environmental economists of sleight of hand. On the one hand they state that environmental benefits should be included in the analysis in numerical form to avoid being overlooked. Campen quotes a congressional committee:

> Whenever some quantification is done—no matter how speculative or limited—the number tends to get into the public domain and the qualifications tend to be forgotten . . . The number is the thing.[48]

Then, on the other hand, they claim that CBA is merely one input into the decision-making process and that other values will play a part.[49] This is having one's cake and eating it. If environmental values need to be included in numerical form to avoid being forgotten, then surely CBA will dominate the other non-numerical inputs? Either CBA and its numbers take centre stage or they do not.

Risk-benefit analysis and the precautionary principle

Although it is often applied to known risks,[50] strictly speaking, the term risk-benefit analysis need be used only when there is uncertainty about the relevant costs. With known risks, a cost figure can in theory be provided and measured against benefits within cost-benefit analysis. However, in areas of uncertainty—for example with EMFs or global warming—it is more a matter of trying to put

[46] L. H. Tribe, "Ways Not to Think About Plastic Trees: New Foundations for Environmental Law" (1974) 83 *Yale LJ* 1315, p. 1330.

[47] C. M. Rose, "Environmental Faust Succumbs to Temptations of Economic Mephistopheles, or, Value by Any Other Name is Preference" (1989) 87 *Mich. LR* 1631.

[48] J. T. Campen, *Benefit, Cost, and Beyond: The Political Economy of Benefit-Cost Analysis* (Cambridge, Mass., Ballinger Publishing, 1986), p. 68.

[49] Pearce, *supra* n.25, p. 35.

[50] See e.g. DoE, *A Guide to Risk Assessment and Risk Management for Environmental Protection* (London, HMSO, 1995).

a figure on an unknown risk and then comparing this with the benefit. This practice of risk-benefit analysis is closely associated with a *specialised*, *weak* approach to the precautionary principle. It is weak because, unlike the strong version, it places considerable emphasis on the balancing of costs and benefits. And it is specialised because it aims for an optimal risk strategy based on a fully monetised assessment of risks and benefits using CVM and other economic valuation tools.

Republicanism

The discursive approach to standard-setting builds on two traditions which have much in common—European critical theory (particularly the work of Habermas),[51] and US civic republicanism.[52] It involves setting standards on the basis of a public consensus reached via undistorted discussion. Legitimacy here is a participatory democratic legitimacy rather than the legitimacy of science relied on in the scientific ideal type discussed earlier. And unlike with CBA, legitimacy is conferred via community consensus: CBA does not involve discussion and consensus by the community—it merely aggregates existing preferences without testing these through the process of rational debate. The legitimacy of decisions reached via CBA is therefore open to question.[53] Republicanism is also hostile towards pluralism, which sees politics as a struggle among interest groups in a poltical market place.[54] Pluralism involves participation by interest groups in the political process but, as with CBA, private preferences are simply asserted without being shaped by discursive debate.[55]

There are, however, problems with setting standards on the basis of civic republican deliberation and consensus.[56] The first is that, from the point of view

[51] See e.g. D. Held, *Introduction to Critical Theory: Horkheimer to Habermas* (London, Hutchinson, 1980); for some practical applications of some of Habermas' ideas, see J. Forester (ed.), *Critical Theory and Public Life* (London, MIT Press, 1985); on Habermas' relevance to public law, see T. Prosser, "Towards a Critical Public Law" (1982) 9 *Jo. of Law & Soc.* 1; for discussion of critical theory, Habermas and ecology, see J. S. Dryzek, *Rational Ecology: Environment and Political Economy* (Oxford, Basil Blackwell, 1987), ch. 15, and R. Eckersley, *Environmentalism and Political Theory: Toward an Ecocentric Approach* (London, UCL Press, 1992), ch. 5.

[52] See M. Seidenfeld, "A Civic Republican Justification for the Bureaucratic State" (1992) 105 *Harv. LR* 1511; C. Sunstein, "Beyond the Republican Revival" (1988) 97 *Yale LJ* 1539 and F. Michelman, "Law's Republic" (1988) 97 *Yale LJ* 1493.

[53] Seidenfeld, *ibid.*, p. 1637; Sagoff, *supra* n.43.

[54] Sunstein, *supra* n.52, p. 1542.

[55] *Ibid.*, pp. 1542–5; Note, "Civic Republican Administrative Theory: Bureaucrats as Deliberative Democrats" (1997) 107 *Harv. LR* 1401.

[56] Both Seidenfeld and Sunstein (*supra* n.52) make it clear that civic republican deliberation to achieve consensus is not the same as negotiation (see Seidenfeld p. 1529, note 89; Sunstein, p. 1549). Perhaps the best known advocate of negotiation of environmental standards is P. Harter (see "Negotiating Regulations: A Cure for Malaise" (1982) 71 *Georgetown LJ* 1). Seidenfeld and Sunstein state that negotiation assumes a trade-off between competing private interests so that a compromise can be reached. Civic republicanism differs from negotiation in that it "involves an ongoing attempt at persuasion that has the potential to alter how all participants view the contested

of ecologism, the consensus reached may fail to respect the ethical imperative to achieve sustainability. As Dryzeck observes:

> Is it not conceivable that the individuals involved in discursive designs would reflectively and competently choose to downgrade environmental concerns in comparison with (say) economic prosperity or social integration?[57]

Reviews of Mark Sagoff's book, *The Economy of the Earth* have noted that author's tendency to denigrate working class tastes as against those of the middle classes.[58] They have also noted that, while he supports the idea of deciding environmental goals discursively, "he repeatedly characterizes deliberation in terms that reveal a systematic disdain for the uneducated or lower classes: 'a pack of yahoos'".[59] Yet while he is forced by his commitment to democracy to allow the "yahoos" to enter the discussion, he blithely assumes that they will not win.[60] While the possibility of downgrading cannot be ruled out (and it is by no means obvious that this would be instigated by the working class rather than the non-environmentalist, materialistic middle classes), Dryzek claims that this is unlikely if there is a sufficiently wide number of interests present and if communication is truly undistorted by ideology and strategic behaviour.[61] He also cites Paehlke, who believes that the experience of democratic participation so far has been on the side of environmental improvement rather than downgrading.[62]

A further difficulty with setting standards discursively comes in deciding who should attend the relevant deliberative fora.[63] At a local level, there is some evidence that public deliberation can be made to work[64] and because of the small numbers involved, there is no need to limit attendance. However, there are many other issues which need to be addressed, such as how representative the participants are of the local population, how to ensure that discussion is even-handed, how to ensure non-middle class involvement, and what counts as con-

subjects of debate". In other words, the process aims at acceptance rather than compromise. The UK Royal Commission on Environmental Pollution adopts a similar approach in rejecting a "stakeholder" model (which has much in common with negotiation) in favour of discursive approaches to eliciting public values (Twenty-first Report, *Setting Environmental Standards*, Cm 4053, London, TSO, 1998), ch. 7.7).

[57] J. S. Dryzek, "Ecology and Discursive Democracy: Beyond Liberal Capitalism and the Administrative State" (1992) 3 *Capitalism, Nature, Socialism* 18, p. 38.

[58] See e.g. E. A. San Juan, book review of *The Economy of the Earth* (1991) 15 *Harv. Env. LR* 307, p. 308.

[59] *Ibid.*

[60] *Ibid.*

[61] Dryzeck, *supra* n.57, p. 39.

[62] *Ibid.*, p. 27, citing R. Paehlke, "Democracy, Bureaucracy, and Environmentalism" (1988) 10 *Env. Ethics* 305.

[63] P. Wald, "Negotiation of Environmental Disputes: A New Role for the Courts?" (1985) 10 *Col. Jo. of Env. Law* 1, p. 20. It is details like this that many of the more theoretical writings on critical theory and civic republicanism fail to address. As with proponents of economic instruments, there is a tendency to call for something which sounds very attractive at a level of abstraction but which runs into problems when it comes to moving from theoretical abstraction to practical application (see J. Mashaw, "Imagining The Past, Remembering The Future" [1991] *Duke LJ* 711, pp. 726–8).

[64] See e.g. Reich, *supra* n.43.

sensus (majority vote or unanimity?).[65] If environmental groups are to attend discursive fora, there are potentially further problems of how to ensure that their expertise does not drown out the voices of ordinary citizens, which fora they select to attend (assuming there are too many for them to attend them all), whether they should be granted funding to do so and, again, their representativeness.[66] And of course, not all standards can be set locally because many pollutants have regional, national or transnational effects. Here, the above problems are compounded.[67] Where standards have to be set at a national, European or international level, problems of selection are likely to arise because of the large numbers who might wish to be involved.

Another, public choice-inspired point to be made is that this discursive form of decision-making is extremely unlikely to be introduced—at least in a "pure" form—because it takes power away from existing regulatory decision-makers.[68] Where experiments with republican-type techniques such as citizen juries have been tried, these have tended to be partial rather than "pure": the final decision-maker has remained the same; the thoughts of the citizenry have simply been included as yet another input into the decision-making process.

Finally, in line with the other sections, it is worth noting the discursive approach to risk. Decisions on risk and uncertainty would be treated in the same way as other types of decision: the risk would be discussed in a discursive forum and the process of rational debate would lead to a consensus on the appropriate risk management option.[69] This has the advantage of allowing public perceptions of risk to be aired, but also to be contested and possibly altered after rational debate. Decisions reached in this way may be as risk averse as the ecological approach to risk in the strong version of the precautionary principle, but they could equally end up being tolerant in relation to a particular risk. In any event, unlike with the ecological approach, the public get to decide. With CBA of course, the public could be asked how much they were willing to pay in relation to a particular risk, but the point is that this again just aggregates existing perceptions of risk, without subjecting these to critical scrutiny.

UK AND EC LAW AND POLICY

Having considered three ideal types for setting regulatory standards, this section will examine whether the UK government and the EC subscribe to the above principles as a matter of general policy and, if so, the extent to which their

[65] Wald, *supra* n.63, pp. 20, 24.

[66] See R. B. Stewart, "Regulation, Innovation, And Administrative Law: A Conceptual Framework" (1981) 69 *Cal LR* 1256, pp. 1346–7.

[67] See Dryzeck, *supra* n.57. On p. 37, he describes the question of unrestricted participation at this level as "more problematical" than at the local level, "though not intractable". Unfortunately, he gives no indication of how to solve these problems.

[68] Stewart, *supra* n.66, p. 1346.

[69] What O'Riordan and Jordan label "civic science" (*supra* n.21, p. 200).

conceptions of these principles differ. Where appropriate, it will also seek to provide some concrete policy examples where the principles have been put into practice.

Sustainable development

The EC commitment to sustainability is clearly stated in *Towards Sustainability*, the Fifth Environmental Action Programme adopted in 1992.[70] Alterations made by the Treaty of Amsterdam also place sustainable development at the heart of the EC Treaty. Article 2 now includes, as one of the tasks of the Community, the promotion of a "harmonious, balanced and sustainable development of economic activities",[71] and Article 6 states that environmental protection requirements must be integrated into Community policies, in order to promote, in particular, sustainable development. Sustainable development is not defined in the Treaty. The Fifth Environmental Action Programme adopts the Brundtland definition,[72] and adds that sustainable development entails, *inter alia*, "preserving the overall balance and value of the natural capital stock".[73] It is an anthropocentric account, which stresses the need to protect the environment in order to maintain and improve the quality of human life.[74] That said, in the context of the section on water resources for example, it states that the aim of Community policy is to prevent pollution and to restore surface and ground waters to an ecologically sound condition.[75] Although again, this is stated to be for human, instrumental purposes,[76] it is nevertheless a strong sustainability approach in that it stresses the need to restore ecological quality.

The UK government's first key espousal of sustainable development came in 1990 in the White Paper on the environment, *This Common Inheritance*.[77] Sustainable development was stated to mean "living on the earth's income rather than eroding its capital. It means keeping the consumption of renewable

[70] Commission of the EC, *Towards Sustainability: a European Community Programme of Policy and Action in Relation to the Environment and Sustainable Development* [1993] OJ C138/1. See further S. Baker *et al.* (eds.), *The Politics of Sustainable Development: Theory, Policy and Practice within the European Union* (London, Routledge, 1997).

[71] Pre-Amsterdam, Art. 2 spoke of "sustainable and non-inflationary growth respecting the environment". This was ambiguous, as the term "sustainable growth" is a term used by finance ministers independently of the environment, but is also suggestive of the need for economic growth to respect the environment. The new Amsterdam wording keeps "sustainable and non-inflationary growth", expunges "respecting the environment" and adds "sustainable development" as a separate element. This clears up the ambiguity because sustainable development is now clearly and uniquely associated with environmental considerations.

[72] "Development that meets the needs of the present without compromising the ability of future generations to meet their own needs"—World Commission on Environment and Development, *Our Common Future* (Oxford, OUP, 1987).

[73] *Supra* n.70, p. 21.

[74] *Ibid.*

[75] *Ibid.*, pp. 50–1.

[76] E.g. to provide a suitable source for drinking water.

[77] Cm 1200, London, HMSO, 1990.

natural resources within the limits of their replenishment. It means handing down to successive generations not only man-made wealth (such as buildings, roads and railways) but also natural wealth, such as clean and adequate water supplies, good arable land, a wealth of wildlife and ample forests."[78] This was followed by a dedicated policy document on sustainable development in 1994,[79] and—reflecting the change in government—by yet another in 1999.[80] The 1999 strategy refers to the Brundtland definition of sustainable development and states that "[a]t its heart is the simple idea of ensuring a better quality of life for everyone, now and for generations to come".[81] In line with Blairite concerns about social exclusion, sustainable development is expressly stated to be a people-centred concept,[82] which requires a careful balance of environmental, economic and social capital[83]—an approach that has been criticised on the ground that it risks "deprioritising" the environment.[84] In so far as the environment is singled out, the government's approach is stated to be based on "achieving overall improvements in environmental quality and, where overall standards are already relatively good, ensuring that they do not slip back".[85] Since this says nothing about respecting assimilative capacities or restoring ecological quality, it cannot be labelled a strong sustainability stance.

A clear policy application of a strong sustainability approach can be found at EC level in the shape of the new water policy and the proposed Water Framework Directive.[86] While first generation water directives adopted an environmental quality standard (EQS) approach,[87] and second generation directives

[78] *Ibid.*, p. 47. Although this mentions man-made and natural capital, it does not suggest that they are substitutable and thus it cannot necessarily be considered to represent a "weak" version of sustainability.

[79] *Sustainable Development: The UK Strategy* (Cm 2426, London, HMSO, 1994).

[80] *A Better Quality of Life: A Strategy for Sustainable Development for the United Kingdom* (Cm 4345, London, TSO, 1999). For the sustainable development functions of the newly devolved administrations, see e.g.: s.121 of the Government of Wales Act 1998 (which imposes a specific duty on the Assembly to make a scheme setting out how it proposes to promote sustainable development); s.4 of the Regional Development Agencies Act 1998 (which states that one of the statutory purposes of regional development agencies is "to contribute to the achievement of sustainable development in the United Kingdom where it is relevant to its area to do so"; s. 41 of the Greater London Authority Act 1999; Scottish Office, *Down to Earth: A Scottish Perspective on Sustainable Development* (Edinburgh, The Scottish Office, 1999).

[81] Cm 4345, *supra*, n.80, para. 1.1.

[82] *Ibid.*, para. 4.1, which goes on to state that "[s]ustainable development must enable people to enjoy a better quality of life, now and in the future. In the words of the Rio Declaration, 'human beings are at the centre of concerns for sustainable development. They are entitled to a healthy and productive life in harmony with nature'."

[83] *Ibid.*, paras. 1.2 and 4.2–4.6. "Sometimes discussion of sustainable development, particularly in richer countries, has focused mainly on environmental limits. But economic and social boundaries must also be recognised. An economy in long term recession is not sustainable. Nor is a situation where many people are denied opportunity and face poverty and exclusion. Development which ignores the essential needs of the poorest people, whether in this country or abroad, is not sustainable development at all" (para. 4.2).

[84] 292 ENDS Report (1999) 2.

[85] *Supra* n.80, para. 8.3.

[86] COM(97)49 final, COM(97)614 final, COM(98)76 final and COM(99)271 final.

[87] E.g. the Bathing Water Dir. 76/160 [1976] OJ L31/1, the Drinking Water Dir. 80/778 [1980] OJ L229/11, and the Surface Water for Drinking Dir. 75/440 [1975] OJ L194/26.

took a limit value line,[88] the new, third generation directive adopts a combined approach, using both limit values and EQSs.[89] The directive also differs from previous water directives in two key respects. First, unlike previous directives, it stresses the need for sustainable use of water in terms of both quality and quantity (consumption),[90] And secondly, it focuses on ecological quality with particular reference to biological elements of the ecosystem (flora and fauna). Previous directives were either explicitly aimed at other objectives (such as providing clean bathing and drinking water areas) but at the same time managed to achieve a degree of ecological quality incidentally, in some designated areas; or they were specifically aimed at ecological quality, but only in relation to a limited class of the biological community (for example freshwater fish), and again only in designated areas. The new directive, in contrast, makes *general* ecological quality a specific objective and applies it to *all* surface waters. It sets not just physico-chemical parameters,[91] but also hydromorphological parameters,[92] and biological ones which spell out the organisms that should be present. Member States will thus be required to monitor all of these. The former two are described as "supporting" standards, in that it is the status of those elements which affects the health of the biological community. One of the principal aims of the directive is that all surface[93] waters should achieve "good" status in ecological and chemical terms by the end of 2010—with "good" ecological status being defined as that "achieved by a body of surface water which is demonstrated to be significantly influenced by human activity, but which nevertheless has a rich, balanced and sustainable ecosystem". The aim can, in other words, be seen as one of respecting assimilative capacities in order to achieve a good ecological balance in line with strong sustainability.

In the UK, section 4(1) of the Environment Act 1995 states that:

> It shall be the principal aim of the Agency (subject to and in accordance with the provisions of this Act or any other enactment and *taking into account any likely costs*) in discharging its functions so to protect or enhance the environment, taken as a whole, as to make the contribution towards attaining the objective of achieving sustainable development.[94]

In acccordance with the remainder of section 4, statutory guidance with respect to sustainable development and other objectives was issued by ministers in

[88] E.g. the Urban Waste Water Treatment Dir. 91/271 [1991] OJ L135/40, and the IPPC Dir. 96/61 [1996] OJ L257/26.

[89] http://www.europa.eu.int/water/.

[90] Previous dirs. focused only on quality. The new approach recognises the fact that the latter (through excessive abstraction) can impinge on the former (reduced dilution means greater pollution).

[91] I.e. in relation to pollution factors such as heat, chemical oxygen balance, acidification and dangerous substances.

[92] I.e. ones affecting flow. Hydromophology can of course have a significant effect on biology, both in pollution terms (since decreased flow generally means increased pollution) and through the sheer presence of e.g. flood control systems.

[93] The dir. also covers groundwaters.

[94] Emphasis added.

November 1996.[95] The non-statutory explanatory document which accompanied this statutory guidance draws attention, at one point, to the central role of ecological criteria and the concept of carrying capacity.[96] However, the emphasis in section 4 on the need to take into account likely costs means that this is far from a licence for the Agency to adopt a strong sustainability approach. And in any case, the guidance is far from clear or consistent: carrying capacity is just one principle among many that are regarded as important for sustainable development; and at one point the guidance seems to support weak sustainability.[97]

Finally, it is worth considering the justiciability of the sustainable development objectives in the EC Treaty and the UK Environment Act 1995. Given that neither defines what it means by sustainable development, this will be a matter of interpretation for the courts. If the latter adopt the vague definitions of the Brundtland variety, then the objectives will clearly be non-justiciable: it would be virtually impossible for a court to decide if a particular policy action had achieved the wrong balance between current and future generations.[98] However, if the courts were to adopt an ecological carrying capacity interpretation, then review would in principle be available. However, neither the ECJ nor UK courts would be able to adopt a cost-oblivious strong sustainability interpretation: in the case of the UK, section 4 of the Environment Act 1995 makes it clear that the Agency must take account of costs in the context of its sustainable development objective, and Article 174 of the EC Treaty requires Community enviromental policy to take into account costs and benefits. The presence of these cost considerations means that it is extremely unlikely that anyone could successfully challenge a policy on the ground that it failed to achieve strong sustainability: the relevant authority would simply reply that the costs were considered too great, and it is hard to see any court interfering lightly with a discretionary judgement of that kind.

Critical loads

A critical loads approach has been explicitly endorsed as policy by the UK government[99] and by the EC[100] in relation to the control of air pollutants causing acid

[95] DoE, MAFF, Welsh Office, *The Environment Agency and Sustainable Development* (London, DoE, 1996).

[96] *Ibid.*, Part II, para. 3.7. See also the Environment Agency's own guidance on its sustainable development objective, which summarises the government guidance: SD1, *Introductory Guidance on the Agency's Contribution to Sustainable Development* (Bristol, Environment Agency, 1996, para. 7.6).

[97] DoE, *supra* n.95, para. 3.8; Environment Agency, *supra* n.96, para. 7.6.

[98] Though *cf.* S. Tromans, "High Talk and Low Cunning: Putting Environmental Principles into Legal Practice" [1996] *JPL* 779, p. 793.

[99] See e.g. *This Common Inheritance*, *supra* n.77, p. 144; *This Common Inheritance: The Second Year Report*, (Cm 2068, London, HMSO, 1992), pp. 99–101; and more recently, the 1999 strategy for sustainable development, *supra* n.80, paras. 8.26–8.27.

[100] See the Fifth Environmental Action Programme (*supra* n.70), reaffirmed more recently in e.g. Art. 11(2) of European Parliament and Council Decision 2179/98 on the review of the European

rain.[101] However, both are united in their support for what is effectively a weak version of critical loads; while they support critical loads as a target—conscious of the costs involved—they wish to move towards this target gradually rather than quickly. As the UK government's 1999 stategy on sustainability states:

> [i]n the EU and internationally, the Government presses for emission reductions based on sound science and a thorough assessment of all the costs and benefits. The Government supports the long term EU goal of not exceeding "critical loads" for acidification—levels of pollutant deposition below which significant harmful effects to the environment do not occur. The Government supports a gradual movement towards this goal, which could not be achieved quickly without unacceptable social or economic impacts, in this country and elsewhere.[102]

Initial EC legislation on acid rain was not based on critical loads. While the aim of the Large Combustion Plants (LCP) Directive[103] was to reduce the damage caused by acid rain, the stucture of the programme was such that emissions were not directly linked to critical loads under the Directive. All Member States were required to reduce their emissions of sulphur dioxide by 60 per cent by 2003 and nitrous oxides by 30 per cent by 1998, beginning from a 1980 baseline. Commentators noted the Directive's ability to over-regulate, citing the example of Spain, which had to cut emissions by the same amount as other countries despite the fact that it produces little sulphur which falls into neighbouring countries.[104] The 1994 UNECE[105] Second Sulphur Protocol was a partial improvement, in that it set individual, national targets linked to the contribution a state's sulphur emissions made to exceedances of critical loads.[106] However, the Protocol did not aim at bringing sulphur deposition below critical loads across the board, because this was considered to be too expensive; instead, a 60 per cent "gap closure" was to be the goal.[107] Having ratified the protocol in 1996, the UK's individual target was set as a 50 per cent reduction in sulphur dioxide emissions by 2000, 70 per cent by 2005 and 80 per cent by 2010. While the Second Sulphur Protocol is an international law instrument rather than an EC one,[108] it has provided a model for more recent EC policy on com-

Community programme of policy and action in relation to the environment and sustainable development "towards sustainability" [1998] OJ L275/1, and in the Commission Communication to the Council and the European Parliament on a Community Strategy to Combat Acidification, COM(97)88.

101 Although not explicit, the proposed water framework dir. (*supra* n.86) can be seen as endorsing a critical loads approach.

102 *Supra* n.80, paras. 8.26–8.27.

103 Dir. 88/609 [1988] OJ L336/1.

104 *The Economist,* 4 Sept. 1993, p. 18.

105 United Nations Economic Commission for Europe.

106 33 ILM (1994) 1540. The Protocol was introduced under the 1979 Convention on Long Range Transboundary Air Pollution (CLRTAP) 18 ILM (1979) 144. Earlier protocols, like the LCP Dir. had set a general percentage reduction target for all signatories.

107 See 233 ENDS Report (1994) 41, pp. 41–2.

108 A further protocol has recently been adopted (EB. Air/1999/1). The 1999 Protocol to Abate Acidification, Eutrophication and Ground Level Ozone is multi-pollutants (covering nitrogen oxides, VOCs and ammonia) and as its title suggests—multi-effects.

bating acidification.[109] The Commission is similarly of the view that the ultimate target of no breach ever of critical loads is too costly in the short term, and has thus proposed an interim target of 50 per cent gap closure by 2010. This requires the gap or difference between the level of ecosystem protection in 1990 and the ultimate target of total protection to be closed by 50 per cent by 2010. What this means in practice is that in each "grid cell" across the Community, the total area where critical loads were exceeded in 1990, should be reduced by a half by 2010.[110] Again, as with the 1994 Protocol, binding national emission ceilings for the various acid gases will be a key part of the strategy to achieve this target.

However, in setting *national* emission ceilings for acid pollutants, one might argue that even this more recent policy is still not sufficiently focused. Just as the LCP Directive tended to under- or over-regulate *between* nations, so the newer policy may still under- or over-regulate *within* the emission ceilings. Regulation *within* emission ceilings is, as one might expect, the province of national policy. So has UK regulation aimed at critical loads? In the UK, the 1994 Protocol, like the LCP Directive, was implemented via the national plan[111] and BATNEEC within IPC.[112] The national plan essentially shared out the national emission ceiling among the key players, in particular the power generators. Not surprisingly therefore, fulfilling the national plan did nothing to prevent breaches of critical loads at local level—as the Orimulsion controversy at National Power's Pembroke power station illustrates. National Power admitted that burning the fuel would spread acid rain over Wales, but argued that it was reducing emissions at other plants in Britain to meet the overall reductions required by the national plan.[113]

With BATNEEC, there is potential for tying plant emissions of acid gases directly to critical load levels. After all, section 7(2)(a) of the Environmental Protection Act 1990 requires that BATNEEC be used to "render harmless" any prescribed substances[114] that are released, and the concept of critical loads presupposes lack of harm. However, BATNEEC has the potential to under-regulate because all firms may be applying BATNEEC, but critical loads may still be exceeded: section 7 imposes a duty only to use BAT*NEEC* to render harmless, not BAT; it could be argued that while fitting BAT (such as flue gas

[109] See Commission Communication to the Council and the European Parliament on a Community Strategy to Combat Acidification, COM(97)88.

[110] *Ibid*., p. 31.

[111] DoE, *The United Kingdom's Programme and National Plan for Reducing Emissions of Sulphur Dioxide and Oxides of Nitrogen from Existing Large Combustion Plants* (London, DoE, 1990.

[112] Environmental Protection Act (EPA) 1990, s.7. Pt. I of the EPA 1990 has now been replaced by the Pollution Prevention and Control Act 1999 which implements the IPPC Dir. However, there is a transitional period for existing plants, which will be brought under the new regime in phases between 2001 and 2007 (the final date for implementation of the dir.). Until that time, plants subject to IPC will continue to be regulated under the existing system.

[113] 201 ENDS Report (1991) 7, p. 8.

[114] Which include the main acid gases.

desulphurisation) might achieve critical loads, this would come at an excessive cost in relation to the environmental benefit. BAT on the other hand may over-regulate: imposing BAT may be regarded as an excessive cost if there is no threat to critical loads. While HMIP seem to have been aware of these issues, they did little to clarify the uncertainty surrounding them and the Environment Agency does not appear to have taken matters any further. In 1993, the ENDS Report reported an HMIP consultation paper on BATNEEC and environmental harm, which suggested that there might be an attempt to "provide a mechanism to relate long-range environmental damage, such as acid deposition and low-level ozone formation, to emission controls on the numerous point sources".[115] However, according to ENDS, this idea was scrapped because HMIP felt it would be too difficult to disentangle the effects of numerous distant point sources.[116]

The precautionary principle

The first significant commitment to the precautionary principle as UK government policy took place in *This Common Inheritance* in 1990,[117] which stated that:

> [w]here there are significant risks of damage to the environment, the Government will be prepared to take precautionary action to limit the use of potentially dangerous materials or the spread of potentially dangerous pollutants, even where scientific knowledge is not conclusive, if the balance of likely costs and benefits justifies it. This precautionary principle applies particularly where there are good grounds for judging either that action taken promptly at comparatively low cost may avoid more costly damage later, or that irreversible effects may follow if action is delayed.[118]

In stressing the need to consider the costs and benefits of taking action, this is a weak version of the precautionary principle. There is, however, nothing to indicate that it is a *specialised* weak version: there is no suggestion that the costs and benefits taken into account must be fully monetised using CVM and related techniques. More recent government policy is similarly weak. The 1999 strategy on sustainable development begins by quoting the Rio definition, which states that where there are threats of serious or irreversible damage, lack of full scientific certainty shall not be used as a reason for postponing cost-effective measures to prevent environmental degradation, before adding that "[p]recau-

115 222 ENDS Report (1993) 16, p. 17.
116 231 ENDS Report (1994) 38, p. 39.
117 See further Haigh, *supra* n.14.
118 *Supra* n.77, p. 11. See also Cm 2426, *supra* n.79, which states that "[w]here appropriate (for example, where there is uncertainty combined with the possibility of irreversible loss of valued resources), actions should be based on the precautionary principle if the balance of likely costs and benefits justifies it".

tionary action requires assessment of the costs and benefits of action, and transparency in decision-making".[119]

EC support for the precautionary principle can be found in both the Treaty[120] and the Fifth Environmental Action Programme,[121] although neither provides a definition of the principle. Nevertheless, it is at least clear from the Treaty that the EC version too is weak: although Article 174 EC states simply that "Community policy on the environment . . . shall be based on the precautionary principle", it goes on to state that "[i]n preparing its policy on the environment, the Community shall take account of . . . the potential benefits and costs of action or lack of action".

The main area in which the precautionary principle has explicitly been held to apply at both UK and EC levels is in relation to policy concerning hazardous chemicals (otherwise known as dangerous substances).[122] This is true of legislation controlling the presence of such chemicals in drinking water,[123] release of such chemicals to the environment as waste,[124] and prior controls on the manufacture, marketing and use of chemicals as raw materials.[125]

The question arises whether the precautionary principle is a justiciable one. First, is the precautionary principle—along with the other principles in Article 174 such as the preventive principle and the polluter pays principle—justiciable as a principle of EC law? In *Peralta*, which involved the preventive principle, the ECJ ruled that "Article 130r is confined to defining the general objectives of the Community in the matter of the environment".[126] In *ex parte Duddridge*,[127] the English courts referred to *Peralta* in reaching a similar decision specifically on the precautionary principle. Both decisions seemed to suggest that the precautionary principle is a only a guide for Community legislative action, and is neither justiciable nor directly applicable in the Member States themselves.[128] However, more recent ECJ case law has indicated that review of the principles in Article 174 are justiciable in so far as review will lie against Comminty

[119] Cm 4345, *supra* n.80, para. 4.1.

[120] The principle was first introduced at Maastricht.

[121] *Supra* n.70, p. 24. See further Haigh, *supra* n.14. And see now COM(2000) 1.

[122] See, respectively, paras. 4.2 and 8.6 of Cm 4345, *supra* n.80, and Art. 11(7)(c) of Decision 2179/98, *supra* n.100.

[123] See the revised Drinking Water Dir. 98/83 [1998] OJ L330/32.

[124] E.g. chemicals released to surface and marine waters: see e.g. DETR, *Sustainable Production and Use of Chemicals: Consultation Paper on Chemicals in the Environment* (London, DETR, 1998), para. 5.12–5.13, and Cm 4345, *supra* n.80, para. 8.35. For a recent EC example, see the preamble to the proposed Water Framework Dir. (*supra* n.86), which states that "[w]hereas the precautionary principle and the principle of prevention at source require that pollution through the discharge of various dangerous substances be eliminated".

[125] However, few *existing* items of chemicals legislation refer explicitly to the principle, which is not surprising given the principle's relatively recent introduction into the Treaty (*cf. supra* n.120).

[126] Case C–379/92 [1994] ECR I–3453 at para. 57.

[127] *R.* v. *Secretary of State for Trade and Industry, ex parte Duddridge* [1995] Env. LR 151, (1996) P & CR 350 (CA).

[128] See J. Holder, "Safe Science? The Precautionary Principle in UK Environmental Law" in J. Holder (ed.), *The Impact of EC Environmental Law in the United Kingdom* (Chichester, Wiley, 1997), p. 123 at 130–1.

institutions if there has been a manifest error in applying the principles in the context of a particular measure.[129]

Since the precautionary principle is also a UK principle, is it justiciable as a matter of UK law? In *ex parte Duddridge*, the relevant statement of the principle was that found in *This Common Inheritance* described above. The applicants contended that the requirement there that action be taken only where there are "significant risks" (from EMFs) was the wrong interpretation of the precautionary principle. Instead, they argued that it required action as soon as *any possible* risk was demonstrated, even though the science was uncertain and no causal connection between EMFs and leukaemia could be proved. Although the courts rejected this argument, holding that the government was free to choose whatever interpretation of the principle it wanted, the case does suggest that future decisions could be declared unlawful, not just on the basis of irrationality, but also if the government failed to follow its own interpretation of the principle. However, it will be very difficult in most cases to show that a particular judgement on risk was unreasonable and—given the breadth of the various policy definitions—no easier to show that a decision was contrary to policy.

Cost-benefit assessment

Cost-benefit assessment (whether CBA or CBB) can be applied at different levels of the regulatory process. The principal distinction is between assessment of costs and benefits of general policy or specific legislative proposals on the one hand, and assessment of the costs and benefits of operational regulatory decisions on the other.

In relation to the former, the Single European Act first introduced a cost benefit duty for EC environmental policy in 1987. This is now to be found in Article 174 of the Treaty, which states that "[i]n preparing its policy on the environment, the Community shall take account of . . . the potential benefits and costs of action or lack of action". This wording raises a number of questions. First, does policy mean just general policy or does it include every item of legislation? Although Kramer suggests the former,[130] it is submitted that the term policy can easily include the latter, and that this is preferable in terms of ensuring the cost-effectiveness of all Community measures. Secondly, is the duty to take account of costs and benefits a justiciable one? Although there have been no specific cases on the matter, the logic of the *Bettati* case, considered earlier,[131] suggests that it should be. However, it seems likely that only procedural and not substantive review would be available. In other words, a Commission policy introduced

[129] Case C–284/95 *Safety Hi-Tech* v. *S & T* [1998] ECR I–4301, para. 64; and Case C–341/95 *Bettati* v. *Safety Hi-Tech* [1998] ECR I–4355, para. 35 (*Bettati*).

[130] L. Krämer, *EC Treaty and Environmental Law* (2nd edn., London, Sweet & Maxwell, 1995), p. 78. He makes a similar point about the other principles in Art. 174—see p. 63.

[131] *Supra* n.129.

with no account taken of costs and benefits might be annulled, but the Court would be most unlikely to interfere with the Commission's discretionary assessment of the relative balance of costs and benefits.

And, finally, does the duty require a specialised CBA or only a more general CBB? It is submitted that the latter is all that is required.[132] However, for quite some time after the introduction of the duty in 1987 the answer remained rather academic, as *neither* was being *explicitly* and transparently undertaken.[133] As late as 1992, in its Sixteenth Report, the UK Royal Commission on Environmental Pollution (RCEP) was calling for EC environmental directives to be subject to some form of cost-benefit assessment.[134] In the same year, the Fifth Environmental Action Programme stated that "although the value of many environmental assets is difficult to measure in monetary terms and, in the case of particularly important or rare elements should not be priced in any event, valuations, pricing and accounting mechanisms have a pivotal role to play in the achievement of sustainable development",[135] before proceeding to advocate the "development of meaningful cost/benefit analysis methodologies and guidelines in respect of policy measures and actions which impinge on the environment and the natural resource stock".[136] In recent years, this process has been aided by an economics unit that has been established within DG XI. This unit assists the technical units (covering air, water pollution and so on) in determining the costs and benefits of policy proposals—with benefits including figures derived from contingent valuation studies.[137]

However, while this economic unit carries out specialised CBAs, that does not mean that this is required by Article 174 or that the Commission uses these to justify its decisions. Indeed the Commission tends to justify its measures publicly by reference to a more general CBB: there are now a number of examples of pollution policy where the costs and benefits are transparently set out in the

[132] Krämer notes that in other languages, the Treaty speaks not of costs and benefits but of "advantages and charges" (*supra* n.130, p. 80), which would seem to support this view.

[133] See further D. W. Pearce, "Environmental Appraisal and Environmental Policy in the European Union" (1998) 11 *Environmental and Resource Economics* 489. *Cf*. Krämer (*supra* n.130, p. 80), who seems to imply that the *implicit* judgement made on adopting a policy—that its advantages outweigh its disadvantages—is sufficient, and that the duty to consider "advantages and charges" is one that can ignore *explicit* consideration of *any* monetary costs and benefits, or indeed any *explicit* consideration of advantages and disadvantages. This cannot be right. Why include the duty if an implicit assessment is all that is required? And surely if monetary costs and benefits are easily identifiable, they should be included.

[134] Sixteenth Report, *Freshwater Quality* (Cm 1966, London, HMSO, 1992), ch. 8.14.

[135] *Supra* n.70, p. 70.

[136] *Ibid*., p. 71. A view supported by the Council at the time—see e.g. Council Resolution concerning the relationship between industrial competitiveness and environmental protection [1992] OJ C331/5, para. 8.

[137] http://europa.eu.int/comm/dg11/enveco/index.htm. Reports prepared by the economic unit assessing the costs and benefits (including WTP elements) of specific legislative proposals include: *Economic Evaluation of the Draft Incineration Directive* (Luxembourg, Office for Official Publications of The European Communities, 1996); and *Economic Evaluation of Air Quality Targets for Sulphur Dioxide, Nitrogen Dioxide, Fine and Suspended Particulate Matter And Lead* (Luxembourg, Office for Official Publications of The European Communities, 1998).

proposal, but where contingent valuation figures have not been included.[138] The Commission is, it seems, happy to see these figures in the reports prepared by the economic unit, but is wary of using them as an explicit basis for policy. In the case of the policy on acidification mentioned earlier for example, one cannot help feeling that the reason for leaving contingent valuation figures out is that it would have made the benefits side much greater. This might have made the high cost of reaching critical loads rapidly appear worthwhile, because matched by large benefits. No doubt the Commission's view was that, whatever figure CBA put on the benefits, the costs of a stricter timetable were politically unacceptable.

The UK government's 1999 strategy on sustainability stresses its commitment in overall policy terms to some form of cost-benefit assessment, although it is difficult to see whether this is CBA or CBB, since the policy states, rather ambiguously, that "[d]ecisions must take account of a wide range of costs and benefits, *including those which cannot easily be valued in money terms*. In pursuing any single objective, we should not impose disproportionate costs elsewhere".[139] In practice, economic appraisal is carried out in the UK at both the legislative and operational stages of the regulatory process. Under the previous Conservative Government, economic appraisal of legislative[140] proposals was introduced as part of the deregulation initiative, in the form of Compliance Cost Assessment (CCA).[141] The initial focus was very much on considering the compliance *costs* to business of new regulation.[142] Only latterly was there a recognition of the importance of considering within CCA the potential *benefits* to business of environmental regulation such as waste savings and promotion of the environmental technology sector.[143] Proper consideration of benefits to humans and the environment similarly came rather later, with the introduction of a requirement to carry out a separate regulatory appraisal incorporating a risk assessment.[144] The present Labour Government has now replaced the separate CCA and regulatory appraisal procedures with a single procedure called regulatory impact assessment (RIA), in which the risks, costs and benefits of regulatory proposals are considered in one document.[145] While all government

[138] See e.g. para. 4 (economic analysis) of the initial proposal for a Water Framework Dir., COM(97)49 final; paras 2.2, 5, 6.5 and para. 4.4 of the Annex to the Commission Communication to the Council and the Euopean Parliament on a Community Strategy to Combat Acidification, COM(97)88.

[139] Cm 4345, *supra* n.80, para. 4.1, emphasis added. See also para. 8.26.

[140] In latter years, this was extended to non-legislative proposals such as codes of practice.

[141] DTI, *Checking the Cost to Business: A Guide to Compliance Cost Assessment* (London, DTI, 1992); Cabinet Office, Deregulation Unit, *Checking the Cost of Regulation: A Guide to Compliance Cost Assessment* (London, Cabinet Office, 1996).

[142] A. I. Ogus, *Regulation: Legal Form and Economic Theory* (Oxford, Clarendon, 1994), pp. 164–5.

[143] 266 ENDS Report (1997) 22.

[144] Cabinet Office, Deregulation Unit, *Regulation in the Balance: A Guide to Regulatory Appraisal Incorporating Risk Assessment* (London, Cabinet Office, 1996).

[145] See Cabinet Office, Better Regulation Unit, *The Better Regulation Guide* (London, Cabinet Office, 1998); and *Modernising Government* (Cm 4310, London, TSO, 1999).

departments are subject to the RIA duty, there is no guarantee that non-environmental departments will fully consider the environmental costs and benefits of their proposals. For that reason, as part of the Greening Government Initiative,[146] all departments must now consider any significant environmental costs and benefits of proposals in papers for Cabinet committees.[147]

In operational terms, the most visible cost-benefit requirement is to be found in section 39(1) of the Environment Act 1995, which places the Environment Agency and SEPA under a duty to take into account the likely costs and benefits of the exercise or non-exercise of their powers. There are a number of points to note here, many of which are similar to those raised in the context of Article 174 EC earlier. First, the subsection speaks only of "powers", with subsection (2) making it clear that the cost-benefit duty does not apply in relation to "duties" imposed on the agencies such as the duty to achieve existing statutory water quality objectives. CBA cannot, in other words, be used to revise the existing, predominantly EC-based pollution standards. Secondly, there is the question whether the cost-benefit duty is justiciable in judicial review terms. It seems likely that procedural review would be available—in other words, judicial review would lie if the Agency had failed to consider costs and benefits at all—although such cases are likely to be rare.[148] However, it seems unlikely that substantive review would be available—either to those who disagree with the Agency's assessment of costs and benefits or to those who wish to argue that the Agency has not chosen an efficient strategy. With the latter, all the Agency has to do is "take account" of costs and benefits, it is not under a duty to aim for an efficient solution where the benefits outweigh the costs.[149] With the former, judicial review courts are likely to want to steer clear of controversy, although, as in the Kennet case considered in the next paragraph, such matters may be challengeable by parties on administrative appeal.

Finally, there is the question whether the duty requires a *specialised* CBA to be used. It seems unlikely that section 39 requires this, although, equally, it would not appear to prevent it.[150] Although specialised CBA has been used in practice by the Environment Agency, recent experience in the context of water abstraction cannot have filled it with confidence. In the River Kennet case,[151] Thames Water was abstracting water from the River Kennet in Wiltshire, affecting its flow and ecology. As a result, the Environment Agency sought to

[146] Which seeks to integrate environmental considerations into other policy areas: see HC Environmental Audit Committee, *The Greening Government Initiative*, Second Report, 1997/98, HC 517; *The Greening Government Initiative 1999*, Sixth Report, 1998/99, HC 426; http://www.environment.detr.gov.uk/greening/index.htm .

[147] DETR Press Release, 16 Nov. 1998.

[148] Environment Agency, *Taking Account of Costs and Benefits*, SD3, Nov. 1996, para. 3.2 suggests that the Agency will seek to ensure that an audit trail is available as evidence that costs and benefits have been considered in appropriate cases.

[149] *Ibid.*, para. 3.2.

[150] *Ibid.*, paras. 3.3 and 4.5.

[151] See further 278 ENDS Report (1998) 16, to which I am indebted for what follows in this paragraph.

reduce the level of abstractions, and Thames Water appealed. At the appeal, the cost of replacing the abstraction with water from other sources was estimated by Thames at £6.2 million. The Environment Agency, in assessing the benefits of reducing abstraction, attempted to capture the use and non-use values of the river (the value to those using the river for angling, boating, walking etc., on the one hand, and the value to those not using it, but valuing its existence on the other). However, faced with a potential bill of around £80,000 for a full WTP study to measure these,[152] it opted instead for "benefit transfer"—borrowing WTP figures from studies carried out on similar rivers. As a result, the Agency assessed the use value of the river as £0.4 million and the non-use value at £13.2 million. The latter figure was based on a sum of 32 pence per household per year, multiplied by the three million customers in the Thames area, together with an appropriate discount rate. However the Inspector at the appeal inquiry, whose findings were endorsed by the Secretary of State in allowing Thames' appeal, followed Thames' figure for non-use value of only £0.3 million. This figure was based on multiplying the 32 pence sum by a much smaller number of people—the 100,000 living in the river catchment area. Obviously, using this figure meant that the costs to Thames were much greater than the benefits, whereas with the Agency's much larger non-use value figure, the benefits would make the costs worthwhile. As ENDS notes, "the arbitrary assumptions employed by all parties to the Kennet decision have underlined the shortcomings of cost-benefit analysis as a basis for policy-making".[153]

Republicanism

Public participation in environmental decision-making exists at both Community level and within the UK. Public participation can take place at all stages of the regulatory process—in determining general policy, at the legislative stage, and in agency policy and rule-making. At all of these stages, there are generally two sides to the participation coin. On one side is consultation, where relevant interest groups are consulted by public officials[154] for their views on proposals. And on the other side of the coin, there is lobbying, which may be directed at public officials in direct response to consultation, or which may be directed elsewhere, independently of formal consultation. In the case of legislation for example, lobbying is likely to take place not just at the agenda-setting and initial proposal stages,[155] but throughout the legislative process, and will be

[152] *Cf.* the observation in the Agency's guidance on the s.39 cost-benefit duty (*supra* n.148) that "the cost of applying this [cost-benefit] duty should be proportionate to the benefit to be gained" (para. 3.4). Paras. 9.4–9.5 suggests that a "full" CBA should be carried only out in "special cases" such as those involving high levels of expenditure.

[153] *Supra* n.151, p. 18.

[154] Whether in the Commission, the UK civil service, or the environment agencies.

[155] N. Hanley, "Britain and the European Policy Process" in P. Lowe and S. Ward (eds.), *British Environmental Policy and Europe: Politics and Policy in Transition* (London, Routledge, 1998), p. 57 at 61–3.

directed at Members of Parliament[156] as well as public officials, in the hope of securing amendments.

Formal consultation by UK national government and environment agencies is relatively well-established, with the DETR in particular consulting widely on policy and legislative proposals[157] with both industry and environmental interest groups. At Community level, formal consultation has historically been less well-established. In its 1998 report, the UK Royal Commission on Environmental Pollution (RCEP), for example, commented on the "general impression that the European Commission has not undertaken enough consultation in the past before submitting formal proposals to the Council of Ministers".[158] However, the protocol on subsidiarity in the Amsterdam Treaty now states that "[w]ithout prejudice to its right of initiative, the Commission should:—except in cases of particular urgency or confidentiality, consult widely before proposing legislation and, wherever appropriate, publish consultation documents". Experience with the new European water policy suggests that the Commission had already begun the process of change before the introduction of this new presumptive duty: the Commission adopted a Communication on Community water policy in 1996 which, though formally addressed to the Council and the European Parliament, invited comment from all interested parties; and a conference on the issue was also held.[159]

Lobbying, in contrast, is well-established at both national and EC levels. At UK level, lobbying on pollution regulation by industry and environmental groups has typically been directed at the DETR and the environment agencies: the former because this government department has been the initiator of most significant UK policy[160]; and the latter because most of the important detail will be implemented by them. Lobbying of Parliament is obviously important when Bills are going through, but this tends to be much more intermittent. Of course the majority of industry and environmental groups have now woken up to the fact that most UK pollution regulation now stems from the EC, so lobbying at that level is now regarded as being equally, if not more, important.[161] Again, most lobbying is directed at DG XI within the Commission as the initiator of

[156] Whether the European Parliament, the UK Parliament (MPs and peers) or the newly devolved parliaments/assemblies.

[157] In relation to both primary and secondary legislation.

[158] Twenty-first Report, *supra* n.56, ch. 7.35.

[159] http://europa.eu.int/water/water-framework/index_en.html.

[160] Although with devolution, lobbying can be expected to shift to the devolved administrations. In addition, with the increased emphasis on integration of environmental considerations into other policy areas as part of the Greening Government Initiative, one might expect a shift towards environmental lobbying within other UK government departments.

[161] Though this may involve lobbying of *national* officials and ministers attending Council meetings, or national officials attending expert groups assisting the Commission. With the former, even if convinced by your line, ministers may of course be persuaded by other Member States to vote against your interests in return for support from them on another more important issue; and even if they vote in line with your interests, majority voting in most areas on the environment means that they may be outvoted.

environmental policy proposals,[162] although as legislative proposals progress through the system, lobbying of the European Parliament also takes place. Some, rather limited, efforts have been made in recent years to prevent abuses of this Community lobbying.[163]

At national level, most industry lobbying is carried out by national trade associations such as the Environmental Services Assocation[164] or the Chemical Industries Association, although large companies will typically also lobby on their own account to ensure their particular interests are represented. Environmental lobbying at national level is almost exclusively the preserve of large national interest groups such as Greenpeace, Friends of the Earth (FOE), the Worldwide Fund for Nature (WWF), the Royal Society for the Protection of Birds (RSPB) and the Council for the Preservation of Rural England (CPRE). At Community level, many national groups join forces to create a European umbrella organisation, such as FEAD[165] in the case of the waste industry, or the European Environmental Bureau (EEB) in the case of environmental groups.[166] This obviously makes it easier for the Commission, which has a single point of contact to deal with, although it can lead to problems. On the one hand, a lowest common denominator approach may be taken by the European organisation, which means that the Commission may end up with rather anodyne, generalised information;[167] on the other hand, a highest common factor approach may be adopted, which ignores the interests of some of the organisation's national member groups. Such problems explain why many national groups (industry and environmental) and large companies also lobby the Commission directly and why the latter is often receptive to such lobbying.

However, public participation at both UK and EC levels is currently more pluralist than discursive. First, the consultation and lobbying process is dominated by interest groups, with private citizens rarely being involved.[168] Secondly, the process tends to be dominated by industry interest groups at the

[162] Although a duty to integrate environmental considerations into other policy areas has existed for some time now at Community level (Art. 6 EC introduced by Amsterdam just emphasises its importance by placing it at the start of the Treaty), environmental lobbying of other DGs remains rather limited—see P. Lowe and S. Ward, "Domestic Winners and Losers" in Lowe and Ward, *supra* n.155, p. 87 at 101.

[163] http://europa.eu.int/comm/sg/sgc/lobbies/index_en.htm.

[164] The waste industry trade association (formerly NAWDC).

[165] The European Federation of Waste Management.

[166] Although the EEB is regarded by some as more of an information source than a true lobbyist—see Lowe and Ward, *supra* n.162, p. 101. For a practical example of interest group lobbying, see M. Porter and A. Butt Philip, "The Role of Interest Groups in EU Environmental Policy Formulation: A Case Study of the Draft Packaging Directive" (1993) 3 *European Env*. 16.

[167] S. Mazey and J. Richardson, "Introduction: Transference of Power, Decision Rules, and Rules of the Game", and R. Hull, "Lobbying Brussels: A View for Within", both in S. Mazey and J. Richardson (eds.), *Lobbying in the European Community* (Oxford, OUP, 1993), p. 3 at 22, and p. 82 at 86 respectively.

[168] The one exception being town and country planning at local level—in many ways the first stage of pollution regulation. Here, there is a long tradition of individual involvement in the context of development plans, individual planning applications and environmental assessments, including participation in public inquiries.

expense of more diffuse environmental interests, whereas republicanism would stress the need for equality of opportunity for all voices. And thirdly, while consultation with industry and public interest groups occurs at both levels, this is sequential rather than discursive: decisions are far from being decided in a round-table discussion by all interested parties.

That said, there are signs that things are beginning to change. Within the UK, the RCEP, in its Twenty-first Report, has for example emphasised the need to move beyond traditional forms of consultation in order to ensure that public values are fully articulated.[169] Though it does not label it as such, the RCEP is clearly calling for a more civic republican approach when it states that:

> The failure to provide an opportunity for interaction, and for clarifying the values underlying the reponses made, is a major shortcoming of traditional forms of consultation. There is little scope for opinions to be developed as a result of exchanging views with others and considering issues in the light of growing understanding. It is unrealistic to suppose that values are fixed, and waiting to be uncovered by questionnaires or other types of analysis. For most people it is more accurate to think of their values emerging or taking shape as they are brought to face important choices between competing options.[170]

The Environment Agency has also issued guidance on consensus building as part of its sustainable development series.[171] Like the RCEP report, this stresses the limitations of traditional top-down forms of consultation, noting that these are all too often a means of legitimising a preferred decision that has already been made, with little real chance of major alterations being introduced.[172] Instead, the guidance recommends a more bottom-up engagement of stakeholders—not just at this late stage, but also at the very start of the policy process when drawing up initial proposals.[173] This engagement would consist of dialogue and consensus,[174] with the former enabling the values and views of different stakeholders to be heard and incorporated into a decision,[175] and the latter implying majority support as a result of informed debate.[176] However, while suggesting that consensus building techniques are best placed to meet increased public expectations of more direct involvement in decision-making, the guidance also emphasises the fact mentioned earlier—that bottom-up techniques can feel threatening for regulators and politicians alike.[177] For this reason, it stresses that the agenda is still set by the original decision-maker[178] and

[169] *Supra* n.56, ch. 7, in particular sections 7.19–7.23.

[170] *Ibid.*, ch. 7.20.

[171] Environment Agency, SD12, *Consensus Building for Sustainable Development* (Bristol, Environment Agency, 1998).

[172] *Ibid.*, para. 2.3.

[173] *Ibid.* The RCEP make a similar recommendation in their report, *supra* n.56, ch. 7.22.

[174] *Supra* n.171, para. 6.1.

[175] *Ibid.*, para. 5.2.5.

[176] *Ibid.*, para. 6.1.

[177] *Ibid.*, para. 2.3.

[178] *Ibid.*

that consensus techniques are designed to reinforce established decision-making processes, not to replace them.[179]

Both the RCEP report and the Environment Agency guidance provide concrete examples of pilot projects involving community dialogue at a local level, including the use of a citizen jury to aid with development of the Hertfordshire county waste strategy and community advisory committees in relation to the Hampshire waste strategy.[180] The Agency guidance also provides details of its own pilot exercise using a stakeholder group as part of consultation on the New Forest Local Environment Agency Plan (LEAP).[181] At national level, the RCEP points to the establishment of a People's Panel as part of the UK government's *Better Government* initiative, as well as experiments with citizens' juries on NHS issues. The RCEP suggests that experience at Community level is rather more limited. It cites the establishment of the Consultative Forum on the Environment established in 1996,[182] but notes that this is made up of "eminent personalities" from a wide range of interest groups including industry, the unions and environmental *groups*, and not *individual* members of the public. A similar criticism could be made of the the Economic and Social Committee (ESC), which provides a similarly wide range of interest groups with an opportunity to discuss and comment on all draft Community legislation.

CONCLUSION

Fashions in the policy-making *literature* change over time. Critical loads was the buzzword of the 1980s in the context of the acid rain debate, then along came the influential "Pearce Report"[183] and CBA became the favoured model for decision-making in the late 1980s and early 1990s. With the recent RCEP report's stress on public values, it looks as though the end of the 1990s and the start of the new millenium could see republicanism taking over as the dominant model. Of course, the degree to which policy-making is changed in *practice* by such fashions is debatable: the fact that government guidance on economic techniques such as CBA abounds is no indication that is being used in practice.

It was noted at the start of the chapter that the outcome of one of these approaches to policy-making may, in some circumstances, be consistent with the outcome of another. One would, for example, expect a majority democratic decision to be reasonably efficient in economic terms, because they can both be analysed in a similar utilitarian light. However, as has been seen, more often than not the outcomes will conflict. This tension or conflict is particularly visi-

[179] Environment Agency, SD12, *Consensus Building for Sustainable Development* (Bristol, Environment Agency, 1998) para. 7.

[180] *Ibid.*, para. 5.5, and ch. 7.26 of the RCEP report, *supra* n.56.

[181] *Supra* n.171, para. 3.2.

[182] Commission Decision 93/701 [1993] OJ L328/53.

[183] D. Pearce *et al.*, *Blueprint for a Green Economy* (London, Earthscan, 1989).

ble as between ecologism and republicanism-inspired democracy, which poses problems for broad conceptions of sustainable development and for green political theory.[184] Broad conceptions of sustainable development, such as that formulated at Rio, espouse a commitment both to bottom-up citizen participation (Agenda 21) and to ecological sustainability. Greens also tend to be committed not only to respect for ecology, but also to participatory forms of democracy. However, the two will often be irreconcilable. Local discursive politics may stop "don't wants" like landfill sites from being built, which greens may support; however, the prospect of discursive democracy tackling "wants" like cars and energy consumption seems more remote.

[184] On the former, see Jacobs, *supra* n.1. On the latter, see e.g. M. Saward, "Green Democracy" in A. Dobson and P. Lucardie (eds.), *The Politics of Nature* (London, Routledge, 1993), p. 63.

6

Regulatory Techniques

INTRODUCTION

While previous chapters have analysed the legitimacy of regulatory institutions and decision-making tools, the aim of this chapter is to analyse the legitimacy of the regulatory instruments utilised by those institutions. Space precludes a comprehensive examination of all of the different instruments available.[1] Instead, the chapter will focus on three separate types: command-and-control techniques, economic regulatory instruments and voluntary mechanisms. Although a wide range of instruments could be included under economic instruments—including for example subsidies[2]—only pollution charges and tradable permits will be examined. Similarly, while tools such as deposit-refund schemes might be included within voluntary mechanisms, analysis will be limited to just three: eco-labelling, the EC eco-management and audit scheme (EMAS) and voluntary agreements. All of the above instruments will be analysed in terms of the key legitimating values of cost-effectiveness, equality before the law, equity, accountability, effectiveness, and legal certainty. However, it is necessary first to provide a brief introduction to the various instruments, so that they can be placed in context.

COMMAND-AND-CONTROL

Most existing EC and UK pollution regulation is of a command-and-control type. But what do we mean by command-and-control regulation? For present purposes, the regulatory process can be divided up into three stages: first, the setting of general policy; secondly, the setting of ambient targets and national waste[3] or energy reduction targets; and, finally, the setting of mandatory individual plant pollution standards,[4] company waste[5] or energy reduction targets,

[1] I do not, for example, examine education as an informational instrument.

[2] See further OECD, *Economic Instruments for Environmental Protection* (Paris, OECD, 1989).

[3] An example of the latter would be the national packaging waste targets set out in Dir. 94/62 on packaging and packaging waste [1994] OJ L365/10.

[4] These will only effectively tackle point-source pollution.

[5] Although note that existing company obligations under the Producer Responsibility Obligations (Packaging Waste) Regs. 1997 (SI 1997 No. 648) are not strictly speaking command-and-control because trading of packaging recovery notes (PRNs) is permitted.

and product standards.[6] The final three in this list should ideally be set to meet the ambient or national reduction targets, but they may be set independently of these. Strictly speaking, the term command-and-control should be used only in relation to these individual plant pollution standards, reduction targets and product standards, for it is individual companies or product specifications and uses that are being commanded and controlled. It is easy to see how the overall framework, encompassing all three stages, might equally be described as one of command-and-control. However, to slip into this way of viewing things is dangerous, because the setting of policy goals and ambient or reduction targets is just as likely to be a feature of a system based on economic instruments or voluntary mechanisms such as voluntary agreements.

Historically, of all three types of command-and-control standard, plant pollution standards have received the most attention,[7] and will be the focus of the sections that follow. These may take a variety of forms. *Emission* standards specify what releases are permissible from an industrial plant. *Process* standards specify the types of technology or techniques that must be used in an industrial process. *Performance* standards are effectively a combination of the two: they lay down emission standards associated with a particular, presumptive technology or technique, but leave the operator free to choose an alternative technology or technique, as long as it is capable of meeting the relevant emission standards.[8] Performance standards are, in this way, more flexible than process standards.

Though not strictly necessary to a discussion of command-and-control standards *per se*, it is worth examining for a moment the relationship between plant and ambient standards. The relationship is a complex one. In the UK, plants emitting non-dangerous substances are generally controlled by emission standards; for these substances, which can be assimilated by the environment, it makes sense to link plant emission standards *directly* to ambient standards. To make plants cut back on their emissions by more than is necessary to achieve the relevant ambient standards is not cost-effective. Plants emitting dangerous substances are generally governed by process or performance standards associated

[6] Product standards are more effective than plant pollution standards for controlling diffuse pollution. They may be "content" standards, governing e.g. the levels of dangerous substances in a product or minimum standards of energy efficiency, or "use" standards. An example of the latter is a ban or controls on the use of pesticides or other chemicals in a given river catchment area via water protection zones (WPZs) under s.93 of the Water Resources Act 1991 (for the first WPZ, see 290 ENDS Report (1999) 11). *Cf.* Nitrate Sensitive Areas under s.94: since these typically involve the payment of compensation, controls there are effectively subsidies—a form of economic instrument: see T. Jewell, "Public Law and the Environment: The Prospects for Decision-Making" in T. Jewell and J. Steele (eds.), *Law in Environmental Decision-Making* (Oxford, Clarendon, 1998), p. 73 at 100.

[7] The other two types (mandatory company waste and energy reduction targets and product use standards) have often been ignored in discussions of command-and-control regulation—principally because they have been little used in practice.

[8] BATNEEC within IPC (see *infra* n.9) is typically expressed as a performance standard: see DETR/Welsh Office, *Integrated Pollution Control: A Practical Guide* (London, DETR/Welsh Office, 1998, para. 7.12.

with BATNEEC under IPC, or BAT under IPPC.[9] In this case, since the environment cannot assimilate dangerous substances, one wants the ambient standard to provide a maximum level for such substances, but for BATNEEC or BAT to continue striving for a minimum level below this in line with the precautionary principle. In other words, BATNEEC/BAT should be *linked* to ambient standards, in the sense that if the ambient target *will not* otherwise be met, then *more* than BATNEEC/BAT may be required.[10] However, BATNEEC/BAT standards should not be *directly* linked to ambient targets, in that firms should not be allowed to use *less* than BAT (in the strictest, cost-oblivious, sense) just because the ambient target *will* still be met without such a strict standard.[11]

ECONOMIC REGULATORY INSTRUMENTS

Economic instruments or market mechanisms cannot be equated with "market forces",[12] as it is these unco-ordinated forces which have helped to produce many of the problems in the first place.[13] They are still regulation, albeit of a different *form* from command-and-control. Non-regulatory or voluntary approaches will be dealt with in the next section.

The two principal types of economic instrument that will be considered in this section are pollution charges or taxes and tradable permits. Pollution charges may take one of three forms corresponding to their equivalent command-and-control relations considered earlier: an emissions charge, a waste or energy charge and a product charge. Trading may similarly be applied to emissions, to waste or energy reduction obligations and even to product controls. However, just as plant pollution standards have tended to dominate discussion of command-and-control regulation, so plant pollution-based instruments, such as emissions trading and emission charges, have tended to dominate discussion of economic instruments and will, similarly, be the focus of the sections that

[9] BATNEEC (best available techniques not entailing excessive cost) and IPC (integrated pollution control) are associated with Pt. I of the Environmental Protection Act 1990. BAT (best available techniques) which despite its strict-looking nature still contains a cost-balancing element, is an element of the IPPC (Integrated Pollution Prevention and Control) Dir. 96/61 [1996] OJ L257/26. With full implementation of the Pollution Prevention and Control Act 1999, the latter will replace the former.

[10] See e.g. Art. 10 of the IPPC Dir., *supra* n. 9.

[11] The *strictest* version of the precautionary principle would require an immediate ban on all discharges of dangerous substances. A *strict* version would require BAT (in the strictest, cost-oblivious, sense) to be used to control all such emissions. Current policy—reflected in the cost elements of IPC's BATNEEC and the BAT of IPPC—implements a *weak* version of the precautionary principle. However, while this requires the costs of control to be balanced against the benefits, this is not the same as saying that a cost is excessive just because it is not necessary to achieve an ambient target—after all, that ambient target represents a maximum rather than an efficient ideal.

[12] Although they do of course make use of these.

[13] M. Jacobs, *The Green Economy: Environment, Sustainable Development and the Politics of the Future* (London, Pluto Press, 1991), p. 24.

follow. Emission charges tax the discharger on each unit of pollution he emits. The assumption is that because he has to pay for his pollution he will cut down on his emissions to cut costs and maximise profits. Emissions trading or tradable pollution permits operate in a similar way to existing regulation, except that firms are able to trade their permits. Allocation of permits can be made on the basis of existing command-and-control entitlements ("grandparenting") or via an auction in which firms have to bid for their share. After allocation, permits can be traded, which provides firms with an incentive to reduce emissions because firms can sell any that are surplus to requirement.[14]

Despite support in the EC Fifth Environmental Action Programme,[15] the direct use of economic regulatory instruments at EC level is currently non-existent.[16] Concerns about the competitiveness of Community industry,[17] together with the requirement for unanimity on fiscal measures, have been key barriers, which notably put paid to the proposal for a Community carbon/energy tax.[18] Nevertheless, in the spirit of subsidiarity, the EC has been emphasising the key role that such instruments may play in Member States—including their use as a means of implementing Community obligations.[19]

In the UK, use of economic instruments is gradually increasing.[20] Existing environmental taxes[21] are product- or waste-related rather than emissions taxes.[22] Examples include the landfill tax[23] and differential duties on leaded and unleaded petrol.[24] There are also developed proposals for a business energy tax or climate change levy,[25] and a pesticides tax.[26] As for tradable permits—while

[14] See further T. Tietenberg, "Economic Instruments for Environmental Regulation" (1990) 6 *Oxford Review of Economic Policy* 17.

[15] *Towards Sustainability: A European Community Programme of Policy and Action in Relation to the Environment and Sustainable Development*, COM(92)23 final [1993] OJ C138/5, ch. 7.4.

[16] Though there are proposals in the pipeline: an energy products tax has been proposed, COM(97)30; and Art. 12 of the proposed Water Framework Dir. (COM(97)49 final, COM(97)614 final, COM(98)76 final and COM(99)271 final) would introduce water use charging.

[17] Particularly energy-intensive industries such as the steel industry.

[18] COM(95)172 final.

[19] See e.g. Annex VI, Pt. B, of the proposed Water Framework Dir., *supra* n.16, and *Environmental Taxes and Charges in the Single Market*, COM(97)9 final [1997] OJ C224/6.

[20] For early support, see *This Common Inheritance* (Cm 1200, London, HMSO, 1990), Annex A; *This Common Inheritance: The Second Year Report* (Cm 2068, London, HMSO, 1992), pp. 33–5, 101, 112, 115; and DoE, *Making Markets Work for the Environment* (London, HMSO, 1993).

[21] The various UK cost-recovery, regulatory charging schemes cannot be described as pollution charges, because they are not designed to have an incentive effect, but rather to reflect the regulatory costs associated with particular processes.

[22] Emission charges for point source discharges to water, although mooted in a DETR consultation paper (DETR, *Economic Instruments for Water Pollution* (London, DETR, 1998)), were not subsequently taken up: see 290 ENDS Report (1999) 21.

[23] Pt. III of the Finance Act 1996; the Landfill Tax Regs. 1996 (SI 1996 No. 1527) and other associated Orders. See further J. Powell and A. Craighill, "The UK Landfill Tax" in T. O'Riordan (ed.), *Ecotaxation* (London, Earthscan, 1997), p. 304.

[24] S.13A of the Hydrocarbon Oil Duties Act 1979 (inserted by s.1 of the Finance Act 1987).

[25] HM Customs and Excise, *Consultation on a Climate Change Levy* (Manchester, HM Customs and Excise, 1999). See further 290 ENDS Report (1999) 19.

[26] DETR, *Design of a Tax or Charge Scheme for Pesticides* (London, DETR, 1999). See further 290 ENDS Report (1999) 21. But see now 301 ENDS Report (2000) 32.

discussion about their use in the context of water pollution[27] and acid rain[28] has come to little—a version of them is present in relation to packaging waste,[29] and they may yet be used in the context of the new climate change levy[30] and in relation to limiting the disposal of biodegradable municipal waste to landfill.[31]

VOLUNTARY MECHANISMS

At EC level, the increase in the use of voluntary mechanisms can be traced back to the Fifth Environmental Action Programme, which encourages voluntary agreements and self-regulation as part of a concept of "shared responsibility" between all of the relevant actors in the environmental sphere.[32] It stresses a "bottom-up" approach rather than a "top-down" approach,[33] stating that:

> Whereas previous environmental measures tended to be proscriptive in character with an emphasis on the "thou-shalt not" approach, the new strategy leans more towards a "let's work together" approach.[34]

In other words, instead of regulatory law attempting—in a number of cases unsuccessfully—to impose solutions on organisations from the outside, the idea is to look to a more "reflexive" type of law that can harness knowledge and self-control on the inside.[35]

[27] See DoE, *supra* n.20.

[28] London Economics, *The Potential Role of Market Mechanisms in the Control of Acid Rain*, DoE Environmental Economics Research Series (London, HMSO, 1992). See further S. Sorrell, "Why Sulphur Trading Failed in the UK" in S. Sorrell and J. Skea (eds.), *Pollution for Sale: Emissions Trading and Joint Implementation* (Cheltenham, Edward Elgar, 1999), p. 170.

[29] As noted *supra* in n. 5, trading of packaging recovery notes (PRNs) is permitted—see further DETR, *Review of the Producer Responsibility Obligations (Packaging Waste) Regulations 1997—A Consultation Paper* (London, DETR, 1998), and 277 ENDS Report (1998) 17. Trading brokers include Evidex and the Environment Exchange (http://www.environmentexchange.co.uk/).

[30] 293 ENDS Report (1999) 3; 294 ENDS Report (1999) 16; 297 ENDS Report (1999) 19. Note also the new power to introduce emissions trading granted to the Secretary of State by para. 1(3) of Pt. I of Sched. 1 to the Pollution Prevention and Control Act 1999.

[31] DETR, *Limiting Landfill: A Consultation Paper on Limiting Landfill to Meet the EC Landfill Directive's Targets for the Landfill of Biodegradable Municipal Waste* (London, DETR, 1999). See further 297 ENDS Report (1999) 23.

[32] *Supra*, n.15, chs. 3, 4 and 8.

[33] *Ibid.*, executive summary, para. 34, p. 17.

[34] *Ibid.*, para. 19, p. 14.

[35] See M. Power, *The Audit Society: Rituals of Verification* (Oxford, OUP, 1997), p. 62; G. Teubner *et al.*, *Environmental Law and Ecological Responsibility: The Concept and Practice of Ecological Self-Organisation* (Chichester, Wiley, 1994), p. 395. Systems theory—on which reflexive law is based—would not appear to support wholesale deregulation. It does, however, favour instruments which seek to combine external constraints with internal potential: L. Farmer and G. Teubner, "Ecological Self-Organisation" in Teubner, *ibid.*, p. 3 at 8).

Environmental management and auditing

There are two principal environmental management systems available to organisations in the UK and EU.[36] The first is the international environmental management systems standard, ISO 14001.[37] The second—and the focus here—is the EC Eco-Management and Audit Scheme (EMAS) introduced by Council Regulation 1836/93.[38] The Regulation was agreed in 1993, came into force in 1994 and was launched in the UK in April 1995. Since Regulations are directly applicable in Member States, there was no need for national implementing legislation to be passed, and the scheme therefore automatically became a part of UK law. The scheme is nevertheless a voluntary one; organisations are not compelled to participate.

What does EMAS actually require? To secure registration, an organisation is required to implement an environmental management system, and also to provide for legal compliance[39] and continual improvement of environmental performance.[40] It must also carry out periodic environmental audits to assess the environmental performance of the organisation, and publish environmental statements to provide interested parties with information on its environmental policy, impact and performance. Finally, it must have the management system, audit procedure and environmental statement verified to ensure that the requirements of the Regulation have been met. Once the Member State's competent body[41] has received a registration form together with a validated environmental statement and a registration fee—and assuming it is satisfied that the organisation complies with all of the Regulation's requirements—then the site will be registered.

As noted above, organisations are not compelled to participate in EMAS. Those that choose to do so are likely to be drawn by the prospect of the increased profits and competitiveness that the scheme may bring. There are two principal means of increasing profits: cutting costs and increasing sales. With

[36] The chemical industry has its own industry-specific initiative called "Responsible Care": see further N. Gunningham and P. Grabosky, *Smart Regulation: Designing Environmental Policy* (Oxford, Clarendon, 1998); 222 ENDS Report (1993) 14; and 233 ENDS Report (1994) 16.

[37] See further R. Krut and H. Gleckman, *ISO 14001: A Missed Opportunity for Sustainable Global Industrial Development* (London, Earthscan, 1998). The precursor of ISO 14001 in the UK was the British Standard on Environmental Management Systems, BS 7750. This was developed by the British Standards Institution, but withdrawn in 1997 to give way to ISO 14001 (*ibid*., p. 20).

[38] [1993] OJ L168/1. The Reg. is currently being revised: see COM(99)313 final. For differences between the requirements of ISO 14001 and (the old) EMAS, see Krut and Gleckman, *supra* n.37, pp. 16–22.

[39] If a competent body is informed by a competent enforcement authority of a breach of relevant regulatory requirements, it must refuse or suspend registration of the site, and is required to reinstate it only if satisfied that the breach has been rectified and that suitable arrangements are in place to prevent a recurrence.

[40] Under the proposed revision (*supra* n. 38), an organisation will also be required to conduct an open dialogue with interested parties with regard to the environmental impact of its activities.

[41] In the UK, the Institute of Environmental Assessment (http://www.emas.org.uk/) took over this role from the DETR on 1 May 1998.

the former, EMAS may produce cost savings from identifying and hence avoiding potential legal liabilities,[42] and from identifying resource, energy and waste-minimisation opportunities—savings that may not have arisen without an environmental management and audit system in place. In addition, the idea has been mooted for some time that registered firms might expect to receive fewer monitoring visits and thus pay lower cost-recovery charges to regulators as a result.[43]

As for increasing sales, organisations may be able to secure more business by demonstrating their green credentials to potential purchasers[44]—a number of whom have become increasingly concerned about the environmental performance of their supply chains.[45] It was originally thought that many large companies would simply not deal with suppliers who were not registered under a formal environmental management scheme.[46] Although some firms have moved towards requiring registration of their suppliers,[47] others have been of the view that formal environmental management systems may, if anything, impede the greening of the supply chain, and are therefore choosing to continue with their own criteria for judging suppliers.[48]

EMAS has not been without its detractors. Besides general criticisms of formal environmental management systems touched upon above, a specific criticism that has been levelled at EMAS is that it is procedural rather than substantive in nature.[49] It does not tell organisations what target they have to reach—only that they must set up procedures to set and keep track of their own targets.[50]

[42] Although there has also been concern that publication of environmental statements may create liabilities—see e.g. 231 ENDS Report (1994) 25.

[43] See e.g. ENDS Reports 231 (1994) 23; 265 (1997) 5; 266 (1997) 3; 271 (1997) 32; see also the preambles to the new proposed Reg., which talk of organisations gaining benefits "in terms of regulatory control".

[44] Aided by the ability of participating organisations to sport the EMAS logo on their registered letterheads and on certain types of organisational publicity, though not on products or their packaging, or in advertising (because this would create confusion with the eco-labelling scheme).

[45] B&Q, BT and British Gas are just three examples of firms which have taken steps to check the environmental credentials of their suppliers (see e.g. 239 ENDS Report (1994) 23). BT has 20,000–30,000 regular suppliers and 50,000 occasional ones (242 ENDS Report (1995) 28).

[46] If lenders and insurers start to require registration, then another advantage besides winning tenders will be the ability to secure loans and insurance. With insurance, even if registration is not made a compulsory feature of cover, insurers may offer reduced premiums to registered firms or sites.

[47] See e.g. 242 ENDS Report (1995) 20, p. 22.

[48] This is true, for example, of B&Q, which is of the view that time spent on implementing the bureaucratic management systems and procedures under formal systems is better spent on addressing the environmental issues themselves (246 ENDS Report (1995) 24).

[49] Power, *supra* n.35, pp. 84–7.

[50] Although this may change with the revised Reg.—see *infra* n. 103.

Eco-labelling

Green consumerism[51] can be analysed in terms of the economics of supply and demand: the theory is that, as consumers demand less-polluting products, so producers will supply them.[52] However, to continue with an economic framework of analysis, there are two potential sources of failure in this market. The first is a lack of full information on the part of consumers,[53] and the second is the failure of product prices to internalise the external costs imposed on society.

For this market to operate effectively, consumers must first therefore be in possession of accurate and easily comprehensible information. In the UK during the 1980s, consumers were confronted by a bewildering array of environmental information on a relatively limited range of products.[54] Furthermore, the information that was provided did not give consumers a full picture of the pollution associated with those products. Washing powders, for example, may have displayed information on disposal aspects such as biodegradability and phosphate content, but they did not give details of pollution caused by the original production process. While inaccurate or misleading claims could to an extent be controlled by laws on trades descriptions and misleading advertising,[55] this did nothing to confront the problems of consumer overload (in the sense of consumers having to compare often incompatible environmental information provided by different manufacturers) or consumer underload (in that only use and disposal information, and not process information, was typically provided).

The EC eco-labelling scheme[56] was designed to overcome these problems. The overload problem was tackled by the provision of a simple label. Rather than consumers doing the work, the scheme does it for them by identifying products which are less damaging to the environment than alternatives serving the same purpose.[57] The scheme sought to tackle the underload problem by subjecting a large range of products to detailed "life-cycle analysis" (LCA) in order

[51] See generally S. Irvine, *Beyond Green Consumerism* (London, Friends of the Earth, 1989).

[52] Of course, while green consumerism usually conjures up thoughts of retail consumers, industry and government can also be green consumers.

[53] On this source of market failure, see further A. I. Ogus, *Regulation: Legal Form and Economic Theory* (Oxford, Clarendon, 1994), p.38.

[54] E.g. aerosols, washing powders and tissues.

[55] *Cf.* 288 ENDS Report (1999) 30 and J. Holder, "Regulating Green Advertising in the Motor Car Industry" (1991) 18 *Jo. of Law & Soc.* 323. On the regulation of green claims, see DETR, *Green Claims Code* (London, DETR, 1998); DETR, *Consumer Products and the Environment* (London, DETR, 1999) (responses to the consultation), paras. 60–64; 292 ENDS Report (1999) 46; Prospect C&S, *Study on Verification and Control of Environmental Product Claims: Final Report* (Brussels, Commission of the European Communities, DG on Health and Consumer Protection, 1998); and ISO 14021.

[56] Council Reg. 880/92 on a Community eco-label award scheme [1992] OJ L99/1. This is currently being revised—see 292 ENDS Report (1999) 46. On eco-labelling, see further DoE, *Giving Guidance to the Green Consumer: Progress on an Eco-Labelling Scheme for the UK* (London, DETR, 1991); HC Environment Committee, *Eco-Labelling*, Eighth Report, session 1990/91, HC 474-I, and *The Government's Response* (Cm 1720, London, HMSO, 1991).

[57] DoE, *supra* n. 56, para. 3.1.

to examine the pollution associated with them "from cradle to grave". Products are divided into product groups and specific criteria are set for each group, which a product must meet if it is to be awarded a label. The criteria reflect a cradle-to-grave, life-cycle assessment and include such factors as the choice of raw materials, distribution, consumption and use of the product and disposal after use. Criteria have now been agreed at EC level for a number of product groups including, for example, dishwashers, washing machines, soil improvers, tissue products and laundry detergents.

The scheme—like EMAS—is a voluntary one. For firms that do wish to apply, applications for a label are made to the competent body[58] of the Member State in which the product is manufactured, or imported from a non-Member. A fee for applications (currently £500) is payable to the competent body to cover administrative costs. In the UK, testing to see whether the product satisfies the criteria can be done either by an independent, accredited laboratory, or by the firm itself as long as its test results are externally verified.[59] The competent body then decides whether to award a label. Products awarded a label are entitled to sport a logo on the product and an annual fee is payable for this privilege.[60] Very few companies currently apply for eco-labels in the UK and their visibility in the shops is therefore low. The key reason for this appears to be that many companies think that the cost of securing the eco-label outweighs the economic benefits it may bring—particularly when they may still attract environmentally conscious consumers with their own, unofficial environmental information.[61]

One of the weaknesses of the current scheme is its single label, pass/fail nature. Not only does this reduce the information given to the consumer,[62] it has also created a difficult balancing act: if too many products pass, the scheme is virtually meaningless; on the other hand, if too many fail, it becomes difficult to secure the backing of industry.[63] Proposed revisions to the Regulation may yet solve this problem by introducing additional information beyond the single label.[64] However, other problems remain. The first is that the scheme merely seeks to rank alternatives within the same product category. In doing so, it fails to emphasise the choice of not consuming or consuming a totally different alternative. An eco-label for batteries, for example, will rate only batteries; it will not mark down batteries in relation to more environmentally friendly mains

[58] In the UK, having previously been the Ecolabelling Board, this is now the DETR (see further DETR, *Prior Options Review of the UK Ecolabelling Board* (London, DETR, 1998).

[59] 223 ENDS Report (1993) 24.

[60] The fee is currently 0.15% of annual sales within the EU. However, since this might put-off large producers (who could end up paying significant sums), current proposals include the placing of a ceiling on the total amount payable.

[61] 234 ENDS Report (1994) 27. However, this balance of costs and benefits may change if the proposed ceiling mentioned in n.60 *supra* is introduced.

[62] Although reducing information was identified earlier as a strength of the scheme—indeed one of its key rationales—the existing scheme arguably goes too far in this direction.

[63] There is apparently an unofficial target that 10–20% of the market share in a product group should pass (227 ENDS Report (1993) 26).

[64] See 292 ENDS Report (1999) 46.

electricity. And neither will it give out a signal that not consuming vast quantities of power at all may be better still for the environment.[65] Next, a green consumer may wish to avoid buying apparently environmentally friendly products from companies with, say, a poor record in relation to accidental pollution incidents and environmental prosecutions. However, this type of information is not taken into account in an eco-label life-cycle analysis, which is based on consented rather than actual emissions and effects.

But perhaps the greatest problem facing eco-labelling is consumer apathy: most consumers will not make consumption decisions on the basis of environmental performance—even if there are labels to guide them.[66] Instead, most purchase on the basis of quality and price. While the days of being forced to trade-off quality for greenness are now behind us with many (though not all) products, price remains a critical barrier to the further development of green consumerism.[67] As long as products generally fail to reflect the full environmental costs of their production, use and disposal, then prices will convey the wrong information to consumers, leaving little hope for meaningful consumer pressure. Recent UK and EC policy moves towards developing an "integrated product policy"[68] have implicitly recognised that eco-labelling schemes address only one source of market failure, and that additional mechanisms will be needed to tackle the other major source—product externalities. In many ways, the problems have now been reversed: for a long time, labelling reflected only the use and disposal stages of a product's lifecycle, but the eco-labelling scheme has now tackled the production stage; however, while the external costs of production have long been internalised to a degree through regulation, the external costs of use and disposal have remained largely uninternalised. Product taxes and other mechanisms will be needed to ensure that a full life cycle approach[69] is taken towards regulation of products, just as it is with eco-labelling.

Environmental agreements

Environmental agreements between government and industry involve the latter agreeing to meet specified environmental objectives. These agreements can

[65] However, to an extent this may be taken into account by excluding certain product groups altogether, e.g. in Germany air fresheners are not considered for their national version of an eco-label because opening the window is seen as more environmentally friendly (HC 474–I, *supra* n.56, p. xvii).

[66] Irvine, *supra* n.51, p. 14.

[67] The Fifth Environmental Action Programme, *supra* n.15, ch. 3, p. 27.

[68] Ernst & Young and SPRU, *Integrated Product Policy* (Brussels, Commission of the European Communities, 1998) Commission of the European Communities, *Workshop on Integrated Product Policy*, 8 Dec. 1998, and http://europa.eu.int/comm/dg11/ipp/home.htm; DETR, *Consumer Products and the Environment* (London, DETR, 1998) (consultation paper) and DETR, *Consumer Products and the Environment* (London, DETR, 1999) (responses to the consultation).

[69] The life cycle approach is at the centre of an integrated product policy—the idea is that, just as integrated pollution control ensures a balanced view across all environmental media, so an integrated product policy ensures that all aspects of a product's life cycle are considered.

either be legally binding and contractual in nature, or they can be non-binding unilateral commitments on the part of industry recognised by the public authorities.[70] The former are sometimes referred to as "negotiated" agreements, and the latter "voluntary" agreements, in that only with the latter is compliance truly voluntary. However the term voluntary agreements is often used to refer to both, because both involve a voluntary entering into the agreement (although how voluntary is debatable given that the threat of legislation is typically in the background). One of the key risks with binding agreements is that of free riding by companies that have not signed up to the agreement. A way around this is actually to legislate (or lay down specific proposals), and then allow those signing up to an agreement in advance to secure some sort of advantage.[71]

At EC level, environmental agreements with the car industry lie at the centre of the Community's strategy on reducing carbon dioxide emissions from new passenger cars. A binding agreement to reduce carbon dioxide from new passenger cars by 25 per cent by the year 2008 was made by the European Commission and the European Automobile Manufacturers Association (ACEA) in July 1998.[72] In the UK, non-binding environmental agreements have recently been used in relation to energy efficiency in the chemical industry,[73] and in relation to HFC greenhouse gases.[74] The government is also currently looking into using environmental agreements in the context of the climate change levy, with sectors that agree to tougher targets benefiting from lower tax rates.[75]

COST-EFFECTIVENESS

Efficiency would require ambient standards to be set by reference to CBA. However, given the difficulties of assessing environmental damage costs, most ambient standards are not set in this way, but rather politically. Many economists are resigned to this fact, but insist that the most *cost-effective* method should nevertheless be used in meeting these ambient targets. They thus advocate the use of *cost-effectiveness analysis*, which requires an assessment of different policy instruments to see which can reach the relevant ambient standard at least cost.

[70] *Commission Communication on Environmental Agreements*, COM(96)561 final.

[71] See e.g. the Climate Change Levy (*infra* n.75).

[72] COM(1998)495 final; http://europa.eu.int/comm/dg11/co2/co2_agre.htm. There has also been a negotiated agreement between the Commission and TV/VCR manufacturers to reduce energy consumption by TVs/VCRs in standby mode [1998] OJ C12/2; and the Commission is looking into the use of such agreements for other consumer electronic equipment (COM(1999)120 final).

[73] 274 ENDS Report (1997) 38.

[74] 252 ENDS Report (1996) 31.

[75] See 291 ENDS Report (1999) 3.

Command-and-control

For non-dangerous substances, geographically uniform command-and-control emission standards are not cost-effective.[76] Geographically uniform standards will not achieve a given level of environmental quality at least cost because, in areas with a high assimilative capacity, the same level of environmental quality is likely to be achievable with less strict (and thus less costly) emission standards.[77] For dangerous substances, which cannot be assimilated by the environment, geographical location is irrelevant and it thus makes little sense to speak of locational cost-effectiveness where such substances are concerned.

However, for *all* substances, uniform command-and-control emission standards are also not cost-effective in marginal abatement cost (MAC)[78] terms. If an agency wishes, say, to reduce emissions by 15 per cent and there are two plants, A and B, it will seldom be cost-effective to make both plants cut back by 15 per cent. This is because MACs typically differ between firms, so that if, for example, A's are five times that of B's, the lower cost solution will obviously be to make B cut back more than A.[79] The least cost solution will be the point where the marginal abatement costs of the two plants are equalised.[80]

In practice a number of the existing UK pollution command-and-control regimes do vary emission standards for non-dangerous substances according to location and are thus cost-effective in this sense.[81] However none appears to consider marginal abatement costs systematically. One reason is that the informational cost to the agency of doing so would be huge. Another is that agencies do not have ready access to firms' MACs; and, even if they did, firms would have an incentive to overstate these. Nevertheless, under most of the pollution control regimes, abatement costs *are* considered on a more *ad hoc* basis.

[76] See Royal Commission on Environmental Pollution, Sixteenth Report, *Freshwater Quality* (Cm 1966, London, HMSO, 1992), para. 8.6. However, most commentators analyse the issue in efficiency rather than cost-effectiveness terms. In other words they argue that uniform standards are inefficient because damage costs vary with location (see e.g. B. A. Ackerman *et al.*, *The Uncertain Search for Environmental Quality* (New York, Free Press, 1974), pp. 236–7; and C. D. Kolstad, "Uniformity versus Differentiation in Regulating Externalities" (1987) 14 *Jo. of Env. Economics and Management* 386).

[77] However, a geographically uniform pollution charge will be no different. That too will not be cost-effective because in some areas it will lead to greater cutbacks than are necessary to achieve the desired ambient standard.

[78] The cost to a firm of reducing its discharge by one more unit of pollution. A good explanation of marginality is given in R. Kerry Turner *et al.*, *Environmental Economics: An Elementary Introduction* (London, Harvester Wheatsheaf, 1994), pp. 66–72.

[79] This example is based on one given in W. J. Baumol and W. E. Oates, *The Theory of Environmental Policy* (2nd edn., Cambridge, CUP, 1988), p. 164. See also T. Tietenberg, *Environmental and Natural Resource Economics* (4th edn., New York, Harper Collins College Publishers, 1996), p. 333.

[80] *Ibid.*, p. 334.

[81] For some old examples, see e.g. Y. Brittan, *The Impact of Water Pollution Control on Industry: A Case Study of Fifty Dischargers* (Oxford, Oxford Centre for Socio-Legal Studies, 1984), p. 20; G. M. Richardson *et al.*, *Policing Pollution: A Study of Regulation and Enforcement* (Oxford, Clarendon, 1982), p. 101. Practice today in the case of water pollution and discharge to sewers appears to remain much the same in this respect.

First, abatement costs may be considered at the standard-setting stage. The most explicit example of this is integrated pollution control (IPC), where inspectors are specifically required to consider cost when deciding on what is BATNEEC (best available techniques not entailing excessive cost) for a particular industrial process. This is far from a systematic calculation, in that inspectors consider costs in relation to each application separately; they do not compare costs across all processes to ensure that the precise, least cost allocation is adopted. However, the *ad hoc*, individualised approach taken does at least ensure that those with lower control costs are likely to be subjected to higher standards than those with high costs. It is thus an approximation of a least cost approach.

There is evidence that abatement costs have—in the past at least—also been considered in some other pollution control regimes, which did not specifically require their consideration. With discharges to sewer for example, Richardson *et al.* found that those discharging very small volumes of dangerous substances were often given similar limits by the old water authorities to those emitting larger amounts, because the abatement costs per litre were lower for small volumes (as manual treatment was possible).[82] Officers would also typically set stricter consents for new dischargers than for existing ones if the sewage treatment works were near capacity. Existing firms might have had their consents tightened slightly, but the greater burden was borne by the new arrival. Here officers explicitly justified their action by reference to cost-effectiveness, arguing that new arrivals would usually be able to control emissions at much less cost than existing firms which might have to install expensive bolt-on equipment or make expensive process modifications.[83] In the National Rivers Authority, costs tended to be considered in setting consent conditions only if they might lead to the firm going out of business. The danger with this approach is that cost-effectiveness may actually be undermined. This is because a firm that has hit hard times may be the least-cost abater and thus, by not loading a greater proportion of the controls on it, the least cost solution will be missed.

Secondly, abatement costs can be considered at the enforcement stage as well as during standard-setting[84] (in fact the two are quite similar in that non-enforcement *de facto* sets a new standard[85]). However cost is likely to be a factor here only if strict enforcement of the standard would lead to the firm going

[82] However, as Richardson *et al.* argue (*ibid.*, pp. 54 and 103), if it is the case that large volumes (of dangerous substances) typically issue from large firms, then the most cost-effective allocation is likely to be to impose stricter standards on the larger volume discharger because large firms are usually the lower cost abaters.

[83] *Ibid.*, p. 104.

[84] For example, G. M. Richardson and A. I. Ogus' research into trade effluent control showed that for large companies cost would often play a part in negotiations at the consent setting stage, while for small companies with less bargaining power, cost might be a factor in enforcement decisions (see "The Regulatory Approach To Environmental Control" (1979) 2 *Urban Law & Policy* 337).

[85] For an example, see Brittan, *supra* n.81, p. 17; Brittan also notes that differential enforcement can be cost-effective if it takes into account differences in abatement costs (p. 67).

out of business. And as stated above, considering costs in this manner is unlikely to produce a cost-effective outcome. Finally, if, as has been suggested, agencies tend to concentrate their enforcement efforts on large firms, allowing small firms to continue with their non-compliance,[86] this may be cost-effective to the extent that large firms enjoy economies of scale which are likely to make them lower cost abaters. If, on the other hand the converse is true and agencies concentrate their fire on small firms, then regulation is unlikely to be cost-effective.[87]

Economic regulatory instruments

Economists have made a strong case for the cost-effectiveness advantages of switching to economic regulatory instruments such as pollution charges and tradable permits. For a pollution charge scheme to be cost-effective, market forces need to operate so that those who can reduce emissions at least cost actually do so. In a charge system, a producer has an incentive to reduce emissions until he reaches the point where it is cheaper to pay the charge; the firms with the lowest control costs will reduce emissions the most, whilst those facing higher costs may prefer to pay the charge. This produces a cost-effective result because the greater burden of reducing emissions is taken on by those who can do so at least cost. In fact, if firms face the same charge, marginal abatement costs will automatically be equalised, which is a condition for cost minimisation.[88] As Tietenberg comments:

> This is a rather remarkable finding. We have shown that as long as the control authority imposes the same emission charge on all sources, the resulting allocation *automatically* minimizes the costs of control. This is true in spite of the fact that the control authority may not have any knowledge of control costs.[89]

While, as we have seen, it is theoretically possible for a command-and-control regulator to achieve a least cost allocation of emission reductions, in practice it is unlikely. With charges in contrast, the least cost solution achieved via equalisation of marginal costs is arrived at automatically.

The cost-effectiveness case for tradable permits is very similar: as a permit market develops, firms with high abatement costs will find it cheaper to buy permits than to cut back their emissions; firms with low abatement costs will be able to make cut-backs easily and then sell some of their permits. Because all

[86] See S. Breyer, *Regulation and Its Reform* (London, Harvard UP, 1982), pp. 277, 280.

[87] P. Yeager, *The Limits of Law: The Public Regulation of Private Pollution* (Cambridge, CUP, 1991), pp. 45–6, 292, 311.

[88] Tietenberg, *supra* n.79, p. 336. See also Baumol and Oates, *supra* n.79, p. 164.

[89] Tietenberg, *ibid.*

firms have to pay the same market price for a permit, marginal abatement costs are equalised across all firms and a least cost solution will be achieved.[90]

Voluntary mechanisms

Voluntary mechanisms such as eco-management and audit, eco-labelling and voluntary agreements between government and industry are also likely to be more cost-effective than command-and-control regulation. There are two senses in which this may be true. First, they are likely to be more cost-effective than command-and-control standards that require specific types of technology or techniques to be adopted. This is because firms have detailed knowledge of their own costs and processes and are likely to choose a more cost-effective method for controlling pollution than one imposed by an outside regulator which lacks such detailed knowledge. Thus with eco-management and audit, firms set their own pollution reduction targets and choose the most cost-effective method of achieving these. Eco-labelling similarly leaves decisions in the hands of firms, which can choose what process and product changes to make to attract the green consumer, rather than have these imposed by a regulator. With voluntary agreements, companies are able to choose the most appropriate time at which to introduce improvements since the target approach provides them with reasonable lead-times; and again, rather than regulatory agencies imposing costly solutions without first-hand experience, the system relies upon industry knowledge.

However, this particular cost-effectiveness advantage has arguably been rather overstated, since few UK command-and-control regimes lay down prescriptive technology conditions. BATNEEC within IPC for example, has typically been defined in terms of a performance standard—leaving firms free to choose the technology to achieve the relevant emission standards—rather than a process or technology standard.

A separate cost-effectiveness argument would be one more in line with that typically offered in relation to charges and tradable permits, which relates not to savings *within* firms (as considered in the previous two paragraphs[91]), but to savings *across* firms. The argument here would be that one would expect those firms with lower control costs to adopt a greater proportion of reductions under a voluntary approach than those with high control costs. As we have seen, command-and-control regulators—lacking such information—are unlikely to apply the least cost method.

[90] Baumol and Oates, *supra* n.79, p. 177. This is the theory. In practice, if for example markets are thin, or permits are hoarded and little trading takes place, then the cost-effectiveness advantages of tradable permits will not be realised.

[91] Although taxes and tradable permits are also likely to be cost-effective in this sense, since they too leave decisions in the hands of firms rather than having a regulator impose costly solutions on them.

EQUALITY

Command-and-control

Assessing standard setting-in terms of fairness or equality before the law is far from straightforward.[92] Fairness or equality can be seen as requiring like cases to be treated alike. The difficulty comes in establishing when plants are like cases. A very basic view would be that plants are like cases when they are of the same type and size. Fairness on this view would thus require plants of the same type and size to be treated alike in the sense of being given the same standards. However, a more sophisticated version would point to other factors, which mean that apparently similar plants are not in fact like cases. One such factor would be location. Hawkins quotes a field officer thus:

> if people perhaps in the same industry are situated in different places in the estuary, y'know, if one was to point the finger at the other and say "But you allow him to discharge such and such and you only let us do this", then we should be able to turn round and say, "Ah yes, but you're discharging in a different place and the river quality in this different place needs different treatment." . . . I think you can only treat them similarly if all other things are equal, if they're discharging into the same sort of watercourse in the same sort of position.[93]

Another factor could be marginal abatement costs (MACs). If cost-effectiveness is regarded as a legitimate aim, then setting apparently similar firms different standards on the basis of their differing MACs cannot be considered unfair. Take the example of two competing firms, A and B. Assuming, as is quite likely, that A and B have differing MACs, then giving them both the same standard would not be cost-effective. Equality in cost-effectiveness terms may thus be seen as requiring the grant of standards which differ to the extent necessary to ensure equalisation of A's and B's MACs.[94]

[92] See generally Kolstad, *supra* n.76; T. O. McGarity, "Media Quality, Technology, and Cost-Benefit Balancing Strategies For Health and Environmental Regulation" (1983) 46 *Law and Contemporary Problems* 159, pp. 219–20; R. A. Leone and J. F. Jackson, "The Political Economy of Federal Regulatory Activity: The Case of Water Pollution Controls" in G. Fromm (ed.), *Studies in Public Regulation* (Cambridge, Mass., MIT Press, 1981), p. 231 at 264; and C. J. Koch and R. A. Leone, "The Clean Water Act: Unexpected Impacts on Industry" (1979) 3 *Harv. Env. LR* 84, pp. 104–5.

[93] K. Hawkins, *Environment and Enforcement: Regulation and the Social Definition of Pollution* (Oxford, Clarendon, 1984), p. 26; see also p. 31. However, in certain circumstances it seems, the scientific judgment apparent in the sophisticated version gave way to the more basic reading of equality: "[f]ield men, however, are constantly reminded that industrialists and farmers work on a principle of equity: they can readily discover the standards which their competitors must observe and may complain if they are being handicapped. But the agencies prefer to avoid complaints wherever possible, and this encourages an administrative inclination for equity of treatment, even though 'scientific' judgement may dictate otherwise. Negotiating about standards, especially when there is some disparity between apparently similar dischargers, though an infrequent event, can be one of the field man's trickiest tasks" (p. 26).

[94] However, if the only reason one of the firms has low marginal abatement costs is that it has had an easy ride in the past and has not installed basic equipment that the other has, it would

However, if equality between firms is seen as important for competition reasons, then it will be necessary to equalise, not the *marginal* abatement costs of A and B, but the *total* control costs so that they feel "equal pain".[95] If one of them ends up paying out more in total costs than the other, it may be placed at a competitive disadvantage. Were A to ask why its standards differed from those of B, the agency could thus reply that it is because it has differing total abatement costs.

Where command-and-control regulation is process-based (such as IPC/IPPC), there will also be a question of trying to ensure fairness *between* industrial sectors. Unlike unfairness *within* an industrial sector, this is unlikely to be significant in competition terms (unless the products from different sectors are closely interchangeable). However one industrial sector can be said to have a legitimate grievance in fairness terms if it is suffering a greater burden than that of another, which is seen as "getting off lightly".[96]

Equality is also relevant in relation to the enforcement of standards. The issue of enforcement has potentially serious implications for competition, because some firms could end up facing prosecution (with all the associated costs in terms of management time, legal fees and so on) and fines more regularly than others.[97] Perhaps more importantly, non-enforcement is effectively the setting of a less stringent standard—one that may be lower than that held by a competitor.[98]

Economic regulatory instruments

With tradable permits, there will be no question of equality between firms if the initial allocation of permits proceeds by way of auction because the market is responsible for the resulting differences in the distribution of permits. If, on the

arguably be more equal for it to bear the burden now rather than aiming for an equalisation of marginal abatement costs (see RCEP, Sixteenth Report, *Freshwater Quality* (Cm 1966, London, HMSO, 1992), report 8 of the additional reports undertaken for the RCEP, "Appraisal of the Potential Role of Market Mechanisms in Water Quality Issues", p. 351, at para. 6.63).

[95] Leone and Jackson, and Koch and Leone, *supra* n.92.

[96] Unless the disparity reflects historical levels of effort by the two industries (*cf. supra* n.94). An example of quite the reverse happening can be found in the context of the national plan for the reduction of acid gas emissions under s.3 of the Environmental Protection Act 1990. The oil refinery industry and "other industry" categories were unhappy with the fact that they had been given a much larger burden under the plan than the electricity generating industry, given that they had already done a great deal to reduce their emissions as against the poor efforts of the power generators (see (1990) 1 *Utilities Law Rev*. 120). It is difficult to see a way round this problem, other than perhaps to allocate each industry a presumptive base-line—what Baumol and Oates call a "hypothetical 'raw waste load'": see W. J. Baumol and W. E. Oates, *Economics, Environmental Policy and the Quality of Life* (Englewood Cliffs, NJ, Prentice-Hall, 1979), p. 236.

[97] EC Fifth Environmental Action Programme, *supra* n.15, p. 81.

[98] Brittan, *supra* n.81, pp. 27, 68. On p. 68, she gives an example of the metalwork finishing industry, where different consents *and* differential enforcement meant that firms in a lax area had won orders from those in a strict area (a 20% difference in prices is mentioned).

other hand, permits are grandparented, then—as far as existing sources are concerned—equality is dependent on the pre-existing command-and-control standards. There is also, of course, the question of equality between those existing sources and new entrants. If the permits are grandparented, this may produce inequality in that existing sources gain a significant asset while new entrants will have to buy permits before they can commence production.[99]

After the initial allocation, and once a market has developed, tradable permits may be regarded as satisfying equality in that the marginal abatement costs facing firms will be the same. Charges satisfy equality not only in ensuring that marginal abatement costs are equalised, but also in that all firms face the same charge rate. There may of course be differences in the charge rates between locations, but this will not conflict with equality because this differentiation can be justified on cost-effectiveness grounds. However, again, if equality is seen as important for competition reasons, then equality will require the equalising not of marginal but of *total* control costs proportionate to size of output, which neither a charge nor a tradable permit system will achieve.[100] That said, both would get closer to the competitiveness ideal than an attempt to achieve a cost-effective standard-setting system. Kneese and Bower comment on a flexible command-and-control system as follows:

> Perhaps the scheme that would strike one as most inequitable is the efficiently programmed effluent standards approach because it emphasises waste reduction by dischargers with low marginal waste reduction costs. In effect, it could penalise those with low costs and present the high-cost waste discharger with a free property right to continue his waste discharge unmodified.[101]

In contrast, with both charges and tradable permits there is a much more even distribution of total costs among firms. With a flexible command-and-control approach aiming at the equalisation of marginal costs, costs would be loaded on firms with low abatement costs. However, with charges, the high cost abater would have a charge bill to pay, and with a tradable permit system, the low cost abater would be able to sell permits and the high cost abater would have to buy them.[102] In other words the total costs are much more evenly spread, which is likely to be beneficial from a competition point of view.

Of course, although economic instruments switch the question of equality from that under a command-and-control system—of whether the standards are in accordance with the principle of equal treatment—to the question whether the charge or the initial allocation and results of permit trading are equal, they will not affect the issue of equality in enforcement. Unequal enforcement may have just as much, if not more, of an impact on competitiveness in a system

[99] DoE, *supra* n.20, p.14.

[100] McGarity, *supra* n.92, p. 220.

[101] A. V. Kneese and B. T. Bower, "Standards, Charges, and Equity" in R. Dorfman and N. S. Dorfman (eds.), *Economics of the Environment: Selected Readings* (New York, W. W. Norton & Co, 1972), p. 159 at 168–9.

[102] Although again, how fair this is depends on historical levels of effort: see *supra* nn.94, 96.

based on economic instruments, as it does in one based on command-and-control.

Voluntary mechanisms

Equality is not an issue if firms are acting independently in the market. It is only an issue if there is an external, official body doing some "treating" (as in "treat like cases alike"). However, the important point to note is that treatment can just as well involve carrots (*dominium*) as the more familiar sticks (*imperium*) of regulation. And voluntary mechanisms such as EMAS and eco-labelling supply such carrots in the form of the ability to sport the eco-logo and the eco-label respectively. Equality or fairness is thus a legitimate concern in relation to these instruments.

As with process-based command-and-control regulation, fairness here may apply both between and within industries. With EMAS, external verification of the commitment to continuous improvement currently proceeds on the basis of a subjective assessment by the verifier, rather than by reference to quantitative performance targets or benchmarks for particular industry sectors set out in sector application guides (SAGs).[103] With subjective assessment, consistency of treatment is unlikely. A situation may, for example, arise where there are widely differing standards of improvement between two similar firms and yet both qualify for the carrot. Only if SAGs are used is there likely to be any equality within industry sectors. However, even SAGs would not necessarily ensure fairness between sectors since, as the ENDS Report notes, "[t]here is . . . a clear potential for the SAG for one sector to be more demanding on companies than SAGs for others".[104]

Similar problems arise with eco-labels. There may be unfairness between industries if criteria for some product groups are much more stringent than those for others.[105] As for equality within sectors, the arrangement of products into groups appears, at first sight, to guarantee this. However, on closer inspection this turns out not to be the case. The main reason for this lies in the imprecise nature of life-cycle analysis (LCA). For example, the greater weighting of one factor rather than another in the LCA (for example, with washing machines, weighting electricity consumption rather than powder usage) may be

[103] However, the revised Reg. (*supra* n.38) looks set to change this. The preamble to the proposal states that "the Commission should, according to a Community procedure, establish guidelines in partnerships with EMAS stakeholders for ensuring a consistent implementation of the EMAS requirements across the Member States". Annex III also provides for the reporting of environmental performance against "sector, national or regional benchmarks". On SAGs (in relation to BS 7750), see e.g. 218 ENDS Report (1993) 20.

[104] *Ibid*. Though if one sector has made much more effort historically, then giving it a less demanding SAG may not be regarded as unfair: see *supra* nn.94, 96, 102.

[105] Though again, this may not be unfair if the application of less stringent criteria reflects an already significant head-start in terms of effort on the part of the industry manufacturing the product concerned.

seen as unfair on the part of a manufacturer whose product fails to secure a label because of that weighting, but who would have been awarded one had the weighting been slightly different. One cannot level the same accusations at regulatory orders to install pollution control equipment, because, unlike LCA, that is at least a reasonably precise science. At worst, the skewing of eco-labelling product assessment criteria may be deliberate rather than simply a natural result of LCA's imprecision. To begin with, responsibility for establishing ecological criteria was shared out amongst different Member States, which created a risk that a particular Member State would deliberately place a greater weighting on criteria which favoured its national products in a group.[106] However, the need for final agreement on criteria in the Regulatory Committee by qualified majority voting meant that, even back then, this was not a particularly significant risk.

EQUITY

So far, we have considered only equality or fairness between firms. While this can be described as an equity issue, the term equity in the regulatory context is normally used to refer to other concerns. First, it may be used in relation to the distribution of pollution damage costs between polluter and the public. This is the concern of the "polluter pays principle" (PPP)—a broad equitable principle, which requires the polluter to pay for the damage costs rather than letting these fall on the public. With command-and-control regulation, the "polluter" pays for the technological costs of process design or pollution abatement equipment to enable him to keep within the levels specified by his permit.[107] However, while he pays for these *control* costs, he does not pay for the *damage* costs of emissions within his permit levels.[108] Under a charge system, the "polluter" does pay for these, because he is charged on each unit of his emissions.[109] However, in so far as a charge system also charges for non-polluting emissions, then it too can be said to conflict with the PPP.[110]

Where command-and-control costs or pollution charge costs are significant, producers will often seek to pass these on to consumers. Indeed the whole point of some pollution taxes is to seek to alter not producer but consumer behaviour, in order to reduce consumption of the good in question. Of course, in so far as

[106] For example, intended or not, the effect of the proposed criteria for paper drawn up by Denmark favoured Scandinavian mills. The criteria included CO_2 and SO_2 emissions from energy usage. British paper manufacturers, which used high sulphur content British coal to generate in-house energy would have been placed at a disadvantage compared to Scandinavian mills which used biomass, with its lower CO_2 and SO_2 emissions (219 ENDS Report (1993) 24).

[107] What Kerry Turner *et al.* refer to as the "standard" PPP (*supra* n.78, p. 146).

[108] *Ibid.*

[109] What Kerry Turner *et al.* refer to as the "extended" PPP, *ibid.*

[110] *Ibid.*, pp. 172–3. One way round this would be to adopt what Field terms a "two-part emission tax"—allowing an initial quantity to go untaxed and applying the tax only to emissions above this quantity—B. Field, *Environmental Economics: An Introduction* (London, McGraw-Hill, 1994), p. 231.

consumers of polluting products are also polluters, making consumers pay can be seen as fulfilling an equitable distribution of damage costs between polluters and the general public in accordance with the PPP. However, doing so may bring regulatory policy into conflict with a separate equity concern, which relates to the distribution of costs between rich and poor. For example, some pollution taxes such as VAT on domestic fuel—while perfectly in accordance with the PPP—are considered potentially regressive, and hence inequitable, because the poor spend a higher proportion of their income on fuel. If such taxes are to be introduced, then alterations to other taxes or social security may be needed to ensure an equitable result. Besides distribution of costs, equity can also be applied to the distribution of benefits between rich and poor. For example, if green consumption can be seen as providing a "virtue" benefit to those who practise it, then eco-labelling may be considered inequitable—at least where green products are more expensive than non-green alternatives, meaning that only the better off can afford them.

Finally, equity can also be used to refer to the incidence of pollution between rich and poor and between different races, although this is more commonly referred to as a matter of "environmental justice".[111] The argument—which is made particularly vociferously in the USA—is that the poor and ethnic minorities have historically suffered the greater burden of pollution and that efforts must be made to redress this injustice. Applying this to economic instruments, Ann Powers has suggested that tradable permits may raise environmental justice concerns. Citing proposals to adopt a nitrogen trading programme between sewage treatment works discharging into Long Island Sound, she claims that wealthier counties may choose to upgrade their works because they can afford to. Poorer areas, unable to afford this, would instead have to purchase credits from the wealthy counties—effectively redistributing wealth the wrong way.[112] In addition, as we shall see, to the extent that economic and voluntary instruments suffer from effectiveness problems, then a greater reliance on such mechanisms—far from redressing injustice—may well end up exacerbating it.

ACCOUNTABILITY

Accountability can be either *ex ante* or *ex post*. *Ex ante* accountability—often referred to as "participation"—ensures that the public and others have some input into regulatory decision-making; *ex post* accountability enables them to hold decision-makers to account after the event for the practical exercise of their

[111] See further K. Sexton and R. Zimmerman, "The Emerging Role of Environmental Justice in Decision-Making" in K Sexton *et al.*, *Better Environmental Decisions: Strategies for Governments, Businesses, and Communities* (Washington, DC, Island Press, 1999), p. 419.

[112] A. Powers, "Pollution Trading: A 'Sound' Strategy?" (1998) 2(1) *Environmentally Friendly* 6 at 7 (see further A. Powers, "Reducing Nitrogen Pollution on Long Island Sound: Is There a Place for Pollutant Trading?" (1998) 23 *Col. Jo. of Env. Law* 137).

powers—for example through administrative appeals, the ombudsman or judicial review.[113]

Command-and-control

Jewell has noted a shift in emphasis in UK pollution control regimes away from what he terms "tactical", site-specific, technical controls towards more formalised "strategic" decision-making such as environmental quality objectives.[114] His concern is that this shift has worrying implications for accountability because, traditionally, most accountability mechanisms (in particular the public registers) have been directed at the tactical level.

This is an important observation, but to appreciate its specific significance for command-and-control regulation, we need to recall what was said right at the start of this chapter about the scope of the term command-and-control. The regulatory process can generally be separated into three stages: the setting of policy; the setting of ambient environmental standards[115]; and the setting of plant and other standards needed to achieve these ambient goals.[116] Strictly speaking, the term command-and-control should be used only in relation to plant standards, for it is plants that are being commanded and controlled. It is easy to see how the overall framework, encompassing all three stages, might equally be described as one of command-and-control. However, to slip into this way of viewing things is dangerous,[117] because the setting of policy goals and ambient standards is just as necessary in a system based on economic instruments.

With the above in mind, one might be tempted to conclude that accountability for command-and-control regulation, *stricto sensu*, is currently very good, but that it does not deserve the level of accountability with which it is currently lavished (for example through the registers). However, this is true only of *ex ante* accountability: few people are really going to be interested in, or able to offer a viewpoint on technical details about, plant design or precise emission levels.[118] It is less true of *ex post* accountability. Registers offer an important third arm to enforcement of environmental laws. Although few people actually use them for this purpose, that may not be due to lack of interest, but rather to difficulty in accessing and understanding the registers.[119] One cannot, however,

[113] The definition of *ex ante* accountability in this chapter thus differs from that in Ch. 4. The reason for this is to enable Jewell's argument (below) to be mirrored more closely here.

[114] T. Jewell, "Public Law and the Environment: The Prospects for Decision-Making" in T. Jewell and J. Steele (eds.), *Law in Environmental Decision-Making* (Oxford, Clarendon, 1998), p. 73.

[115] These two corresponding to Jewell's "strategic" decision-making.

[116] Corresponding to Jewell's "tactical" controls.

[117] Not that Jewell does this.

[118] *Cf.* the equivalent level of decision-making in planning law, where people typically have very firm ideas about the desirability of particular developments.

[119] See further Ch 4. As noted there, this may change with the Internet-based pollution inventory introduced by the Environment Agency.

argue that command-and-control is poor in terms of accountability (*ex ante* or *ex post*) for the setting of policy goals and ambient standards. Accountability at these levels *is* inadequate,[120] but they are not levels of decision-making unique to command-and-control.

Economic regulatory instruments

In a US context, Ackerman and Stewart have suggested that economic instruments might enhance *ex ante* accountability for the setting of standards:

> BAT focuses Congressional debate, as well as administrative and judicial proceedings, upon arcane technological questions which rapidly exhaust the time and energy that most politicians, let alone the larger public, are willing to spend on environmental matters. In contrast, the marketable permit system will allow the policymaking debate to take a far more intelligible shape. Rather than debating the difference between the "best available control technology" and "lowest achievable emission rate", citizens may focus on a different question when the environmental acts come up for revision: During the next n years, should we instruct the EPA gradually to decrease (or increase) the number of pollution rights by x percent?[121]

What then should one make of this argument that the introduction of economic instruments (specifically tradable permits) will "enhance the democratic accountability of environmental policy decisions"?[122] Mintz is surely correct in concluding that the argument is misguided, since it is not clear that the level of debate would be made any easier by a switch to economic instruments.[123] Deciding on the appropriate ambient standards is necessary under both command-and-control and market-based systems. Just because arguments over the means would become less technical under a tradable permit system (or rather non-existent, since decisions on means would be left to market actors), it does not follow that deciding on what the end should be will be any less problematic than at present.[124]

Despite Mintz's cogent criticisms, Sunstein has also recently argued for the "democracy-reinforcing" feature of economic instruments. He begins in much the same vein as Ackerman and Stewart in drawing a distinction between the opacity of means and the clarity of ends:

> Economic incentives focus democratic attention on the question of ends: "How much clean-up at what price?" Incentives do not focus on the question of means: "Which

[120] Jewell, *supra* n.114.

[121] B. A. Ackerman and R. B. Stewart, "Reforming Environmental Law: The Democratic Case For Market Incentives" (1988) 13 *Col. Jo. of Env. Law* 171.

[122] R. B. Stewart, "Controlling Environmental Risks Through Economic Incentives" (1988) 13 *Col. Jo. of Env. Law*, 153, p. 160.

[123] J. A. Mintz, "Economic Reform of Environmental Protection: A Brief Commentary on a Recent Debate" (1991) 15 *Harv. Env. LR* 149, p. 160.

[124] *Ibid.*

> technology is best?" . . . The issue of ends forces representatives to make the tradeoff between environmental and other values explicitly and openly in a way that the current attention to means does not.[125]

However, the novelty of his argument lies in his subsequent claim that there is also a democratic advantage in avoiding the deals between special interests which arise when the focus is on means. If the focus is on means—the example he gives is whether one ought to use ethanol, methanol, nethanol or thethanol—then it is likely that groups with a stake in the outcome will each argue for one of those.[126] If, instead, the issue is on the level of reduction sought, then the generality of the issue is likely to reduce the influence of factions.[127] His argument thus appears to be that economic instruments enhance democratic accountability by posing a question more amenable to civic republican discussion. In response to this, one critic noted that interest groups and deals are also present in deciding on the ends—citing the example of global warming, where the natural gas companies have lobbied for tougher reductions in global warming emissions than some other sectors.[128] Sunstein's reply is that:

> If the issue is what means of technology is appropriate, then it is an invitation for interest group deals. Whereas, if the question is what aggregate level of acid rain is desirable, you will have interest group manoeuvring—as you say it is unavoidable—but the risk is diminished because there is more generality in the question. It is a little harder for factions to turn the debate to their advantage.[129]

In the end, although they are making slightly different points, both Ackerman and Stewart on the one hand and Sunstein on the other are essentially arguing that discussion of ends is more suited to democratic debate, and that discussion of means is technical and thus inimical to such debate. However, this is no different from our conclusion in the previous section on command-and-control, to the effect that *ex ante* accountability for command-and-control plant standards is actually relatively unimportant. What is important is accountability for policy decisions and for ambient standards adopted within an overall regulatory framework. One can still have command-and-control plant standards but argue that debate should be shifted to prior decisions about ends; it is not necessary to adopt economic instruments to secure such a shift, as Ackerman, Stewart and Sunstein appear to imply.

We have thus rejected the argument that economic instruments will increase accountability because they shift the argument from means to ends: they may, but this can equally be done without them. However, there remains a separate argument—that economic instruments may improve accountability for the setting of means (in so far as this is still considered important). With pollution

[125] C. Sunstein, "Panel II: Public Versus Private Environmental Regulation" (1994) 21 *Ecol. Law Qu.* 455, p. 459.
[126] *Ibid.*, p. 457.
[127] *Ibid.*, p. 459.
[128] *Ibid.*, pp. 470–1.
[129] *Ibid.*, p. 471.

charges, one might argue that the problem of accountability for the power to set plant standards is solved by removing command-and-control standard setting and replacing it with pollution charges. Under a pure charge system, decision-making is decentralised from the agency to individual firms. In other words, firms are free to choose their own output levels (constrained of course by the charge). This removes all power for the setting of standards from the agencies and therefore makes the issue of accountability irrelevant in this respect. Charges therefore appear to lead to an increase in accountability over a system of command-and-control regulation because they remove a decision from the agency for which it needs to be accountable (both *ex ante* and *a fortiori, ex post*).[130]

However, while taxes may remove the need for accountability for standard-setting decisions, accountability will now be required in respect of the tax-setting decision. Although this is obviously only one decision (which may need to be retaken occasionally), as opposed to the many involved in standard-setting, the impact of this one decision will be so significant that one cannot easily conclude that an accountability gain has been made.

With tradable permits, under an auction system, the market would decide permit allocation, not the agency—removing the latter's allocatory power. If, rather than being auctioned, permits were grandparented, allocation would be based on historical agency power. However, once trading was established, agency power in setting standards would be lost. Future allocation would depend on the outcome of trading decisions made by the firms themselves. Thus, as with a charging system, a system of tradable permits might be thought to lead to an increase in accountability over a system of command-and-control regulation because it too removes a decision from the agency for which they need to be accountable.

However, here too there will be new decision areas for which an agency would have to be made accountable. With tradable permits, there are likely to be two of considerable significance. First, if it were decided that the number of permits should be reduced to improve environmental quality, there would have to be decisions on how to go about achieving this. Secondly, controls on trading in a permit market would be needed to prevent the build-up of "hot-spots". As Tietenberg notes of the existing US trading programme:

> A lot of uncertainty is associated with emission reduction credit transactions since they depend so heavily on administrative action. All trades must be approved by the control authorities. If the authorities are not co-operative or at least consistent, the value of the created emission credits could be diminished or even destroyed.[131]

There is thus a danger of over-idealising markets—thinking that the magic invisible hand will replace the visible hand of administrative decision-making.

[130] See C. K. Rowley and A. T. Peacock, *Welfare Economics: A Liberal Restatement* (London, Martin-Robertson, 1975), p. 173; see also D. Helm, "The Assessment: Reforming Environmental Regulation in the UK" (1993) 9 *Oxford Review of Economic Policy* 1.

[131] Tietenberg, *supra* n.14, p. 27.

However, markets, especially of the type at issue, do not exist in vacuums and require careful administrative control. The power necessary to achieve this control will still need to be subject to accountability.[132]

Neither charges nor tradable permits will, it is submitted, affect the accountability of regulatory agencies for their *enforcement* decisions. Enforcement of economic instruments will still be required, and hence there will continue to be decisions on enforcement for which agencies need to be made accountable.

Voluntary mechanisms

The effect that voluntary instruments have on accountability will depend on whether they totally replace the overall framework of regulation or whether they merely act as a supplement. This is likely to vary between such instruments. Voluntary agreements effectively replace overall regulation in a particular area, and this is likely to have a significant impact on both *ex ante* and *ex post* accountability. With *ex ante* accountability, there is a danger of no public debate taking place on either means[133] or ends,[134] since both of these may be seen as a private contractual matter between government and industry. As for *ex post* accountability, contracts are not well known for providing third parties with effective remedies and administrative or judicial review may prove difficult.[135]

Other voluntary instruments, such as EMAS and eco-labelling, are likely to remain as supplements to the existing regulatory process, and thus accountability is arguably less important. Nevertheless, the need for it does not disappear altogether. In relation to *ex ante* accountability, with EMAS there will be a need for participation by relevant interests in the development of any sector application guides that are drawn up. With eco-labelling, there is already provision through the Consultation Forum for participation by industry, environmental groups and other interests in the setting of product criteria.[136] As for *ex post* accountability, the possibility of judicial review of the competent bodies for EMAS and eco-labelling clearly exists.

[132] To similar effect, see Jewell, *supra* n.114.

[133] Although, given our earlier observations, this is not very significant.

[134] In the Netherlands for example, environmental groups have complained about being left out of the target-setting process—see 224 ENDS Report (1993) 3, p. 5. However, the Commission Communication on Environmental Agreements (*supra* n.70) counsels that general targets should be set through legislation, because "[t]his allows all stakeholders, in particular industry and the interested public, to participate in the target-setting by using the constitutionally or legally established procedures" (para. 10, and see also para. 18).

[135] *Ibid.*, para. 11. For a similar problem in medical law in relation to the private finance initiative, see C. Newdick, "The NHS in Private Hands—Regulating Private Providers of NHS Services" in M. Freeman and A. Lewis (eds.), *Law and Medicine: Current Legal Issues* Volume 3 (Oxford, OUP, forthcoming).

[136] Art. 6 of the Reg. *supra* n.56. The European Environment Bureau (EEB) represents environmental groups in this Forum.

EFFECTIVENESS

Command-and-control

In discussing the effectiveness of different types of instrument at tackling pollution, it is necessary to make a clear distinction between practical and theoretical effectiveness. Command-and-control techniques are *relatively* effective in both senses: there is little inherent in them that limits their effectiveness as a theoretical matter; and overall improvements in environmental quality over the past few decades—during which time command-and-control techniques have reigned—may be considered to attest to their effectiveness in practice.

However, while environmental quality has undoubtedly improved overall, there are specific types of pollution that remain problematic. Generally speaking, visible pollution from stationary, point sources[137] has decreased dramatically; but problems remain with more risk-related, invisible pollution from such sources,[138] with visible and invisible pollution from mobile[139] and diffuse[140] sources, and with pollution from product use and disposal.[141] However, even with stationary, point sources, one cannot easily conclude that this improvement is solely due to the effectiveness of command-and-control techniques: shifts to other fuels[142] and a general decline in heavy industry are also likely to have had a significant effect. But then neither can one easily lay the remaining problem areas at the door of command-and-control: the failure is as much if not more one of political will as it is one of failure of the tool.

Economic regulatory instruments

Charges involve a producer paying a fee for each unit of pollution he produces, leaving him relatively free to choose the level of emissions he desires. Tradable permits, on the other hand, require an initial allocation of permits, which can then be traded between firms. Under a charging scheme, the quantity is determined by the market and the price by the regulatory authority; with tradable permits, the quantity is set by the regulator and the price by the market. This points to one of the advantages of tradable permits over pure charging schemes: the quantity (the level of ambient environmental quality) is relatively certain. If one relies on charges alone, then so-called market "flexibility" may mean that

137 E.g. factories and domestic chimneys.

138 E.g. chemicals and CO_2 emissions.

139 E.g. air pollution from cars and other vehicles, which is both invisible (CO_2) and visible (smog).

140 E.g. diffuse pollution from agriculture, of air (e.g. by cattle), and water (e.g. pesticide and fertiliser run-off).

141 The latter has given rise to recent moves by the Commission to develop an integrated product policy—*supra* n.68.

142 E.g. towards gas and away from coal—both for domestic heating and for power generation.

ambient targets are not met. The process of setting charges will inevitably be one of trial and error—adjusting them up or down to achieve the desired quantity—and irreparable environmental damage could result before the charge is pegged at the correct level. However, while tradable permits enjoy an advantage over charges because they can guarantee a given level of environmental quality (in that the number of permits and hence the level of emissions is fixed), this will be true only at a national[143] level. With certain substances,[144] unless strict controls are placed on trading, the desired level of environmental quality may not be achieved at a local level:

> If the total number of permits is set to meet a single national target, it is possible that, as a result of trading, emissions will increase in sensitive areas. It may be possible for regional variations in environmental sensitivity to be taken into account by means of "exchange rates" so that one unit of emissions in a sensitive area can be traded for more units in a less sensitive area. However, there may be problems in fully reconciling national and local objectives.[145]

Unlike command-and-control techniques, there are thus *theoretical* limitations to the effectiveness of economic instruments—in particular charges. However, *in practice*, charges are not likely to be used as an immediate replacement for command-and-control standards: they are much more likely to be used as a supplement, and increased gradually over time. The problem of irreparable damage is thus unlikely to arise. Similarly with tradable permits: in practice these are not likely to be implemented for substances which could produce "hot-spot" problems without careful controls being put in place.

The previous paragraphs concern claims that economic instruments are theoretically *less* effective than command-and-control standards. However, it has also been argued that economic instruments are, in a limited sense, *more* effective than command-and-control standards, in that they provide firms with a continuous incentive to innovate. With charges, there is an incentive to innovate to control pollution further because this may lead to lower charge payments; a tradable permit system offers a similar incentive through the ability to sell spare permits if emission reductions are made. Command-and-control standards are said not to offer this advantage, because once a standard has been imposed, a firm may have an incentive to keep within it, but it will have little incentive to attempt to move beyond it. However this is arguably an over-generalisation, because some command-and-control standards do attempt to provide an incentive to innovate. Technology forcing standards are a good example and a limited example in a UK context can be found in the "residual" BATNEEC condition in section 7(4) of the Environmental Protection Act 1990, which requires firms to keep up-to-date with developments in BATNEEC.

143 Or whichever other level (e.g. EU or international) is chosen for the scope of the market.

144 E.g. acid gases, where damage is locationally specific; *cf.* certain greenhouse gases such as CO_2, where this problem does not exist.

145 DoE, *supra* n.20, p. 13.

Voluntary mechanisms

Besides the specific problems with them mentioned earlier, the environmental effectiveness of eco-labels and EMAS is ultimately constrained by their voluntary nature. It is somewhat optimistic to expect firms—which are constrained by the need to make a profit—to attend to expensive environmental problems, when doing so would inevitably affect their competitiveness. Firms will take expensive environmental measures only if there is some profit in it for them[146]; they will be unwilling to take unilateral loss-making action for fear of the effect on their competitive position. And a satisfactory level of environmental quality cannot be achieved without some loss-making action on the part of firms. Expensive, unilateral action is therefore unlikely to occur in a market-based system—hence the need for regulation, which imposes constraints multilaterally. Regulation makes loss-making action easier to swallow because everyone is subject to it and thus competition is less of an issue.

Voluntary agreements suffer less from the above constraint because the threat of regulation is always lurking in the background, and because most firms in a particular industry will have signed up to the agreement. Both of these factors mean that loss-making action is much more likely to be undertaken. It has also been suggested that, in relation to certain areas (such as transport, energy conservation and production waste arisings which are sent for outside disposal), voluntary agreements are likely to prove more effective than command-and-control regulation.[147] Again however, while it is true that command-and-control techniques have not so far been successfully used to tackle these areas, this appears to be more a failure of political will than of the instrument.[148]

CERTAINTY

To be able to plan their business and investment strategies effectively, firms need a certain, stable framework within which to operate. The use of discretion can create uncertainty, as can rule-based change. Certainty therefore requires the avoidance of excessive use of discretion and excessive regulatory change.

Command-and-control

In a command-and-control system, uncertainty can arise in two principal ways. First, unstructured discretionary action (in either standard setting or

[146] Whether through e.g. decreased liability risks and waste costs, or increased marketability.
[147] M. Potier, "Agreement on the Environment" (1994) 189 *The OECD Observer* 8, p. 11.
[148] Unless one regards problems of public/industry acceptance as being one of the failures of command-and-control.

enforcement) on the part of regulators is an obvious source of uncertainty.[149] And secondly, the formal ability to change permits may create uncertainty and instability. With the former, uncertainty arises because it is difficult to tell in advance what form discretionary action may take. With the latter, if permits are changeable in a short space of time, then a firm will face considerable difficulties in planning investment.

The solution to the problem of uncertainty caused by discretionary action may be to confine or structure the discretion via rules or policy guidance, so that firms are, to a large extent, able to predict the way in which the discretion will be exercised.[150] Whether discretion can or should be effectively channelled in this manner will obviously depend on the particular regulatory context. The solution to the uncertainty created by altering permits is often to lay down time limits within which permits cannot be changed, except in definable emergencies and perhaps on payment of compensation to the affected company.[151]

Economic regulatory instruments

In relation to pollution charges, the uncertainty in a command-and-control system that resulted from discretion in the setting of standards and their subsequent variation will be replaced by uncertainty as to the initial level of the charge and any subsequent increases needed to cope with new entrants or growth. In other words, there will be little to choose between the two systems in terms of the uncertainty they create for firms.

As for tradable permits, firms will be faced with uncertainty if the initial allocation of standards proceeds by way of auction. Grandparenting will produce a greater level of certainty. As with any other system, increasing public expectations of environmental quality may produce a need to reduce the number of permits. Depending on how and how often this is done, such a procedure could create uncertainty for firms. However, assuming the overall number of permits remains the same then, unlike command-and-control or charging, a tradable permit system will respond automatically to new entrants and growth via the market; there will be no need for an agency to adjust standards or charges. This will mean less uncertainty for existing firms because their allocation will remain the same unless they themselves decide to buy or sell permits.

[149] Besides uncertainty, discretion also gives rise to problems of accountability, effectiveness and fairness and may be a contributor to cost-effectiveness. In other words, many of the administrative values are closely connected, and altering one is likely to have a knock-on effect on the others.

[150] E.g. the IPC and local authority air pollution control guidance notes.

[151] See e.g. ss.124–125 of the Water Industry Act 1991, and Sched. 10 to the Water Resources Act 1991; *cf.* ss. 6(6)–(7), 10 of and Pt II of Sched. 1 to the Environmental Protection Act (EPA) 1990, and s.37 of the EPA 1990.

Voluntary mechanisms

Of all the voluntary mechanisms, eco-labels currently raise the most significant certainty issues. The speed at which the product criteria are reviewed will have a considerable bearing on a manufacturer's ability to plan. Under the existing Regulation, once agreed, criteria for *all* product groups are valid for a period of three years before they are reviewed.[152]

CONCLUSION

It is difficult to conclude, as a result of the above analysis, that one type of instrument is any more substantively legitimate than another. After all, the legitimating values concerned are at once broad, slippery and incommensurable. Economic instruments may appear more substantively legitimate in terms of cost-effectiveness, but if the wider range of values is considered, then command-and-control techniques begin to look unfairly maligned. Legitimacy in the context of regulatory instruments is thus best seen in procedural terms. There is a real need for the policy-design process to include a careful assessment of all of the above values.[153] Only if policy instruments have been thoroughly assessed and debated across all of these values can they be regarded as (procedurally) legitimate.

[152] See Art.5(5), *supra* n.56. See further 223 ENDS Report (1993) 24, p. 25, and also 219 ENDS Report (1993) 24, p. 25, where ENDS notes that the British paper industry "with its long investment lead-times, is also arguing that the period for reviewing—and almost certainly tightening—the initial criteria should be extended to 'substantially in excess of the three years presently envisaged'." Under the proposed revisions, it seems that a more flexible approach may be introduced, allowing different time periods to be laid down for different product groups.

[153] For a good start in this direction, see e.g. DoE, *supra* n.20, which assesses instruments on the basis of environmental effectiveness, efficiency, fairness, revenue, innovation, and competition. It does not however consider accountability, a key public law value.

7

Enforcement I: Enforcing National Command-and-control Regulation

CRIMINAL OFFENCES

Before considering regulatory enforcement practice, logically, one must first consider the substance of the law that underpins enforcement. And at the heart of the enforcement process lie a number of criminal offences, most of which are to be found in specific environmental statutes.[1] These criminal offences not only proscribe certain acts and omissions but also provide one route for the enforcement of these proscriptions—prosecution in the criminal courts. Of course, that is not to say that an agency will always prosecute defendants for committing criminal offences; as will be seen, agencies have at their disposal a range of administrative and other techniques beyond prosecution for enforcing proscribed behaviour. However, the fact that a criminal offence may be involved forms an essential deterrent threat—a reserve force that makes the use of many of these other techniques effective. And the fact that the original proscription is criminal arguably sends out a strong moral message about the unacceptability of the behaviour.[2] It is in this sense that the criminal law can be said to underpin the whole of the enforcement process.

Nevertheless, support for a criminal underpinning of environmental regulation is by no means universal. Critics argue that the criminal law should be reserved for "ordinary" offences or "real" crime (*mala in se*), because its use for regulatory or public welfare offences (*mala prohibita*) dilutes the strength of the moral message about the former. They suggest that a system of civil proscriptions, enforced in civil proceedings, would be more appropriate for most pollution cases, with the criminal law reserved for only the most serious cases of wilful behaviour.[3] This would not necessarily detract from deterrence, since

[1] Though not all—see e.g. public nuisance (a common law criminal offence as well as a tort, and one with which the defendants were charged in the Camelford drinking water case).

[2] As Wells observes, "[d]efinitions of crime reflect a moral agenda; choices are made not only as to which acts to proscribe but also as to the legal mechanism (criminal, civil, or administrative) through which those proscriptions should be communicated": C. Wells, *Corporations and Criminal Responsibility* (Oxford, Clarendon, 1993), p. 11.

[3] For suggestions along similar lines, see Note, "Corporate Crime: Regulating Corporate Behaviour Through Criminal Sanctions" (1979) 92 *Harv. L Rev.* 1227 at 1369–75; R. Burnett-Hall, "Enforcement Through Civil Proceedings" [1997] *Amicus Curiae* 24; and V. S. Khanna, "Corporate Criminal Liability: What Purpose Does it Serve? (1996) 109 *Harv. L Rev.* 1477.

civil penalties could be as high as criminal fines.[4] Indeed, it could improve deterrence, as the chances of having to pay penalties would be higher: regulators reluctant to criminalise defendants by bringing prosecutions might be less reluctant to bring cases to a civil court or tribunal; and the chances of being found liable would be greater, since the greater evidential and procedural protections given to defendants under criminal law (e.g. the higher burden of proof) would be absent.[5] However, decriminalising could also reduce deterrence, as the strong moral message of the criminal law would be missing, as would the social stigma of a criminal conviction.

The criminal offences in environmental statutes can be placed into a number of different categories. First, there are acts or omissions of various kinds which will either in themselves be offences—subject to a separate possible defence of acting in accordance with a permit[6]—or which will constitute an offence in the first place only if these acts or omissions are not under and in accordance with a permit.[7] Next, there are relatively straightforward offences involving breaching the conditions of a permit.[8] And, finally, there are offences committed through impeding monitoring powers allowing for access to premises, and offences involving breaches of the conditions in statutory, administrative enforcement tools such as enforcement notices. While the categories listed above are far from exhaustive, they are arguably the most significant in the context of a general analysis of enforcement.

STRICT LIABILITY

Many of the offences in environmental statutes are ones of strict liability. In other words, it is necessary only for the *actus reus*[9] to be made out; there is no need to establish *mens rea* or fault in the form of intention, recklessness or negligence. With the causing offence in section 85 of the Water Resources Act (WRA) 1991 for example, the House of Lords in *Empress*[10] confirmed that the offence is one of strict liability. According to Lord Hoffmann, this means not only that there is no need for *mens rea*, but also that one can be liable for certain deliberate acts of third parties and for certain natural events. Contrary to suggestions in previous case law, it does not matter if these intervening acts or events were not foreseeable, since foreseeability is a concept associated with

[4] *Ibid.*

[5] *Ibid.*

[6] See e.g. s.85(1), (3) and (6) of the Water Resources Act (WRA) 1991 and the defence in s.88(1).

[7] E.g. ss.6(1) and 23(1)(a) of the Environmental Protection Act (EPA) 1990 and s.33(1)(a) and (b) of the EPA 1990.

[8] E.g. the second halves of ss.33(6) of the EPA 1990 and 85(6) of the WRA 1991.

[9] In this context, generally an act, e.g. causing trade or sewage effluent to be discharged into controlled waters (the *actus reus* of the offence in s.85(3) of the WRA 1991).

[10] *Empress Car Company Ltd.* v. *NRA* [1998] 2 WLR 350.

fault-based liability such as the tort of negligence and liability here is strict.[11] However, liability is invariably strict and not absolute: with the causing offence, there will be no offence if a defendant can establish that the act of a third party or natural event was abnormal or extraordinary[12]; and there are also a number of statutory defences which may allow defendants to escape liability. If liability were absolute, there would be no such exceptions.

It is worth pausing to consider some of the reasons for and against imposing strict liability for regulatory criminal offences. Debates on strict liability can be located within two alternative theories of punishment: consequentialist and deontological.[13] The former, which focus on the effect of punishment on others, look to punishment for deterrence, rehabilitation and incapacitation.[14] The latter, which focus more on the individual rights of offenders, believe that punishment should be a matter of retribution or just deserts. There is obviously a potential conflict between the two theories: for example, locking a thief up for life may be justifiable under a consequentialist model, but would be regarded as unfair under a retributivist approach.

One of the most common arguments in favour of strict liability is that it helps to improve deterrence. There are really two sides to this argument. First, it is more difficult for prosecutors to prove fault. The more difficult it is to secure a conviction, the fewer convictions there will be and thus the level of deterrence will be reduced. The reverse side of this argument is that if you know you may be convicted even if you are not at fault, you will take more care overall to avoid causing pollution. A fault requirement of negligence might lead you to take *reasonable steps* to prevent pollution: if you do not, you may face conviction. However, a strict liability standard may lead you to take the *utmost care* to prevent pollution, because you know that you may be convicted even if you have taken reasonable steps.[15]

The polluter pays principle, which rests on a retributive rationale, may also support strict liability. If convicted of an offence, a polluter will typically pay for the pollution caused in the form of a fine or, in extreme cases, through losing his liberty via imprisonment. If a polluter escapes payment because conviction rests on fault, then the polluter pays principle is jeopardised. With strict liability, in

[11] Thus *NRA* v. *Wright Engineering Co. Ltd.* [1994] 4 All ER 281 and *Impress (Worcester) Ltd.* v. *Rees* [1971] 2 All ER 357 were said to have been wrongly decided.

[12] So that the defendant cannot be said to have caused the pollution. See the main text following n.24 *infra*.

[13] See further J. Braithwaite and P. Pettit, *Not Just Deserts: A Republican Theory of Criminal Justice* (Oxford, Clarendon, 1990), pp. 1–11; and Note, *supra* n.3, pp. 1231–3.

[14] The application of the latter two is perhaps easier in the context of traditional crime. However, with environmental offences, rehabilitation could apply if novel sentencing techniques such as the use of environmental management systems were ordered.

[15] See Lord Salmon in *Alphacell Ltd.* v. *Woodward*, who states that strict liability for water pollution offences "encourages riparian factory owners not only to take reasonable steps to prevent pollution but to do everything possible to ensure that they do not cause it" [1972] AC 824 at 849; *cf.* Lord Reid in *Tesco Supermarkets Ltd.* v. *Nattrass* [1972] AC 153 at 174.

theory at least, the polluter pays in all cases and the social costs of production are, to some extent, internalised.[16]

Those who argue against strict liability point out that there is no empirical evidence that strict liability does increase deterrence. Indeed, since deterrence rests not only on the chances of conviction (to which strict liability is relevant), but also on the likelihood of being prosecuted in the first place and the level of punishment on conviction, one might query whether an increase in the first factor will achieve much without paying some attention to the other two.

Another argument often made against strict liability is that the criminal law is premised on morality and notions of fault, and it is morally objectionable to punish those who are not at fault. However, there are two possible responses to this. First, one might query whether those who have caused pollution are really morally blameless, even if not at fault. It can be argued that those who deliberately set up hazardous activities for profit are not morally blameless: they are exposing the environment to a risk for their own benefit.[17] In these circumstances, it is not unjust or immoral to expect them to pay when something goes wrong, even if they were not at fault. Secondly, the argument is obviously premised on a deontological theory of punishment and, if one prefers a deterrence model, then strict liability may be regarded as legitimate.

Finally, it is worth drawing attention to a point which tends to undermine arguments made by both the pro and anti camps. And that is that, although the offences may be ones of strict liability, fault creeps back in during the various stages of the enforcement process. To begin with, it is clear that not all those who are guilty of strict liability offences are prosecuted: as will be seen, one of the factors taken into account by UK agencies in their decisions whether or not to prosecute is the degree to which the perpetrator was at fault: firms which are at fault are more likely to be prosecuted.[18] Of course that is not the only factor taken into account. The seriousness of the pollution incident is, for example, another important factor considered by the Environment Agency in its prosecution decisions. A firm may not have been at fault, but if the pollution incident was major, it may still find itself being prosecuted. However, even if offenders are prosecuted and convicted, the degree of fault is reflected in sentencing: those not at fault tend to receive lower fines. The *CPC* v. *NRA*[19] case provides a good illustration of this. The firm had acted very conscientiously by having a full survey carried out on purchase of the factory. Nevertheless, when a pipe split, it

[16] In practice, because not all strict liability offences are prosecuted, the principle may end up being breached. This point will be considered further below in the text.

[17] There are parallels with the tort of *Rylands* v. *Fletcher* (1868) LR 3 HL 330 here: one explanation of the case (which has fallen out of favour recently) was that it involved the imposition of strict liability in relation to exceptional risks (see further C. Hilson, "Cambridge Water Revisited" (1996) 7 *Water Law* 126).

[18] In *Alphacell*, *supra* n.15, for example, the defendants were arguably at fault in terms of the design of the system and in the lack of maintenance. In other words, just because the prosecution does not have to prove it, does not mean that the defendant was not at fault.

[19] *CPC (UK)* v. *National Rivers Authority* (1995) 7 JEL 69.

was prosecuted and convicted of the causing offence within section 85 of the WRA 1991. While its lack of fault did not lead to an acquittal, it did lead to it receiving an absolute discharge by way of sentence.[20] The fact that the prosecuting agencies and the courts are thus wedded to notions of fault tends to undermine pro arguments about deterrence: if polluters know that in many cases they will actually be prosecuted only when at fault, the extra degree of deterrence provided by strict liability vanishes. However, it does not vanish altogether: fault is only one factor considered by the Agency; firms may still be deterred because they know, for example, that a serious pollution incident will lead to prosecution regardless of fault. The reintroduction of fault in the process also undermines anti arguments about the morality of punishing those not at fault: in many cases, those prosecuted will have been at fault; and where, as in *CPC*, they were not, this will be reflected in the sentence awarded.[21]

CAUSE, KNOWINGLY CAUSE AND KNOWINGLY PERMIT

The offences which have proved the most difficult to interpret are those which contain the wording of "cause", "knowingly cause" or "knowingly permit" pollution.[22] With causing in particular, there have been numerous reported cases in recent years, culminating in the House of Lords' decision in *Empress*.[23] In that case, Lord Hoffman essentially confirmed previous decisions, which had held that cause requires a positive act.[24] However, he stated that there was no need for the positive act to have been the immediate cause of the escape. The case involved diesel spilling from a tank into a river as a result of a vandal opening up a tap on the tank. On these facts, the defendants were found guilty of the causing offence: maintaining a tank of diesel on their land was a sufficient positive act; it did not matter that the immediate cause had been vandals opening the tap.[25]

[20] See 235 ENDS Report (1994) 41.

[21] Although, as noted in ENDS (*ibid.*), despite the absolute discharge, the company still has the stigma of a criminal conviction to its name.

[22] The wording "causes or knowingly permits" can be found in the water pollution offences in s.85 of the WRA 1991 and s.4(1) of the Salmon and Freshwater Fisheries Act 1975 (and also, in a civil context, with the clean-up provisions of ss.161 and 161A of the WRA 1991). "Knowingly cause or knowingly permit" is wording used in the waste offences in s.33(1) of the EPA 1990.

[23] *Supra* n.10.

[24] However, he stressed that this requirement was not inherent in the notion of causing (and would thus not necessarily apply in other statutes using the term); it was rather a matter of statutory interpretation of the particular subsection involved (s.85(1) of the WRA 1991), which contained two separate offences—one of causing and the other of knowingly permitting. The distinction between the two was that the former required an act, whereas the latter involved an omission (knowingly omitting to prevent pollution when one could have done so).

[25] Lord Hoffmann thus cast doubt on the earlier cases of *Price* v. *Cromack* [1975] 1 WLR 988 and *Wychavon DC* v. *NRA* [1993] 1WLR 125, where the defendants had been acquitted of the causing offence. Although in both there was no positive act in relation to the immediate cause (the immediate cause in *Price* v. *Cromack* was presumably an omission to maintain the lagoons properly and in *Wychavon* an omission to discover the blockage sufficiently quickly), the defendants in both cases were carrying out a positive act (maintaining lagoons on his land in *Price* v. *Cromack* and maintaining the sewer in *Wychavon*).

Having considered the need for a positive act, Lord Hoffmann proceeded to examine the question of causation more closely. He stated that the key question to ask was not "what caused the pollution?" It was rather "did the defendant cause the pollution?"[26] It did not matter if someone or something else could also be said to have caused it. Next, there was the question whether the act of a third party (such as a vandal) or natural forces could break the chain of causation. Lord Hoffmann's approach here mirrors his views on fault mentioned earlier. If the act of a third party or a natural event is abnormal and extraordinary (citing the example of a terrorist attack) then this breaks the chain of causation so that the defendant's act will no longer be said to have caused the escape. If on the other hand it is a normal and familiar fact of life,[27] then, even if not foreseeable in the particular case,[28] the chain will not be broken—the defendant will still be held to have caused the pollution.[29]

"Knowingly cause" will be examined below in the context of corporate liability. The key case on "knowingly permit" in relation to water pollution is *Schulmans* v. *NRA*.[30] Here, oil entered the defendant's drainage system and ended up in a nearby brook. The spillage was brought to the attention of the managing director of the company some time the same day. However, there was no clear evidence on the precise time at which he was alerted—it could have been as late as 7.30pm. The company arranged to have the drain cleaned the following day. Its appeal against conviction for the knowingly permitting offence under the equivalent of section 85 of the WRA 1991 was successful. The court held that for defendant to be convicted of the offence, it would have to have had *knowledge* of the following: first, that the spill had occurred; secondly, that the oil had entered the drain; thirdly, that the drain led to the brook; and fourthly, that unless the drain was cleaned, the oil would soon enter the brook. It seems from the case that *constructive* knowledge is enough for each of these. In other words, the prosecution need not prove *actual* knowledge—it can draw *inferences* about the defendant's knowledge, and the burden is then on the defendant to prove that he did not have such knowledge. Establishing knowledge is one thing—the *permitting* side must then also be established. Permitting involves a failure to prevent pollution when you could have done so. *Schulmans* was acquitted on this ground, because there was no evidence that it could have prevented the escape of oil into the brook (by having the drains cleaned) any sooner

[26] With respect, there seems to be no reason why the first of these questions is inadequate. It would have been otherwise if the question had been "what was *the* cause of the pollution?" (which suggests only one defendant is possible). In *AG's Ref. (No 1 of 1994)* [1995] 1 WLR 599, the court stated that it was a matter of asking not what was *the* cause of the pollution, but whether the defendant was *a* cause (which means there can be more than one).

[27] The question whether something is normal and familiar or abnormal and extraordinary was held to be one of fact and degree.

[28] As with the vandalism in *NRA* v. *Wright Engineering*, *supra* n.11.

[29] As noted earlier, this means that *NRA* v. *Wright Engineering* (*ibid.*) and *Impress* v. *Rees*, *supra* n.11, must now be regarded as having been wrongly decided.

[30] *Schulmans Incorporate Ltd.* v. *NRA* [1993] Env LR 1. Knowingly permit in the waste context is different and, again, will be considered below in the text in the context of corporate liability.

than it did. After all, as we have seen, there was some evidence which suggested that the managing director was not alerted until 7.30pm. At that time of night, it may not have been unreasonable to leave measures until the next day.[31] It thus could not be said to have "permitted" the pollution.[32]

CORPORATE LIABILITY

Most pollution is caused by companies. However, such pollution stems either directly or ultimately from the acts or omissions of individual employees or directors working for such companies. There are two questions which thus need to be addressed at this stage. The first is should a company be liable in addition to the possible individual liability of its employees or directors? And the second is when in law can a company be held criminally liable for the acts of individuals working for it?

There are a number of justifications for holding companies themselves liable, as opposed to individuals working for them. It may be that a general systems failure was responsible for a pollution incident, rather than it being traceable to one or more identifiable individuals within the company. In this sort of situation, prosecution of individuals would be difficult, if not impossible, and yet one clearly wishes to hold someone to account.[33] In addition, placing liability on the company ensures that the attention of *all* senior management is focused on preventing pollution: if only individuals can be prosecuted, then only those with direct responsibility for pollution matters are likely to be deterred. Finally, the names of individuals will typically mean very little to the public, whereas dragging a company's name through the courts ensures that the public becomes aware of its wrongdoing and can take any appropriate action in response (such as avoiding its products).[34] The reverse side of this is that deterrence is increased: it is only if companies themselves are prosecuted that they will be concerned about negative PR associated with prosecutions. One argument made against corporate liability, which rests on a retributive theory, is that it is shareholders who end up paying for fines imposed on the company, and yet they are not at fault (since the reality is that shareholders do not apply any effective control over day-to-day management of companies). However, this is not a

[31] Although *quaere* whether this would always be true.

[32] A number of issues surrounding "permit" remain unresolved. What if it would be *extremely* costly to prevent pollution? If a defendant allows it to go ahead because of this, would this amount to permitting? And what if a defendant is unable to prevent pollution because he has been negligent in having too few staff to deal with it?

[33] Although, as will be seen, in the case of *mens rea* offences, it will not be easy to convict the company in this situation either.

[34] However, with small companies, it may be more appropriate to prosecute the directors (considered further below in the text), and there may be little extra to be gained by charging the company too, as few will have heard of it, and in any case it is likely to fold: see C. Wells, "Corporate Killing" (1997) 147 *NLJ* 1467; and J. Ross, "Corporate Criminal Liability: One Form or Many Forms?" [1999] *Juridical Review* 49, p. 52.

particularly strong argument since, as Glanville-Williams notes, a "shareholder does not feel the punishment in his body or reputation. He suffers it only in his bank account—and perhaps imperceptibly at that".[35]

When therefore will a company be liable for a criminal offence?[36] Until recently, the law on corporate criminal liability was based on two sets of rather rigid distinctions. The first was between "vicarious liability" on the one hand (where a company is held liable for criminal offences committed by its employees in the course of their employment), and "direct liability" on the other (where an offence is committed by someone in the company who is part of its "directing mind and will",[37] and where the acts or state of mind of that individual are then identified as those of the company itself). The second distinction was between strict liability offences and *mens rea* offences. The two distinctions were connected, in that it was said that companies could be vicariously liable only for strict liability offences; with any type of *mens rea* offence—whether ordinary[38] or regulatory—companies could be liable only via the direct liability route.[39]

However, recent case law has moved away from these rigid distinctions, which reflected a common law, precedential approach, towards a more general approach based on a purposive approach to statutory interpretation. With the first distinction, after Lord Hoffmann's Privy Council judgment in the *Meridian* case, rather than being seen as different, "directing mind" and vicarious liability can now be regarded as examples of the same thing; they are both rules of attribution.[40] In other words, they are both rules to tell one whose acts can be regarded as acts of the company: in the case of vicarious liability, it is those of any employee; with directing mind, it is just those of a member of senior management. With the second distinction, Lord Keith in *Seaboard* commented that he did not think it useful to categorise the offence in that case as either one of strict liability or one of *mens rea*.[41] It is submitted that this comment is of general applicability. The cases simply cannot be forced into categories where strict liability equals vicarious liability and *mens rea* equals directing mind. The statutory section in *Seaboard* itself arguably involved strict liability, but it was nevertheless held that the company could be liable only on a directing mind basis

[35] G. L. Williams, *Textbook of Criminal Law* (2nd edn., London, Stevens & Sons, 1983), p. 975.

[36] See further, C. M. V. Clarkson, "Kicking Corporate Bodies and Damning Their Souls" (1996) 59 *MLR* 557; and Ross, *supra* n.34.

[37] See e.g. *Lennard's Carrying Co. Ltd.* v. *Asiatic Petroleum Co. Ltd.* [1915] AC 705; *Tesco* v. *Nattrass*, *supra* n.15.

[38] Such as (corporate) manslaughter.

[39] However authority for this appears far from conclusive (see e.g. the *obiter* remarks of Lord Diplock in *Tesco* v. *Nattrass*, *supra* n.15, at 199; and Wells, *supra* n. 2, pp. 110–11).

[40] *Meridian Global Funds Management Asia Ltd.* v. *Securities Commission* [1995] 2 AC 500. See also Mance J. in *Shanks & McEwan (Teeside) Ltd.* v. *Environment Agency* [1998] 2 WLR 452 at 464, 466. See further R. Grantham, "Corporate Knowledge: Identification or Attribution?" (1996) 59 *MLR* 732.

[41] *Seaboard Offshore Ltd.* v. *Secretary of State for Transport* [1994] 1 WLR 541 at 546.

and not vicariously. And alcohol licensing offences, though requiring *mens rea*, have always been regarded as attracting vicarious liability.[42]

The position thus now appears to be that one must interpret the offence to determine whose acts will be attributed to the company. With some offences, the purpose of the statute will require only that the acts of the directing mind be attributed to the company.[43] With others, the purpose of the statute will be defeated unless the acts of any employee acting within the course of their employment are attributed to it.[44]

Two cases, one environmental and one health and safety, provide examples of the latter. In *McAlpine*,[45] the company was charged with causing pollution of controlled waters within section 85(1) of the WRA 1991. Those responsible for the pollution were two relatively lowly managers, and the company was acquitted in the magistrates' court on the ground that they were not part of the directing mind. On appeal by way of case stated, Morland J. adopted a purposive construction of the legislation. The purpose of the section 85 offence was to control pollution. If a company could be liable *only* if the offence was committed by someone representing the directing mind and will, and could not be vicariously liable for more lowly employees, then the effectiveness of the causing offence would be lost "and the filthiness of rivers increased",[46] because it will usually be the more lowly employees who are responsible for pollution incidents. Similarly, in *R* v. *British Steel Plc*, where British Steel were held vicariously liable for the health and safety breaches of one of its employees, Steyn J. observed that "it would drive a juggernaut through the legislative scheme if corporate employers could avoid criminal liability where the potentially harmful event is committed by someone who is not the directing mind of the company".[47]

In *Shanks & McEwan*,[48] however, Mance J. adopted a rather different approach. The company was charged with "knowingly causing" controlled waste to be deposited in breach of a condition in its waste management licence. Waste had been delivered to the company's landfill site. This was due to be offloaded in a tank and the requisite waste forms had been filled out for this. However the site supervisor changed his mind and had the waste put in a different place, without filling out more forms as required by the waste management licence. The company was convicted in the magistrates' court on the basis

42 *Vane* v. *Yiannopoullos* [1965] AC 486.

43 *Seaboard Offshore*, *supra* n.41.

44 I.e. vicarious liability. In *Meridian* (*supra* n.40) for some reason (perhaps since it was an offence requiring *mens rea*—although it was argued above in the text that this should make no difference), it was held that vicarious liability was not available, but that an interpretation of the statute required a special rule of attribution to be created so that the acts and knowledge of the employee there—though not part of the directing mind—could be attributed to the company. With respect, it is not clear how this differs from vicarious liability.

45 *NRA* v. *Alfred McAlpine Homes East Ltd.* [1994] 4 All ER 286.

46 *Ibid.*, at 300.

47 [1995] 1 WLR 1356 at 1362–3.

48 *Supra* n.40.

that the site supervisor was part of the directing mind of the company. On appeal, the Environment Agency conceded that he could not be so regarded, but this did not prevent the company's conviction from being upheld. Mance J. first stated that, although knowingly cause requires knowledge, it requires knowledge only of waste being deposited and not the breach of a condition in the licence.[49] Thereafter, Mance J. proceeded to follow Lord Hoffmann's approach in *Meridian*, treating vicarious liability and direct liability as rules of attribution. He stated that it was unnecessary to determine the appropriate rule of attribution under section 33(1)(a) because, whatever it was, it was satisfied on the facts of the case.[50] If knowledge of the employee was sufficient in the context of "knowingly cause", then Shanks would be caught by the vicarious liability route. The employee here who had made the decision (the site supervisor) had knowledge of the specific deposit and Shanks would thus be vicariously liable for the conduct and knowledge of their servant acting in the course of his employment. Alternatively, if knowledge had to be shown on the part of senior management, then Shanks would be liable under the directing mind route: knowledge that waste in general was being deposited was sufficient and senior management, running a landfill site, would know that waste in general was being deposited there.[51] However, he stated that, if he was wrong on this point and knowledge of the specific deposit was indeed required, then that would itself be a powerful reason for adopting a wider rule of attribution involving vicarious liability.[52]

The tenor of Mance J.'s reasoning makes sense here. Unlike *British Steel* and *McAlpine*, one cannot say here that a purposive interpretation of the statute requires vicarious liability. In other words, one cannot conclude that the statutory regime on waste would be rendered ineffectual without vicarious liability, since there is the alternative here of holding the company liable via the directing mind route of attribution.[53] Better then to say, as Mance J. does in effect, that a purposive approach requires the company to be liable one way or the other.

[49] However, "knowingly" does serve some purpose here. As Mance J. notes (*Shanks*, *supra* n.40, at 462): "[i]t is possible to conceive of situations where a person may 'cause' controlled waste to be deposited without knowing he is doing so". An example might be a waste delivery where some waste falls off the back of the lorry. If the wording were just "cause" as in s.85 of the WRA 1991, a defendant would no doubt be guilty in that situation, as there is a positive act (of driving the lorry). However, the driver in that situation cannot be said to have "knowingly caused". In a fly-tipping situation, a sender will probably be held to have "knowingly caused" and the driver simply to have "deposited" within s.33(1)(a) (*ibid.*, at 463). However, s.33(5) provides for the situation where the sender claims that the driver has fly-tipped against instructions. Since most senders would no doubt try this on, s.33(5) provides that the sender "shall be treated as knowingly causing the waste to be deposited whether or not he gave any instructions for this to be done" (*ibid.*, at 466–7).

[50] *Shanks*, *supra* n.40, at 464, 466.

[51] *Shanks*, *supra* n.40, at 463–4. Although Shanks had not been charged with "knowingly permitting" controlled waste to be deposited, Mance J. also expressed the opinion, *obiter*, that it could equally have been charged with that offence (at 464). A similar dual approach to corporate liability would operate there.

[52] *Ibid.*, at 466.

[53] *McAlpine* (*supra* n.45) cannot be argued on the same basis: while the knowledge of the directing mind that waste in general is being deposited can be attributed to a landfill company, there will

Where an offence comes with a separate due diligence or absence of knowledge defence,[54] then the defence must similarly be interpreted to determine the appropriate rule of attribution.[55] In some cases, it may be that the due diligence of the directing mind will be attributed to the company (and the lack of due diligence of lesser employees will not)[56]; in other cases, the absence of knowledge of an employee may not be attributed to the company.[57] Although it was not relied upon by the appellants in *Shanks*, section 33(7)(a) of the EPA 1990 provides a due diligence defence to the offence in section 33(1). In future cases, a rule of attribution will thus need to be formulated for the defence to determine whether it is reasonable care on the part of the employee which is being referred to there or reasonable care on the part of senior management. If it is the latter, then it will be interesting to see whether the presence of an environmental management system such as EMAS will be regarded as evidence of reasonable care.

LIABILITY OF EMPLOYEES

Most statutes allow for the prosecution of an employee, either instead of[58] or as well as the company. Section 217(3) of the WRA 1991, for example,[59] states that:

> where the commission by any person of an offence under the water pollution provisions of this Act is due to the act or default of some other person, that other person may be charged with and convicted of the offence whether or not proceedings for the offence are taken against the first-mentioned person.

However, although the acts typically *allow* for this it does not of course mean that it will be used in practice.[60] In the *McAlpine* case,[61] for example, the NRA could have used the above section to proceed against the individual employees,

be no causing acts of the directing mind in most water cases that can be attributed to the company. In *McAlpine* itself, counsel for the appellants had argued that *Alphacell* (*supra* n.15) was in fact a direct liability case—those representing the directing mind had caused the pollution there. Simon Brown J. disagreed, stating that there was nothing in that case to link the failure of the pumps with any senior officer of the company. He considered it to be a straightforward case of vicarious liability.

[54] The presence of a due diligence *defence* may be viewed as a counterweight to, or a reason for, adopting a broad rule of attribution (vicarious liability) for the *offence* (see Lord Diplock in *Tesco* v. *Nattrass*, *supra* n.15, at 194 and 197, and Lord Reid at 174, cited by Mance J. in *Shanks*, *supra* n.40, at 465; see also 466). However the *absence* of a due diligence defence does not mean that vicarious liability cannot exist (*per* Mance J. in *Shanks* at 465, citing *McAlpine* (*supra* n.45) as an example, since vicarious liability was imposed there and yet the WRA 1991 has no such due diligence defence: see also *R.* v. *British Steel*, *supra* n.47).

[55] *Meridian*, *supra* n.40, at 507–8; *Shanks*, *supra* n.40, at 465–6.

[56] *Tesco* v. *Nattrass*, *supra* n.15.

[57] *Tesco Stores Ltd.* v. *Brent LBC* [1993] 1 WLR 1037.

[58] Though here there is an obvious danger of the employee being made a scapegoat for what are actually systemic problems within the company.

[59] See also s.158 of the EPA 1990 and s.36 of the Health and Safety at Work Act (HSWA) 1974.

[60] For reasons mentioned *supra* in n.58.

[61] *Supra* n.45.

but chose instead to prosecute only the company. Prosecution of employees for environmental offences is rare and is likely to be reserved for serious pollution incidents stemming from intentional or reckless malpractice. In these circumstances, if *someone* is to be held liable, it will often have to be the employee: the company will probably escape vicarious liability since acts of this nature may take the employee outside the course of his employment. Here though, prosecution of employees is essentially based on a retributive rationale, as it makes little sense from a deterrence point of view. Ordinary employees are likely to be deterred from acting unlawfully by the prospect of internal disciplinary procedures or dismissal. The threat of criminal prosecution may provide an extra element of deterrence, but this is likely to be marginal.

Finally, there may be occasions where the employee acts intentionally, but does so under orders from his or her employer. In this situation, some statutes provide a limited defence. Section 33(7)(b) of the EPA 1990, for example, provides a defence to a person "that he acted under instructions from his employer and neither knew nor had reason to suppose that the acts done by him constituted a contravention". The second, limiting part of the defence is obviously necessary here, just as it is for more serious war crimes: we all have a personal responsibility to stand firm against things that we know are wrong.

LIABILITY OF DIRECTORS

Most of the key regulatory regimes provide for personal criminal liability of directors. Section 157 of the EPA 1990 for example,[62] states that:

> Where an offence under any provision of this Act[63] committed by a body corporate is proved to have been committed with the consent or connivance of, or to have been attributable to any neglect on the part of, any director, manager, secretary or other similar officer of the body corporate . . . he as well as the body corporate shall be guilty of that offence and shall be liable to be proceeded against and punished accordingly.[64]

One might of course question why it is necessary to provide a specific section for directors and other senior managers, since one might think that they too could fall within the "some other person" provisions mentioned above, which catch ordinary employees. However, it seems that a specific section was introduced for the avoidance of doubt. As Lord Diplock noted in *Tesco* v. *Nattrass*, without this type of section, "it would have been open to doubt whether persons whose acts were in law the acts of the company itself would have been guilty in their personal capacity also of the offence committed by the company".[65] In

[62] See also s.217(1) of the WRA 1991, s.210 of the WIA 1991, and s.37 of the HSWA 1974.

[63] This will include e.g. integrated pollution control (IPC), local authority air pollution control (APC) and waste therefore.

[64] While there may be deterrence grounds for saying that prosecution should proceed against both, this will obviously be more expensive for the prosecuting Agency.

[65] *Supra* n.15, at 201.

other words, it may be that directors would not be regarded as "some other person". If this is indeed the case, it may at first sight appear rather unfair, since personal liability of directors is fault-based (consent, neglect and so on), whereas corporate and employee liability may be strict. However, if senior management were subject to the same provision as that for employees, they would probably seldom be held liable, because in most cases they would be too far removed from the action to come within the original offence. At least their own special section ensures that in these circumstances they will nevertheless be caught if the offence was carried out with their consent, connivance or was due to their neglect.

Who then is a senior manager in this context? In *Woodhouse* v. *Walsall MBC*,[66] a waste site manager was convicted along with the company in the magistrates' court. According to the Divisional Court on appeal, the question to be asked is whether the defendant has the power and responsibility to decide corporate policy and strategy. Since the appellant site manager did not have this power or responsibility, and could not therefore be regarded as a manager within the statutory wording, his appeal against conviction was thus successful.

Waste is the area where personal liability has been used most frequently. And while there have now been cases of personal liability in other fields of pollution regulation,[67] waste appears to be the only area where directors have been *imprisoned* for environmental offences.[68] This is no doubt due to the nature of the waste industry—there are numerous small, "cowboy" outfits where the company amounts to not much more than the directors themselves. In these circumstances, it will not be difficult to establish the requirements of personal liability where the operators have indulged in, for example, the illegal fly-tipping of waste. In large companies, it will obviously be more difficult to establish that offences were committed with the consent, connivance or neglect of senior officers.

The deterrence rationale for prosecuting a member of the directing mind is much greater than for ordinary employees. Senior management, who are in effect the company, are not likely to be disciplined by it for pollution offences. They are also likely to be the ones whom the presumption of a rational economic person underlying the deterrence model best fits, since calculating costs and benefits is their daily bread.[69] In addition, they are in the best position to ensure that controls to prevent pollution are put in place. Corporate liability

[66] [1994] Env. LR 30. For a similar case in the context of health and safety, see *R.* v. *Boal* [1992] 2 WLR 890.

[67] See 281 ENDS Report (1998) 50. The director of an incinerator company was prosecuted using s.157 of the EPA 1990 for breach of conditions in the IPC authorisation and, although convicted, received only 60 hours of community service by way of sentence.

[68] See e.g. 272 ENDS Report (1997) 45. The director of a waste company was imprisoned for offences under s.33(1)(a) of the EPA 1990, having been involved in depositing clinical waste without a waste management licence. Although there is a case where an individual was imprisoned for a water pollution offence under s.85(1) of the WRA 1991 (see 273 ENDS Report (1997) 45), it is not clear whether he was running a company as such, and thus charged as a director using the powers in s.217 of the WRA 1991, or whether he was simply prosecuted as an individual.

[69] Note, *supra* n.3, p. 1235.

and a desire to avoid corporate fines and negative PR may lead them to focus on such controls, but there is evidence that senior management shelter behind the company and are insufficiently deterred by corporate liability[70]; personal liability thus adds an extra element of deterrence. Indeed, they are likely to be very keen to avoid the stigma, both social and professional, which a criminal conviction brings. And for them of course, there is not only the financial and embarrassment deterrent of a fine or imprisonment,[71] there is also the concern that they may as a result become disqualified to act as directors in the future[72]—essentially depriving them of their comfortable livelihood.

MONITORING

There is little point in setting standards if these are not then enforced in practice. The term "enforcement" here is best separated into its two constituent parts: first regulatory agencies must *monitor* to make sure that ambient standards are being met and that firms are not in breach of their permits; and, secondly, they must take some form of follow-up *enforcement* action against those who are in breach. They must of course also monitor and take enforcement action against polluters who have failed to seek the necessary prior authorisation in the first place and thus have no permits at all.

The term "monitoring" can cover a number of different activities in the context of pollution control. First, there is *emissions sampling* which is essentially concerned with ensuring that firms' discharges are complying with the emission standards in their permits. Secondly, there is *ambient environmental quality sampling* which is designed, *inter alia*, to determine whether any ambient environmental quality standards are being met, and which will also provide statistics on environmental quality to enable long-term trends to be identified. And finally, monitoring may also be used to refer to less frequent, but longer and more detailed audit *inspection visits*—which may be used for emissions sampling purposes, but which are principally concerned with assessing compliance with non-emissions-related permit conditions.[73] Environmental regulators are

[70] C. Wells, "Corporate Liability and Consumer Protection: *Tesco* v. *Nattrass* Revisited (1994) 57 *MLR* 817, p. 821.

[71] Note that, on public policy grounds, these cannot be insured against (since that would reduce the deterrent effect): see *MacGillivray & Parkington on Insurance Law* (8th edn., London, Sweet & Maxwell, 1988), p. 189; and V. Finch, "Personal Accountability and Corporate Control: The Role of Directors' and Officers' Liability Insurance" (1994) 57 *MLR* 880, pp. 887–8.

[72] Under s.2 of the Company Directors Disqualification Act 1986, which enables a court to disqualify a director convicted of an indictable offence in connection with the management of a company. The Environment Agency *Enforcement and Prosecution Policy* (Bristol, The Environment Agency, 1998), para.24, states that "[i]n appropriate cases, the Agency will consider seeking disqualification of Directors". For a case example in the health and safety context, see 213 ENDS Report (1992) 40.

[73] These are particularly important with waste and also IPC where there are many such conditions.

typically granted wide powers of entry and inspection under statute to enable them to carry out the above activities on firms' premises.

Under some regulatory regimes such as integrated pollution control (IPC), self-monitoring of emissions by firms is widely relied upon. As Wolf and White note:

> [a]ll IPC authorisations will include conditions which require the process operator to monitor discharges and emissions from the prescribed process in order to ensure compliance with conditions. Moreover it will usually be a condition that where there is a breach of condition the process operator informs the Agency. Failing to tell the Agency that there has been a breach of condition constitutes a further breach.[74]

Delegating this key regulatory task to industry was criticised in some quarters. However, it saves the Agency valuable resources as it is the firm and not the Agency which has to provide and maintain the monitoring equipment and record the data. Howarth suggests that another benefit of self-monitoring may be that it instils in firms a sense that they are responsible for the pollution they create.[75] In addition, there are certain safeguards in place. First, firms are subject to spot-check sampling visits by the Agency or agents appointed by them to make sure that the figures supplied by the firm are accurate. And, secondly, the Agency has introduced a monitoring certification scheme (MCERTS) which provides independent verification of the quality of the monitoring equipment used by firms.[76] This scheme has initially been applied only to *continuous* monitoring equipment used by certain IPC processes, although it is likely to be extended in the future to other monitoring systems and to all IPC processes. While use of MCERTS-approved equipment is not a condition of the IPC authorisation, firms who use such equipment may be subject to fewer spot-check sampling visits.[77]

For emissions sampling where pollution control regimes do not rely on self-monitoring, and for audit-type inspection visits, an agency is likely to wish to target its monitoring activity in an efficient manner. Since monitoring is expensive—involving as it does considerable time spent by officers out in the field—such cost should only be expended where the likely level of risk (benefit) to the environment justifies it. In assessing risk, an agency will need to consider the seriousness of the hazard posed by the site or process (for example, a large chemical plant is likely to constitute a much greater environmental hazard than a small paint workshop) and then the risk associated with this hazard in terms of the likelihood of it occurring. As the Environment Agency's *Enforcement and Prosecution Policy* states, a low-hazard site or activity which is poorly managed can pose a greater risk to the environment than a well managed, higher hazard

[74] S. Wolf and A. White, *Principles of Environmental Law* (2nd edn., London, Cavendish, 1997), p. 258.

[75] W. Howarth, "Self-Monitoring, Self-Policing, Self-Incrimination and Pollution Law" (1997) 60 *MLR* 200.

[76] 279 ENDS Report (1998) 38.

[77] *Ibid.*

site or activity. The Policy makes it clear that, in line with the principle of "targeting",[78] the Agency will target its monitoring activity on high-risk sites and activities, while stating that certain high-hazard sites (such as nuclear installations, some major chemical plants and some waste disposal facilities) will also receive regular visits so that the Agency can ensure that remote risks continue to be effectively managed.

A more detailed risk-based policy exists for the purposes of IPC audit-type inspection visits. Under the Agency's operator and pollution risk appraisal (OPRA) scheme,[79] detailed pollution hazard and operator risk criteria are assessed for each IPC process and scores allocated. Firms which are certified to an environmental management standard (such as EMAS or ISO 14001) may find that this improves their operator risk rating, but this will depend on how demanding the system is that the firm has set for itself.[80] The OPRA scores are used to target IPC inspections, with high-risk sites receiving more frequent visits. The scores may also be linked in the future to the amount in IPC cost-recovery charges paid by firms, with low-risk and hence low-visit sites benefiting from lower charges.[81]

In other words, with OPRA, IPC inspection frequency is now based on site-specific risk assessments, as opposed to the old system of standard inspection frequencies. Until recently, the latter still existed in other regimes such as waste regulation. Although the different inspection targets which applied to different categories of waste facility[82] were broadly based on hazard, sites within these categories were not individually assessed for the risk they posed. It was hard to see how this squared with the concept of targeted, risk-based monitoring outlined in the Agency's enforcement policy described earlier and it is perhaps not surprising therefore that the Agency has recently sought to introduce a scheme based on OPRA for individual waste facilities.[83]

ENFORCEMENT TOOLS, STYLES AND APPROACHES

If, during monitoring, firms are found to be in breach of standards or to have no permit at all, the question is what enforcement action should the regulator take? The temptation for lawyers is perhaps to think only of prosecution, but regulators have a much broader range of enforcement tools at their disposal.

78 Discussed further below, p. 158.

79 See 271 ENDS Report (1997) 32.

80 See ENDS Reports 265 (1997) 5; 266 (1997) 3; 271 (1997) 32.

81 *Ibid.*

82 E.g. eight visits per month for co-disposal landfill site taking special waste, and quarterly visits for in-house waste storage sites (para. B9 of Waste Management Paper No. 4, *Licensing of Waste Management Facilities*, which contained these minimum inspection frequencies).

83 280 ENDS Report (1998) 25–2; DETR, *Waste Management Licensing Risk Assessment Inspection Frequencies; Operator Pollution Risk Appraisal; "OPRA For Waste": A Consultation Paper* (London, DETR, 1999).

Enforcement tools can be divided into formal and informal, statutory and non-statutory, and administrative and court-based. Prosecution or injunctions for example are formal, statutory, court-based tools. Next there are formal, statutory, administrative enforcement tools such as enforcement, works, prohibition, variation and revocation notices. Then there are formal, non-statutory mechanisms like warning letters and cautions. And, finally, there are informal, non-statutory mechanisms such as advice, persuasion, informal warnings, threats and so on. On the subject of formal, statutory, administrative enforcement tools, it should be noted that the Environment Agency has the full range of mechanisms (including enforcement notices) at its disposal across all of the key pollution functions (IPC, water and waste). In the case of water, this is a change from the position with the old National Rivers Authority (NRA), which did not have the enforcement notice at its disposal.

Different enforcement styles and approaches are associated with different enforcement tools. An adversarial *style* is associated with legal prosecution as a tool, while a co-operative *style* is associated with co-operative tools. These co-operative tools lie on a spectrum: at one end of the scale come "harder" formal, statutory, administrative enforcement tools such as enforcement notices; at the other, more obviously co-operative end of the scale, come "softer" informal, non-statutory mechanisms such as advice and persuasion.

An adversarial *approach* involves routine use of the adversarial style. A co-operative *approach* on the other hand will adopt an adversarial style occasionally, but will principally rely on a co-operative style. A "hard" co-operative approach will use prosecution and harder co-operative tools quite frequently. A "soft" co-operative approach will use prosecution and harder co-operative tools rarely if at all—relying almost exclusively on softer co-operative tools.

Work in the Oxford Socio-Legal Studies series emphasises the fact that British agencies have tended to adopt a co-operative rather than an adversarial approach.[84] These agencies are often described as relying on a "compliance" rather than a "sanctioning" strategy: agencies are, in other words, concerned with getting firms on board to comply with the standards and not with punishing firms for breaches; although, as Wells notes,[85] there is an element of confusion here, since the aim of both a co-operative and adversarial approach is compliance—they simply have different ways of going about it.

DESCRIPTIVE EXPLANATIONS FOR THE CO-OPERATIVE APPROACH

Why then has a co-operative approach existed? This is a particularly pertinent question given that most of the regulatory offences are ones of strict liability. The following descriptive theories have been suggested.

[84] E.g. G. M. Richardson *et al.*, *Policing Pollution: A Study of Regulation and Enforcement* (Oxford, Clarendon, 1982); K. Hawkins, *Environment and Enforcement: Regulation and the Social Definition of Pollution* (Oxford, Clarendon, 1984).

[85] Wells, *supra* n.2, p. 28.

The nature of pollution offences

A number of commentators have drawn attention to the fact that pollution offences are a form of "white collar" crime and that, unlike "real" crime, a high degree of moral ambivalence attaches to these and other regulatory offences such as health and safety. Because of this moral ambivalence, regulators were unhappy with the strict liability nature of the offences and would introduce a fault element at the enforcement level: they would only prosecute if pollution were intentional or calculated; with other cases, they would adopt a co-operative style.

This theory can, it is suggested, no longer adequately account for the use of the co-operative approach. In recent years there has been a marked change in attitudes towards environmental crime and corporate crime in general. A number of major health and safety disasters, such as the sinking of the *Herald of Free Enterprise*, have, in particular, played a part in reshaping public opinion. In any event, many pollution incidents with serious environmental effects are now prosecuted, even where the polluter was not at fault.

The poacher/gamekeeper problem

The old water authorities were not only regulators, they also ran sewage works which were one of the most significant water polluters. Similarly, local authority waste disposal authorities were not only responsible for waste regulation, they also operated waste disposal sites which were often well below standard. In these circumstances, it is perhaps not surprising that the co-operative approach was employed by these bodies in their regulatory capacity: it would hardly be acceptable to come down hard on others by prosecuting when your own operations were also in breach of the law and yet escaping prosecution.

However, for a while now, operational and regulatory functions have been separated: with sewage works, the Water Act 1989 saw the allocation of operational functions to the newly privatised water and sewerage undertakers, and regulation of water pollution to an independent regulatory agency—the NRA. Likewise with waste facilities, the Environmental Protection Act 1990 ensured that, while waste regulation remained in the hands of the local authority (with a change in name for the regulatory department from Waste Disposal to Waste Regulation Authorities), any local authority operational disposal facilities now had to be run by commercially owned, arm's-length local authority waste disposal companies (LAWDCs). Both of these regulatory functions—water pollution and waste regulation—were brought under the control of the Environment Agency by the Environment Act 1995, also an independent regulatory agency with no conflicting operational responsibilities in these areas. It is thus difficult to see how the poacher/gamekeeper problem might still account for the continuing use of the co-operative approach.[86]

Capture theory and the revolving door

Unlike the theories above which provide possible explanations for the use of the co-operative approach across *all* types of organisation, the theories to be considered in this section are able to account only for its use in the case of large organisations. According to the capture theory, top-level scientific and regulatory experts employed by large organisations exert their power in the form of knowledge over the more lowly expertise of regulatory enforcement field-staff. The latter, cowed by the superior resources of the former, are thus "captured" by them and negotiate rather than resort to prosecution. Recent changes within the water and waste regulation teams of the Environment Agency,[87] separating permitting from enforcement functions with less experienced staff concentrating on the latter, could have one of two impacts on use of the co-operative approach. On the one hand, it could, as ENDS quotes, "erode the 'dialogue of equals' between inspectors and industry",[88] which might suggest an increase in capture, and thus an increase in the co-operative approach. On the other hand, and this is perhaps more likely, it could as ENDS also notes, lead to a "tickbox" mentality and a "loss of pragmatism" by inspectors.[89] While this might lead to an adversarial approach, it is perhaps more likely to lead to a less soft co-operative approach, with fewer softer tools (persuasion, advice and so on) being utilised within the co-operative spectrum.

The revolving door theory, on the other hand, postulates that regulatory personnel are likely to have half an eye on future, better-remunerated, career opportunities within the large organisations, which they are policing. For this reason, one might argue, they are likely to want to remain on good terms and avoid prosecution.

The problem with such theories is that they are of course difficult to prove. While there is some evidence that smaller companies tend to be prosecuted more than larger ones, one cannot easily conclude that this is because large companies benefit from capture or the revolving door. It may simply be that large companies have more resources at their disposal and are thus better able to comply and avoid any form of enforcement action; it may also be the case that they are more likely to comply because they are more conscious of the PR disadvantages associated with prosecution.

[86] Although one should note that formal institutional change will take time to filter through to alter individual behaviour within institutions: an enforcement officer in one of the new independent regulatory agencies will not overnight lose an affinity with friends and former colleagues in what is now a separate operational organisation.

[87] But not yet in relation to IPC—see 281 ENDS Report (1998) 6.

[88] 266 ENDS Report (1997) 3.

[89] *Ibid.*

Marxist approaches

Another explanation is a Marxist argument that polluters and regulators are predominantly middle class whereas the polluted often tend to be working class.[90] The assumption is thus that those from similar classes will "look after their own"—avoiding prosecution—against the interests of the polluted which may have been better protected by such action. Again, it is one thing to identify the polluted as typically working class, but quite another to draw from this fact the conclusion that regulators are biased against them, or that they are protecting their own class. In the absence of any empirical evidence that regulators adopt such a class-based approach, the class-incidence of pollution must remain as an interesting factual observation rather than as a valid explanation for use of the co-operative approach.

Some more recent explanations and the current position

If the first two of the above (nature of offences and poacher/gamekeeper) are regarded as the most plausible descriptive explanations for the co-operative approach and these are no longer applicable, to what extent has the co-operative approach remained in use in recent years?

In the case of the NRA, the statistics reveal that its use of prosecution increased dramatically soon after its creation in 1989.[91] However, prosecutions were mainly brought for relatively serious one-off "accidents" rather than continuing, more minor breaches of consent conditions.[92] The latter type of breach continued to attract the co-operative style. In contrast, other pollution control bodies had very low rates of prosecution. In 1991–2, waste regulation authorities brought an average of just over ten criminal charges each—a very low figure.[93] One reason for this low use of prosecution may have been the substance of the law itself. Prosecutions at the time were still governed by the Control of Pollution Act 1974,[94] and it seems that a restrictive interpretation by the courts of a key offence in that Act had the effect of deterring legal action.[95] Her Majesty's Inspectorate of Pollution (HMIP) and local authority environmental health departments (in respect of IPC and local authority air pollution control

[90] S. Bell, *Ball & Bell on Environmental Law* (4th edn., London, Blackstone Press, 1997), p. 134 contains shades of this argument. Much of the literature on white collar crime has a Marxist underpinning—see e.g. "Introduction" in E Hochstedler, *Corporations as Criminals* (London, Sage Publications, 1984), p. 9.

[91] For statistics, see Bell, *supra* n.90, pp. 470–1.

[92] *Ibid.*

[93] With 49 English waste regulation authorities, the total number of charges brought was 584, with an average of 5 prosecutions each ending in success (262 in total): 217 ENDS Report (1993) 42.

[94] The waste management licensing regime under the EPA 1990 had not yet been brought into force.

[95] ENDS Report, *supra* n.93. For the difficulties posed by the law, see Bell, *supra* n.90, pp. 378–9.

respectively) also had very low rates of prosecution.[96] It may be that they had at their disposal a better range of formal, statutory, administrative enforcement tools besides prosecution than the NRA (for example the enforcement notice), but since these are arguably not much use in relation to serious, one-off incidents, one could argue that, like the NRA, they should have been prosecuting these.

One reason this may not have been the case is that both HMIP and local authority environmental health departments suffered from a lack of resources, and dealing with applications and setting the new BATNEEC[97] standards was taking up so much of their time that there was little staff time left to spend on enforcement. Another possible explanation for greater use of prosecution by the NRA may lie in institutional structure. Given their routine interaction with companies, one would expect all enforcement officers to adopt a co-operative style. If however, decisions on cases are taken out of their hands, then there may be a greater tendency for an organisation to adopt an adversarial style. It may thus be that in the NRA, enforcement officers had less control over individual cases than officers in HMIP.

With HMIP yet another possible explanation for it adopting the co-operative approach is that there is a close connection between the design and delivery styles of the IPC regulatory system and the enforcement style.[98] Because IPC is very much an anticipatory, process-based regulatory system, it has typically involved a close, consultant-type relationship between the regulator and industry at the standard-setting stage.[99] Not surprisingly, this close relationship is carried over into a conciliatory approach to enforcement.[100]

If one examines the situation more recently, since the creation of the Environment Agency in 1995 the picture is in many ways clearer, in that the statistics provide details not only of prosecution rates, but also rates for the use of harder, statutory co-operative tools such as enforcement notices. This means that one can now see, not just whether a co-operative approach is being adopted, but also whether this approach is hard or soft.

The Environment Agency's prosecution rates for water pollution, like its predecessor's, remain relatively high, with a total of 231 prosecutions concluded in 1997–8. One notable change in the past few years is with waste regulation, where there are now a much greater number of prosecutions.[101] Although with

[96] For HMIP statistics, see Wolf and White, *supra* n.74, p. 117.

[97] Best available techniques not entailing excessive cost, under s.7 of the EPA 1990.

[98] A. Gouldson and J. Murphy, *Regulatory Realities: The Implementation and Impact of Industrial Environmental Regulation* (London, Earthscan, 1998), pp. 51, 141–2.

[99] At first, HMIP stated that it would be adopting a less "cosy" approach to standard-setting, relying heavily on guidance notes and less on individual negotiation of authorisations (see National Audit Office, *Control and Monitoring of Pollution: Review of the Pollution Inspectorate*, 1990/91, HC 6375; and J. Gibson, "The Integration of Pollution Control" (1991) 18 *Jo. of Law & Soc.* 18, p. 28). However, HMIP soon abandoned this arm's-length approach, and the old style of close partnership with industry was reintroduced (223 ENDS Report (1993) 9 and 224 ENDS Report (1993) 7).

[100] Gouldson and Murphy, *supra* n.98.

[101] A total of 345 prosecutions were concluded in 1997–8.

water pollution and now waste, the Agency thus has a relatively strong prosecution record, it is still far from adopting an adversarial approach however, because the number of substantiated pollution incidents with both remains much higher than the number of cases prosecuted.[102] Nevertheless, the relatively high use of prosecution means that a "hard" co-operative approach is being adopted in these areas, although with waste it appears to be "harder", in that a high number of enforcement notices have also been served.[103] In contrast, with IPC, the Agency adopts a "soft" co-operative approach, since the number of prosecutions remains almost non-existent and the use of harder co-operative tools is also relatively low.[104] The same picture emerges with local authority air pollution control—in 1995–6 only eight firms were prosecuted for APC offences and just ten enforcement notices were served.[105]

NORMATIVE ARGUMENTS FOR THE CO-OPERATIVE APPROACH

The descriptive explanations for the co-operative approach outlined above are all very well, but there is a real need to consider normative arguments too. In other words, should the co-operative approach exist? If one examines enforcement from a law-and-economics perspective, one can see that the co-operative approach is justifiable on cost-effectiveness grounds. An economic model of compliance posits that firms will comply with the law only if the expected costs of violation exceed the benefits of violation: they will only comply where $pD>U$ (where p is the perceived probability of getting caught *and* convicted, D the costs of being prosecuted such as defence costs and any fines or other forms of punishment and U the benefits of violation).[106]

One way of increasing deterrence is to raise fine levels or the use of imprisonment and thus raise the level of D.[107] To some extent this has been done. Fine levels provided for in most UK pollution statutes have increased in recent years and many include imprisonment as an option—although there is still some way

[102] Environment Agency *Annual Report and Accounts 1997–98* (Bristol, Environment Agency, 1998) Appendices, pp. 154–5.

[103] *Ibid*. With waste, a total of 1,400 "notices" were issued (looking at columns in the report for the other functions, one assumes these are enforcement notices). With water pollution in contrast, only 3 were issued.

[104] Ibid. Only 12 prosecutions were brought in 1997–8 (11 of these were in the North West region, with many regions bringing no prosecutions at all), and 16 prohibition notices and 34 enforcement notices were served.

[105] ENDS Report 274 (1997) 9. In 1996–7, local authorities brought 9 prosecutions in total for APC offences (ENDS Report 284 (1998) 4 at 5).

[106] See further A. I. Ogus, *Regulation: Legal Form and Economic Theory* (Oxford, Clarendon, 1994), pp. 90–7 and his "Corrective Taxes and Financial Impositions as Regulatory Instruments" (1998) 61 *MLR* 767 at 772.

[107] Note that there may also be *civil* costs associated with pollution, which add to deterrence. In the case of both statutory clean-up costs (under e.g. s.161 and 161(A) of the WRA 1991) and private damages claims, these costs may be much larger than any criminal fine imposed.

to go in persuading courts to *use* the higher penalties available to them.[108] Indeed, the introduction by the Environment Agency of a "name and shame" list of the worst offenders in 1999 was an explicit response to the perceived inadequacy of current fine levels.[109] In effect, this tactic can be seen as an example of raising D by increasing the stigma and PR costs on companies.

Another possibility is to raise p. Increasing monitoring will increase the "probability of getting caught" element of p, and the use of continuous-monitoring equipment will of course increase it considerably. The other way is to increase the "probability of conviction" element of p by, for example, bringing more prosecutions.[110] But that is costly for the regulator because prosecution is expensive. As we shall see, this expense may be warranted for serious, one-off incidents, but in the case of routine breaches, why bother when you can adopt a co-operative style and keep prosecution as a background threat? After all, from the firm's point of view, p—the probability of being caught and convicted—is greater after it has been caught once for a routine breach, because it knows that the agency's eyes are likely to be focused on it in monitoring terms and that any repeat breaches may not attract another co-operative response. If p and thus pD have increased in this way and are now greater than U, then the firm has an incentive to comply.

Many environmentalists would however stress the need not only for deterrence, but also for appropriate retribution in line with the polluter pays principle (PPP). If a company has breached the rules but is not prosecuted, then the polluter does not end up paying. However, this assumes that a breach of consent will always give rise to pollution, which is not the case. Minor breaches will often have a negligible effect on the receiving environmental medium, and hence non-prosecution of minor breaches is not necessarily contrary to the PPP. However, environmentalists will be on stronger ground when a breach *does* give rise to pollution of some kind and a prosecution is not brought; this does appear to be contrary to the PPP.[111] One way around this might be to introduce a small, on-the-spot civil penalty or tax for relatively minor pollution incidents, rather like a

[108] Though in some (rather atypical) cases, the judge cannot be accused of not ensuring that the size of D made up for U. See e.g. the *Shell* case, where Shell was fined £1 million for oil pollution of the River Mersey (181 ENDS Report (1990) 5) and, more recently, the *Sea Empress* case, where Milford Haven Port Authority was fined £4 million for its role in the pollution of the Pembrokeshire coast by oil from the *Sea Empress* tanker (288 ENDS Report (1999) 50). There is of course an obvious danger of company liquidations if fine levels are increased too significantly across the board.

[109] See 290 ENDS Report (1999) 6.

[110] The nature of the criminal laws and laws of criminal procedure and evidence will also affect p: as noted earlier in the chapter, the strict liability nature of the offences increases deterrence by increasing the probability of conviction; laws of evidence and criminal procedure may also provide a hindrance to conviction (e.g. rules against self-incrimination—on which see Howarth, *supra* n.75; and 272 ENDS Report (1997) 46).

[111] Unless of course clean-up powers (under e.g. s.161 and 161(A) of the WRA 1991) are used where pollution has occurred, since this would fulfil the PPP. However, in relatively minor pollution cases, there may be little which can be cleaned-up as such.

parking penalty.[112] This recognises the economic inefficiency of prosecuting in every case while still maintaining the essential principle of the "polluter pays".[113]

There are, in other words, sound economic reasons for adopting a co-operative approach. Assuming the aim of an agency in enforcing pollution standards is to achieve the best level of environmental benefits for the costs spent on enforcement,[114] then it makes sense to reserve prosecution for cases involving serious environmental harm and for the repeat offender who is not responding to co-operative tools. In those cases, the high costs to the agency of prosecution are warranted because of the deterrent signal this sends out to prevent significant harm to the environment.[115] However, prosecuting minor breaches by first or even second time offenders, or by those who are spending money trying to put things right will not produce any significant environmental benefits and thus the high costs of prosecution cannot be justified in these cases. In these circumstances, the use of co-operative tools is more efficient.

ENFORCEMENT POLICIES[116]

If enforcement is examined in terms of legitimacy, then values such as cost-effectiveness, accountability, equality and certainty must all be considered. While the co-operative approach may be cost effective and may secure a contractual-type legitimacy as between regulator and regulated, the policy of selective prosecution involved gives rise to problems of inconsistent decision-making (and hence uncertainty and unfairness)[117] and lack of accountability to third parties. In contrast, an extreme adversarial approach, involving the prosecution of all breaches would solve the problem of fairness and accountability, but would not be cost-effective. A limited way forward is to adopt a policy of selective prosecution, but to structure prosecutorial discretion by way of an

[112] Penalties like this are, it seems, applied in Australia: see D. Robinson, "Regulatory Evolution In Pollution Control" in T. Jewell and J. Steele (eds), *Law in Environmental Decision-Making* (Oxford, Clarendon, 1998), p.29 at 68. For possible disadvantages, see N. Hawke, *Waste Management Law Enforcement* (Leicester, Leicester Polytechnic Law Monographs, 1989), p. 12. Note also that such penalties are not the same as the civil fines system mentioned earlier in the chapter (see text at *supra* n.3): here, most pollution incidents are prosecuted as normal in the criminal courts, but very minor cases which would not normally be prosecuted are dealt with by civil penalties; in the systems mentioned earlier, a significant swathe of cases which would previously have been prosecuted in the criminal courts are diverted to civil proceedings.

[113] Such a tax must be distinguished from a typical pollution tax, under which firms pay for emissions *within* their consents.

[114] And in the case of the Environment Agency, its duty in s.39 of the Environment Act 1995 specifically requires it to take costs and benefits into account.

[115] Harm caused either immediately during a one-off incident, or by everyone getting the message that persistent routine breaches are not prosecuted, and thus creating the potential for numerous minor breaches by individual firms to create significant environmental harm in combination.

[116] This section draws on ideas presented in C. Hilson, "Discretion to Prosecute and Judicial Review" [1993] *Crim. L Rev.* 739.

[117] See K. C. Davis, *Discretionary Justice: A Preliminary Inquiry* (Baton Rouge, Lou, Louisiana State University Press, 1969), pp. 90, 168–70.

internal policy on prosecution.[118] This ensures consistent decision-making and accountability[119] within the co-operative approach. In other words, for the sake of fairness and accountability, a policy *of* selective prosecution should be accompanied by a policy *for* selecting prosecution.

However, if the respective advantages of a policy of selective prosecution and a policy for selecting prosecution are cost on the one hand and fairness and accountability on the other, what are the possible disadvantages? The principal one is a reduction in deterrence: if all crimes are prosecuted, deterrence is maximal; if, on the other hand, there is a policy of selective prosecution, there may be a reduced deterrence to the extent that people can perceive a pattern in the offences that are not prosecuted. If, for reasons of fairness and accountability, an internal policy for selecting prosecution is introduced, deterrence may then be further reduced because much more of a pattern will become discernible. In other words, with selective prosecution, there may be a trade-off between cost-effectiveness and deterrence; with an internal prosecution policy there may be a further trade-off between fairness/accountability and deterrence. If the policy is made *open*, there may be yet another trade-off of this kind. By adopting an open policy, you increase transparency and fairness by allowing people to see that they have been treated fairly, and you increase accountability by enabling them to bring informal[120] and formal action[121] drawing attention to inconsistencies with policy. However, in making the policy public, you also allow everyone to see the pattern of what is prosecuted. This may further decrease deterrence, leading to an increase in offences, because people will be able to see what they can "get away with".[122] Whether this is likely to be true in relation to the environment will be considered later, after an examination of the Environment Agency's public policy.

The Environment Agency first introduced a non-statutory *Enforcement Code of Practice* in 1996.[123] The Code was public, although a more specific and detailed prosecution policy was not.[124] Its origins could be traced in part to two

[118] On structuring discretion, see *ibid.*, p. 97. If all offences were prosecuted, a prosecution policy would obviously be unnecessary.

[119] Albeit of a rather limited, internal kind. If a policy is all that there is, the enforcement discretion of officers is in theory structured by the policy, but the officer is not obliged to account externally for the exercise of his discretion either informally or formally in review proceedings.

[120] See A. Ashworth, "The 'Public Interest' Element in Prosecutions" [1987] *Crim. L Rev.* 595, p. 605.

[121] Such as judicial review, considered further below in the text at n. 148.

[122] Allowing policies to be relied upon in judicial review proceedings might make matters worse still, because if a policy is open but review is not allowed, there is always the chance that the prosecuting body might ignore the policy and decide to prosecute. This uncertainty may serve as a deterrent. If, on the other hand, review is allowed, this deterrent is removed because one can take formal action if the body ignore the policy.

[123] The Code consisted of an enforcement policy statement, an enforcement guide for Agency enforcement officers, and a guide to the rights and appeals procedures of those subject to enforcement action.

[124] Two of the key former regulators—the NRA and HMIP—had enforcement policies. The NRA's policy was public, while HMIP's was not. Adopting open enforcement policies can be seen as reflecting a general trend in environmental law towards the increasing use of formalism (on which

initiatives of the previous Conservative Government: the Citizen's Charter, and the deregulation drive. In relation to the latter, the Code adopted many of the principles outlined in that Government's code for enforcement agencies[125] and in Schedule 1 to the Deregulation and Contracting Out Act 1994.[126]

A new Environment Agency, *Enforcement and Prosecution Policy* was introduced towards the end of 1998. Again, it is public, although more detailed, regime-specific guidance remains internal.[127] The Policy reflects the concerns of the Labour Government and in particular the principles of good regulation set out by the Cabinet Office's Regulatory Impact Unit.[128] While the new Policy is different from the 1996 Code in a number of ways, the general principles which it states are to be used in relation to enforcement remain very similar. These principles are those of proportionality, consistency, transparency and targeting. With proportionality, the Policy states that the enforcement action taken by the Agency will be proportionate to the risks posed to the environment and to the seriousness of any breach of the law. Consistency, according to the Agency, means taking a similar approach, in similar circumstances, to achieve similar ends. However, it stresses that consistency does not mean uniformity. In effect, it is stating that, if consistency is a matter of treating like cases alike, then cases which are unlike may legitimately be treated differently. Cases, it suggests, may be unlike in terms of the scale of environmental impact, the attitude and actions of management and the history of previous incidents or breaches. Transparency is stated to be important for maintaining public confidence in the Agency, and means that the regulated and the public should understand what is expected of them and what they can expect of the Agency. Targeting, finally, means ensuring that regulatory effort is directed primarily towards those whose activities pose the greatest risk to the environment. The Policy effectively states that this requires both monitoring and follow-up enforcement action to be based on risk.

The range of enforcement tools available to the Agency is discussed briefly in the Policy. Powers mentioned include: enforcement notices and works notices (which will be used where contravention can be prevented or needs to be remedied), prohibition notices (where there is an imminent risk of serious environmental damage),[129] suspension or revocation of licences, variation of licence

see R. Macrory, "Environmental Law: Shifting Discretions and the New Formalism" in O. Lomas (ed.), *Frontiers of Environmental Law* (London, Chancery, 1991).

125 DTI, *Working with Business: A Code For Enforcement Agencies* (London, DTI, 1993).

126 S.5 of the Act provides ministers with the power to introduce an Order to improve enforcement procedures by adopting one or more of the principles set out in Sched. 1 (for further details, see Ch. 2). In the Environment Agency's case, the principles in Sched. 1 to the Act were not introduced in legislative form in this way (i.e. by Order); instead the Agency was informally "ordered" by the previous government to incorporate them into their non-statutory Code (see 278 ENDS Report (1998) 39).

127 See para. 5 of the policy.

128 Previously the Better Regulation Unit.

129 Previous guidance has stressed that prohibition notices are not intended for routine use on firms that have breached their permits—they will normally be used only as an emergency measure to shut firms down in order to prevent the aggravation of a serious pollution incident (even one caused by someone else).

conditions, injunctions and the carrying out of remedial works. Where a criminal offence has been committed, the policy states that the Agency will consider bringing a prosecution, administering a caution,[130] or issuing a warning.[131] The aims of a prosecution are stated to be to punish wrongdoing and to act both as an individual deterrent (to the defendant, to prevent a recurrence) and as a general one (to others). The Policy also points out that administrative enforcement mechanisms (such as prohibition notices) may be used in conjunction with formal criminal tools such as prosecution and cautions, and informal tools such as warnings.

Agency decisions about prosecution will take into account the criteria in the Code for Crown Prosecutors, such as evidential sufficiency, the presence of a realistic prospect of conviction and the public interest. Public interest factors that will be considered in deciding whether or not to prosecute include: the environmental effect of the offence, its foreseeability, intent (individual and/or corporate), any history of offending, the attitude of the offender, the individual and general deterrent effect of a prosecution and the personal circumstances of the offender. The Policy further states that there will be a presumption in favour of prosecution, *inter alia*, where: incidents or breaches have significant environmental consequences; operations have been carried out without a relevant licence; there have been excessive or persistent breaches of regulatory requirements in relation to the same licence or site; or there has been a failure to comply adequately with formal remedial requirements. Again, much of this is very similar to the provisions of the former 1996 Code.

Linking principle with tools, proportionality seems to dictate that the ultimate tool of prosecution be reserved for the most serious cases, either environmentally or in terms of offender profile. With less serious cases, the wide range of formal and informal enforcement mechanisms besides prosecution are likely to offer a more proportionate response. As the former 1996 Code stated, there "should be a quick and effective response to serious breaches of the law and a discriminating and efficient approach to other breaches".

At the start of this section, it was suggested that one of the benefits of introducing an enforcement policy is fairness, and a potential disadvantage—particularly of an open one—a decrease in deterrence. Having considered the Agency's policy, it is worth pausing to consider whether these advantages and disadvantages are likely to occur in practice. As it stands, the part of the Agency's enforcement and prosecution policy that is open is very unlikely to reduce deterrence; there is simply not enough concrete information there which will lead dischargers to be able to spot when they can "get away with" something. However, even if its more detailed, internal policy were published, it is still unlikely that this would reduce deterrence: regulatory crimes are not like

[130] A caution can be given only where the offender admits to the offence in writing, and where a prosecution could properly have been brought.

[131] A warning is a written notification that the Agency believes that an offence has been committed. This is recorded and may be referred to in any subsequent proceedings.

crimes such as shoplifting or speeding, where revealing a detailed internal policy might lead people to ignore the law with impunity in cases where the policy has alerted them that they are unlikely to be prosecuted. With pollution, serious incidents will attract prosecution—that much is clear from the open policy. And most dischargers are unlikely to rush to emit small amounts: doing this just once will hardly be worth it financially; and doing it more than once will attract the tools of a co-operative approach. With speeding in contrast, the policy may reveal that you are unlikely to be stopped at all if speeding below certain thresholds, and thus you can carry on doing this; with shoplifting, the policy may indicate that you will be prosecuted a second time, but getting away once with free goods will look worthwhile to some. It is hard to think of an equivalent danger that may lie in the Agency's internal enforcement policy.

As for fairness, an examination of recent statistics on enforcement reveals that, while there may be consistency within regions, the existence of a national Agency enforcement policy is far from achieving consistency across regions, and still less so across pollution control regimes. Prosecution rates, for example, vary wildly between regions. Where the North West region brought 55 prosecutions for water pollution offences and 71 for waste offences in 1997–8, the figures for the South West were just 15 and 16 respectively. And with regimes, while waste and water pollution enjoy high prosecution rates, those processes subject to IPC are much less likely to be prosecuted.[132] In the case of regimes, it is not surprising that differences exist, given that the general policy is supplemented by more detailed, internal, regime-specific guidance.[133]

ACCOUNTABILITY FOR ENFORCEMENT DECISIONS

An open enforcement policy thus provides a degree of transparency both to companies and to the public, providing them with information on how an agency is likely to respond in a particular situation. However, the question then is what can be done if a company or the public is unhappy with the regulator's enforcement decision in an individual case. The most likely (and cheapest) initial option is to make an informal complaint to the regulator, perhaps pointing out, if applicable, that the decision conflicts with the written enforcement policy. If informal routes fail, there are more formal options available to hold the regulators to account for their enforcement decisions. The cheapest, formal option is likely to be to make a complaint to the relevant ombudsman.[134] Otherwise, it will be a matter of pursuing one of the expensive legal options below.

[132] Not only is there inconsistency between IPC and other regimes, but regional inconsistency within IPC is also particularly marked. Six of the eight regions brought no prosecutions at all, one brought 11 and the other brought 1.

[133] See *supra* n.127.

[134] See e.g. [1999] *JPL* 662 for details of a complaint to the Local Government Ombudsman about, *inter alia*, poor enforcement action regarding waste transfer activities that were causing a nuisance to local residents. The complaint was substantially upheld and compensation was recommended and duly paid.

Private prosecutions

Private prosecutions[135] present a mechanism for holding agencies to account for their enforcement decisions, in that if an agency decides not to prosecute, individuals or environmental organisations can step in and bring a prosecution themselves. They are, in other words, a kind of check on the agency's enforcement discretion. Section 6(1) of the Prosecution of Offences Act 1985 provides for a general power of private prosecution,[136] although in some areas of environmental law this power has been circumscribed.[137]

It is worth noting that while the availability of private prosecution in most areas of environmental law upholds the value of accountability, it may come at the expense of another important value—fairness: if an agency is prosecuting then its enforcement or prosecution policy should lead to fairness in the treatment of individual wrongdoers; however, where private prosecutions take place, they are not guided by such considerations. It could be argued therefore that defendants subjected to a private prosecution ought to be able to seek review of a decision to prosecute, even though this is by a private individual against whom judicial review would not traditionally lie, on the grounds that the prosecution is contrary to provisions in the agency's enforcement policy. If a private individual thinks that enforcement policy (or indeed the agency's monitoring policy) is too lax, then the course she ought to take is to seek review of the policy, not to prosecute someone who would not have attracted prosecution under the policy.

The existence of public registers should aid the cause of those bringing private prosecutions: the registers contain actual company performance alongside the standards set out in that company's consent, enabling citizens to take action where the register suggests some irregularity.[138] While registers look like an unqualified good, they are not without their problems. Research has shown that ordinary individuals are unlikely to make effective use of the registers.[139] It has

[135] For a good, though now somewhat out of date, practical guide see M. Polden and S. Jackson, *The Environment and the Law: A Practical Guide* (London, Longman, 1994), pp. 187–90 and 261–72.

[136] Although, under s.6(2), the DPP may take over the proceedings and may also discontinue them.

[137] See e.g. s.216 of the WRA 1991 (in relation to the water *resources* provisions of the WRA 1991, a private prosecution can be brought only with the consent of the DPP); s.211 of the WIA 1991 (written consent of Attorney General required for private prosecution in respect of sewerage offences) and s.4(3) of the Salmon and Freshwater Fisheries Act 1975 (private prosecution requires a person to obtain a certificate from the Minister of Agriculture confirming that he has a material interest in the waters affected).

[138] The exception here is trade effluent consents: details of samples taken do not have to be placed on the register; indeed, it is a criminal offence under s.206(7) of the WIA 1991 for an employee of a sewerage undertaker to provide such information. However, as has been seen, private prosecution is somewhat limited there in any case (see *supra* n.137).

[139] See e.g. T. Burton, "Access to Environmental Information: The UK Experience of Water Registers" (1989) 1 *JEL* 192; J. Rowan-Robinson, A. Ross, W. Walton and J. Rothnie, "Public Access to Environmental Information: A Means to What End?" (1996) 8 *JEL* 18; T. Jewell, "Public

also been suggested that, in practice, only fairly large interest groups such as angling clubs and groups like Friends of the Earth, will be able to afford the cost of bringing private prosecutions—and even they may not find the process a simple one.[140]

Sampling for use as evidence in a private prosecution may pose a particular obstacle. If a group wishes to rely on its own samples, an important question is whether these can be taken only at official sampling points, which may be inaccessible to those without the powers of entry enjoyed by official agencies. In *Greenpeace* v. *Albright & Wilson*,[141] Greenpeace took its sample at the end of the pipe rather than the official sampling point, which was within the site. The company argued that this was unfair because a reaction might occur leading to a technical breach at the pipe's end, and that the official sampling point was more indicative of compliance.[142] The magistrates rejected this argument, convicting Albright & Wilson, although of course a magistrates' court decision has no precedential value.[143] It would therefore be open to a later court to reach a contrary conclusion. If, in a future case, a higher court did rule that samples can be taken only from the official sampling point and, as in the *Greenpeace* case, lawful access is impossible, a group would either have to risk trespassing on the discharger's land[144] or rely on information in the registers.[145] A problem with the latter is that sampling data have not always been put on the register if a prosecution is being considered.[146] This will have no adverse effect if the agency does eventually decide to prosecute, but if it chooses not to, there may be a considerable delay before the information becomes available to third party interests.

Tort

Tort does not provide a significant *direct* mechanism for holding agencies to account for their enforcement decisions, because claims for damages against

Law and the Environment: The Prospects for Decision-Making" in T. Jewell and J. Steele (eds.), *Law in Environmental Decision-Making* (Oxford, Clarendon, 1998), p. 73. However things may improve with the recent introduction by the Environment Agency of the pollution inventory on the Internet.

140 Burton, *supra* n.139. Among the few private prosecutions that have been brought are: *Greenpeace* v. *Albright & Wilson* (1991) 2(9) *Env. Law Brief* 107, (1991) 2(10) *Env. Law Brief* 119; and *Wales* v. *Thames Water Authority* (1987) 1(3) *Env. Law* 3.

141 *Ibid.*

142 See further (1991) 3 *LMELR* 202 and (1992) 4 *LMELR* 23.

143 See 203 ENDS Report (1991) 5, which suggests that pressure from other chemical companies not wishing a binding precedent to be established may have led A&W to drop its appeal by way of case stated from the magistrates.

144 If this course is taken, the evidence may be excluded under s.78 of the Police and Criminal Evidence Act 1984 as improperly obtained, although in police cases the courts will, in their discretion, usually allow such evidence.

145 As in the *Wales* case, *supra* n.140, where the prosecution was successful.

146 See (1991) 2(9) *Env. Law Brief* 104.

regulatory authorities arising from enforcement action are very unlikely to succeed.[147] However, tort does provide a useful *indirect* accountability mechanism, because if an agency decides not to prosecute, plaintiffs are still entitled to bring a civil claim against the polluter. Nevertheless, it will not normally be possible for environmental groups to make use of civil actions to protect the environment, because there is typically a requirement that a plaintiff must possess a proprietary interest or have suffered damage; environmental groups will seldom fall into this category.

Judicial review of enforcement discretion

The alternative to bringing a private prosecution or tort action is to seek judicial review of the agency's enforcement decision.[148] This will not fall foul of the alternative remedies rule in administrative law, because private prosecutions and tort claims cannot be regarded as equally convenient, beneficial and appropriate remedies for checking an agency's enforcement discretion.[149] Judicial review is undoubtedly a stronger accountability mechanism and provides a more effective check, because it has the potential to force the authority to reconsider its actions. Having done so, it may end up doing what you want it to do, rather than, as with private court action, having to take enforcement action yourself.

The enforcement decision under scrutiny in a judicial review case is likely to consist of a decision to prosecute or a decision not to prosecute. Environmental groups are likely to seek review of decisions not to prosecute; some firms may feel that uneven enforcement is putting them at a competitive disadvantage and likewise mount a challenge on the ground that the agency has failed to prosecute, though this is unlikely. Most firms, if they bring a review action, are likely to be challenging a decision to prosecute themselves.[150]

However, this is not to say that decisions to use "lesser" enforcement tools may not be the subject of challenge. In some cases, review of a prosecution decision will effectively be review of a decision to use or not to use a lesser tool. For example, where an environmental group is challenging a decision not to prosecute, the agency may have served an enforcement notice; the group here is in effect challenging the use of this lesser tool, which it considers inappropriate.

[147] At least in relation to formal enforcement tools—see *Harris* v. *Evans* [1998] 1 WLR 1285 (a health and safety case). It may be different where informal advice has been given: see *Welton* v. *North Cornwall DC* [1997] 1 WLR 570 (an environmental health case).

[148] See further Hilson *supra* n.116; P. Osborne, "Judicial Review and the Criminal Process" in B. Hadfield (ed.), *Judicial Review: A Thematic Approach* (Dublin, Gill & Macmillan, 1995), p. 128; Y. Dotan, "Should Prosecutorial Discretion Enjoy Special Treatment in Judicial Review? A Comparative Analysis of the Law in England and Israel" [1997] *Public Law* 513.

[149] C. Lewis, "The Exhaustion of Alternative Remedies in Administrative Law" (1992) 51 *CLJ* 138.

[150] Note that firms may also be able to challenge prosecutions under the abuse of process jurisdiction: see e.g. *R.* v. *Croydon Justices, ex parte Dean* [1993] QB 769; *Environment Agency* v. *Campbell and another* [1998] All ER (D) 199.

Equally, a firm may challenge a decision to prosecute, and be arguing that it should instead have been served with an enforcement order. Other cases may not involve prosecution at all. An environmental notice could, for example, seek review of a decision to use an informal warning when it thinks an enforcement notice should have been served. Similarly, though perhaps unlikely, a firm might challenge the issue of a caution.[151]

There is a growing body of case law on judicial review of enforcement discretion, which includes bodies ranging from the police and the Crown Prosecution Service to the Bar Council and the Inland Revenue. There are, as yet, no cases involving judicial review of the prosecution decisions of an environmental prosecuting body, but the only way to determine what approach the courts might take if such a case were brought is to look at the existing cases, which are predominantly of the more traditional criminal justice type.[152]

It has for some time been clear that the courts will allow review of an enforcement policy[153] or an individual enforcement decision[154] on the ground that it is *Wednesbury* unreasonable.[155] However, the *Wednesbury* hurdle is a very difficult one to cross and, not surprisingly no applications have succeeded on this basis.[156] While a blanket policy of never prosecuting might well be regarded as *Wednesbury* unreasonable, a policy of selective prosecution—as in the co-operative approach—will not be.[157]

The chances of a successful review action were boosted immeasurably by cases such as *ex parte L*[158] and *ex parte Mead* (although neither actually succeeded on the merits). The cases were important in that they introduced the principle of review on the ground that the prosecution had failed to have regard to or had acted contrary to its enforcement or prosecution policy.[159] In *ex parte L*, Watkins LJ considered that a *successful* challenge would be rare because an

[151] Police cautions are subject to (limited) review: see R. Evans, "Challenging a Police Caution Using Judicial Review" [1996] *Crim. L Rev*. 104.

[152] Indeed, it has been suggested that it may be easier to obtain review against "other bodies" than it is against the police or, now, the Crown Prosecution Service (CPS).

[153] *R.* v. *Metropolitan Police Commissioner, ex parte Blackburn* [1968] 1 All ER 763.

[154] *R.* v. *Commissioner of Police of the Metropolis, ex parte Blackburn (No.3)* [1973] 1 QB 241; *R.* v. *General Council of the Bar, ex parte Percival* [1990] 3 All ER 137 (including a decision to prefer a less serious charge than that considered appropriate by an applicant—*ex parte Percival*).

[155] *Associated Provincial Picture Houses* v. *Wednesbury Corporation* [1948] 1 KB 223.

[156] See e.g. *ex parte Percival* (*supra* n.154). In that case, the court found that the Professional Complaints Committee had acted in accordance with the rules, and had not acted unreasonably because there was room for different views on the seriousness of the charge a person should face. In *R.* v. *Inland Revenue Commissioner, ex parte Mead* [1993] 1 All ER 772, relying on *Blackburn*, the applicants might have succeeded had they shown that the prosecution policy was *Wednesbury* unreasonable. However, as Stuart-Smith LJ noted, they were unlikely to establish that a policy approved by the Keith Committee (chaired by Lord Keith) was irrational.

[157] *Ibid.*

[158] *R.* v. *Chief Constable of the Kent Constabulary, ex parte L*, and *R.* v. *DPP, ex parte B* [1993] 1 All ER 756.

[159] In *Ex parte Mead* (*supra* n.156), while Stuart-Smith LJ did not question the policy *of* selective prosecution, he did stress that any decision should be in accordance with the policy *for* selecting prosecution.

applicant would find it hard to demonstrate that a decision had been made in disregard of or contrary to settled policy. However, as Stuart-Smith LJ implicitly recognised in *ex parte Mead*, it would not be as hard as winning a case where no policy exists. In those circumstances, one is thrown back to the grey area of *Wednesbury*, where discretion is not lightly interfered with by the courts. Where there is a policy on the other hand, the issue before the courts is much more black and white: either the decision was contrary to the policy or it was not.[160]

Ex parte L and *ex parte Mead* were both cases involving review of decisions to prosecute contrary to setttled policy. In *ex parte C*,[161] a wife sought judicial review of the DPP's decision not to prosecute her husband for buggery. The application for review was successful because the prosecutor had failed to have regard to the criteria in the Code for Crown Prosecutors. Kennedy J. stated that a court could review a decision not to prosecute if the decision was guided by an unlawful policy or if it was not in accordance with established policy, or if the decision was perverse. The case is significant for two reasons: not only is it the first case where an applicant seeking judicial review of a prosecutorial decision has succeeded on the merits; but it also establishes that applicants can seek review of decisions not to prosecute contrary to an established policy as well as decisions to prosecute made in this way.

That said, the chances of successful review on the grounds that the agency has disregarded or acted contrary to its policy will depend on a number of factors. First, there must obviously be a policy in existence.[162] And next, the policy must be sufficiently detailed. With local authority environmental health departments in respect of local authority air pollution control, it is clear that many do not have enforcement policies.[163] With the Environment Agency, while it has a public enforcement and prosecution policy, the details in this are probably insufficient to ground a successful review action.[164] Much of the detail remains internal and the question is thus what can be done in relation to such material? Obviously, if the details cannot be tracked down, a review action cannot be based on a failure to follow the policy, because one does not know what that policy is. However, if the details are traced, then it is clear that a prosecution

160 Where an environmental group feels that *monitoring* is unduly lax, it will be very difficult to establish that the authority has acted in a *Wednesbury* unreasonable manner, because the court will be especially wary of interfering in such an obviously scientific area. Again, successful review will be much more likely if an environmental group can point to a monitoring policy that sets out monitoring frequencies. Of course, if the group disagrees with the policy itself, it will be back to the difficult task of establishing that it is *Wednesbury* unreasonable.

161 *R.* v. *DPP, ex parte C* [1994] COD 375.

162 *Quaere* whether not having a policy could be regarded as *Wednesbury* unreasonable.

163 Although they are being encouraged to adopt them in accordance with the Cabinet Office, Better Regulation Unit's, *Enforcement Concordat* (London, Cabinet Office, 1998)—see 285 ENDS Report (1998) 40.

164 HMIP's policy on prosecution, which was in an internal manual, was not available to the public. The NRA had a prosecution policy, but decided not to make it fully public because it was "concerned that general disclosure of the policy could encourage defendants to challenge its decisions to prosecute on the grounds that a particular pollution incident fell outside the relevant category": 189 ENDS Report (1990) 28.

decision contrary to an internal policy is in principle reviewable.[165] With environmental agencies, one might argue that the Environmental Information Regulations 1992 require official disclosure of internal enforcement policies.[166] An agency might seek to rely on regulation 4(3)(d) which states that information need not be provided if disclosure would "increase the likelihood of damage to the environment affecting anything to which the information relates". However, we saw earlier that revealing detailed policies in relation to environmental enforcement is unlikely to pose a threat to deterrence.[167]

To conclude, if prosecution is selective, like cases will not be treated alike without a policy to act as a yardstick in each case. Ideally, fairness requires that this policy for selection is rational, visible and of practical use to third parties. Without a sufficiently detailed, open policy, one cannot be sure that fairness exists. If it is unenforceable by third parties, one may see unfairness, but be powerless to take formal action against it. The other value besides fairness that is served by allowing review based on failure to follow a prosecution policy is accountability. Having a policy and making it open both provide a measure of accountability, but for that accountability to be of a worthwhile, active sort, judicial review based on the policy is arguably required. For environmental prosecuting bodies, a requirement that they adopt detailed, open policies which can be relied upon in review actions should pose few problems.

[165] R. v. *IRC, ex parte Allen* [1997] STC 1141.

[166] SI 1992 No. 3240. The Regs. are designed to implement EC Dir. 90/313 on the freedom of access to information on the environment [1990] OJ L158/56.

[167] See text at pp. 159–160 *supra*.

8

Enforcement II: Enforcing EC Regulation, and Alternative Instruments

ENFORCING EC REGULATION

The previous chapter considered the enforcement of national regulation, which includes not only legislation but also administrative rules (such as permits) made under that legislation. As we saw, at the centre of the regulatory process lie a series of proscriptions in the form of criminal offences, which can be enforced by either criminal or administrative means. Breaches of these proscriptions are by individuals or companies, and they are thus the subjects of any such enforcement action.

Enforcement of EC environmental regulation is different in a number of respects. First, the regulation being enforced here is purely legislative in nature. Next, there are no criminally proscribed activities such as causing pollution. Instead, Member States have public law-type obligations or duties, which are laid out in the Treaties and in regulatory legislation (predominantly directives). It is these obligations which are enforced, either through public enforcement action brought by the Commission (or other Member States) under Articles 226–228 EC, or via the private enforcement mechanisms of direct effect, indirect effect and state liability. The former involves proceedings which may end up with the Member State having to appear before the Court of Justice. The latter involve actions brought by individuals in their national courts.

Thus, unlike national regulatory enforcement, the subjects of direct enforcement of EC environmental regulation are not companies, but Member States.[1] Although many pollution directives impose obligations (such as to respect limit values) on individuals—both natural persons and legal ones such as companies—these are not *directly* enforceable against them, either by the Commission under Articles 226–228, or by other individuals in the national courts.[2] Public enforcement action lies only against Member States, not against those directly responsible for breaching the obligations. And since directives are generally not horizontally directly effective, they cannot impose obligations on individuals

[1] *Cf.* other areas of Community regulation, such as competition law, where companies are the subjects of direct enforcement.

[2] From the point of view of the protection of the environment, this is obviously regrettable.

until they have been transposed into national law; this means that individuals and, *a fortiori*, the state have no corresponding direct rights under pollution directives which they can enforce against private polluters in their national courts.[3] Of course the doctrine of indirect effect or sympathetic interpretation—which requires national courts to interpret national legislation as far as possible so as to conform with the directive—may involve an individual enforcing an obligation against another individual. However, here the obligation is a national law one: it stems from ambiguous national legislation and the ambiguity is resolved in favour of the Community interpretation. If this process of interpretation is stretched beyond the "as far as possible", then one would be imposing direct Community obligations on individuals and horizontal direct effect would be introduced by the back door.

That said, the nature of some of the differences outlined above should not obscure many of the essential similarities between national and EC regulatory enforcement. First, Member State obligations in directives have been interpreted by the Court of Justice as strict—excuses other than those explicitly provided for in derogations in the directive will not prevent a Member State from being ruled in breach of its Community obligations.[4] There is thus some parallel with many UK national regulatory offences, where liability (though criminal) is similarly strict but not absolute.

In addition, the aim of Community public enforcement is invariably one of ensuring Member State compliance rather than one of punishing Member States for infractions. In other words, as with national regulation, the underlying theory is more one of deterrence than retributivism. It is worth recalling here the economic model of compliance used in the previous chapter. This suggests that Member States will comply with their Community obligations only if the expected costs of violation exceed the benefits of violation—in other words where $pD>U$ (where p is the perceived probability of getting caught *and* found in breach by the ECJ, D the costs of court proceedings such as defence costs, political embarrassment and any penalties imposed and U the benefits of violation).[5]

Monitoring

With p, the "getting caught" side depends on monitoring of Member State action. Monitoring takes place in two ways. First, Member States are expected

[3] The emphasis on private polluters is important: if the polluter is a public one and can be regarded as an "emanation of the state", then vertical direct effect is possible.

[4] See e.g. Case C–337/89 *Commission* v. *United Kingdom* [1992] ECR I–6103; and Case C–56/90 *Commission* v. *United Kingdom* [1993] ECR I–4109.

[5] The benefits to a Member State of a *practical* breach are likely to be particularly high. It is relatively cheap formally to implement EC norms in national law; however, making things change on the ground (e.g. with drinking and bathing water) costs a great deal: see e.g. H. Somsen, "Dynamics, Process, and Instruments of Environmental Decision-Making in the European Union" in T. Jewell and J. Steele (eds.), *Law in Environmental Decision-Making* (Oxford, Clarendon, 1998), p.161 at 200.

to monitor themselves. They have reporting obligations to the Commission, which are typically found in individual directives, although the Reporting Directive 91/692 has aimed to provide a degree of standardisation.[6] These require them to provide the Commission with details of both formal and practical implementation. Secondly, since the Commission is not equipped to carry out investigations on the ground itself, it relies considerably on complaints of breaches passed to it by private individuals and interest groups in the Member States. In practice, most practical breaches come to the Commission's attention this way,[7] and it may then seek further details from the Member State.

There is an obvious weakness in relying on reporting by the Member State. It is easy for the Commission to tell if a Member State has not implemented directives at all. However, in cases of defective implementation, the Member State obviously has no incentive to declare any potential breaches; it will typically involve considerable work on the part of the Commission to seek out inconsistencies between the national and Community legislation.[8] And with practical breaches, there is an incentive to misreport or under-report. As for the individual complaints procedure, though important, this is also far from perfect: it relies on the vagaries of individual and group mobilisation, and this varies considerably from state to state.[9] A better, though perhaps politically unrealistic, solution would be for a better-resourced Commission or the European Environment Agency to enjoy direct monitoring powers.

A co-operative approach?

With the other, "being found in breach" part of p, the Court's strict approach to Member State obligations obviously helps: Member States know that if they do appear before the Court, the chances of being found in breach are high. The probability of being found in breach by the ECJ obviously also depends on the number of cases involving alleged breaches which are successfully "prosecuted" by the Commission as guardian of the Treaty[10] before the ECJ. At this stage it is worth setting out the Commission's powers under Article 226. The Article states that:

[6] [1992] OJ L377/48.

[7] Some also come to its attention via questions from MEPs, petitions from the European Parliament, from national media, and from meetings with experts from the Member States: see EC Commission, *Fifteenth Annual Report on Monitoring the Application of Community Law—1997* [1998] OJ C250/1 p. 53; and R. Williams, "The European Commission and the Enforcement of Environmental Law: An Invidious Position (1994) 14 *YEL* 351, p. 359.

[8] Some Member States (Denmark, Germany, Finland and Sweden) provide concordance tables with detailed explanations of the match between national and corresponding Community provisions, but this has yet to become common practice: see EC Commission, *ibid.*, p. 52.

[9] R. Macrory and R. Purdy, "The Enforcement of EC Environmental Law Against Member States" in J. Holder (ed.), *The Impact of EC Environmental Law in the United Kingdom* (Chichester, Wiley, 1997), p. 27 at 38.

[10] Under Arts. 211 and 226 EC.

> If the Commission considers that a Member State has failed to fulfil an obligation under this Treaty, it shall deliver a reasoned opinion on the matter after giving the state concerned the opportunity to submit its observations.
>
> If the State concerned does not comply with the opinion within the period laid down by the Commission, the latter may bring the matter before the Court of Justice.

Although the procedure did start out involving just two formal stages, for some time now there have been three—two administrative and one judicial.[11] First, a formal Article 226 letter is sent to the Member State. If there is no reply or if the reply is unsatisfactory, then the Commission may decide to deliver a reasoned opinion. If the reply to that is unsatisfactory or not forthcoming, then the Commission may decide to refer the matter to the ECJ. However, these formal stages are typically accompanied by more informal procedures. For example, Member States are warned in writing on an informal basis some time before a formal Article 226 letter is sent; and informal meetings with Member States, known as "paquet"[12] meetings also take place, in which alleged infringements are discussed.[13]

At first sight, it might be thought that deterrence would be maximised if the Commission were to bring Article 226 proceedings for every alleged breach and to see all of these through to the judicial phase. However, it does not possess the resources to investigate every individual complaint made, let alone to commence and complete Article 226 proceedings on every occasion. In any event, until the introduction of potential penalties at Maastricht under Article 228 EC, it could be argued that enforcing every case in this way would not have been cost-effective, in that it would not actually have produced the greatest deterrence. First, this might have antagonised Member States and made them more obstructive in the future, both in terms of implementation and in terms of other aspects of the Commission's work. And secondly, the rulings given by the Court in Article 226 cases are in many ways symbolic, which stems from their declaratory nature. If too many cases proceeded to the judicial phase, then the sheer number of these rulings may have reduced "D" in the equation by diluting their symbolic and stigmatising effect in terms of political embarrassment.[14]

However, these arguments are only really applicable to over-use of the *judicial* phase. Admittedly, the Commission is caught in a Catch 22 situation in relation to this phase: if it under-uses it, then the level of p will be low—Member States will think they have little chance of having a ruling against them; on the other hand, if the Commission over-uses the judicial phase, then the symbolic capital of the Court's rulings and hence deterrence might also be reduced. High

[11] Williams, *supra* n.7, p. 365.

[12] Variously translated as packet or package meetings.

[13] Williams, *supra* n.7; see also Macrory and Purdy, *supra* n.9, p. 35.

[14] For a similar point, see L. Neville Brown and T. Kennedy, *The Court of Justice of the European Communities* (4th edn., London, Sweet & Maxwell, 1994), p. 107. They state that the Commission should exercise its discretion to "prosecute" sparingly because excessive use will dilute its deterrent effect.

use of the *earlier*, co-operative, administrative phases remains effective however. If Article 226 proceedings are commenced against a particular Member State, then p in relation to that state is increased. The Commission can then negotiate compliance from a position of strength. There is simply no need to proceed to the "adversarial" judicial phase in many cases. That can be reserved for cases where negotiated compliance fails, or where the Commission wants a judgment for clarification purposes or to act as a general deterrent to other Member States.

In any event, as suggested above, arguments about over-use of the judicial phase possibly reducing deterrence due to the dilution factor have now arguably disappeared because of the revisions made to Article 171 (now Article 228) at Maastricht. Now, if a Member State fails to comply with an Article 226 ruling, the Commission is able to bring further proceedings, requesting the imposition of financial penalties in the form of a lump sum or a periodic penalty payment. "D" in the compliance equation has, in other words, been significantly increased. The Commission first used this Article 228 procedure in environmental cases in 1997, recommending "fines" of up to ECU 30,000 per day. However, most cases are settled without actually being heard by the Court and hence without fines. In 1997, 15 environmental cases reached the Article 228 letter or reasoned opinion stage; only eight cases overall[15] reached the stage of being referred to the Court, and only two cases from that year appear to have proceeded further.[16] One of these cases—Case C–387/97, *Commission* v. *Greece*—is in fact the first Article 228 case to be heard by the Court of Justice. The Commission complaint was that Greece had still not complied with a ruling by the Court in an earlier Article 226 case on waste.[17] It thus requested the Court to impose on Greece a penalty payment of Euro 24,600 per day, with effect from notification to Greece of the Court's judgment in that earlier case.[18]

The threat of a fine being imposed under Article 228 is useful in a number of respects: as well as reducing the danger of too many Article 226 rulings diminishing the deterrent to Member States, it is an indirect but powerful background presence in Article 226 administrative stage negotiations, and a direct presence in the context of Article 228 negotiations on compliance.

Accountability

Accountability of the Commission for its enforcement decisions is particularly important given the fact that the enforcement part of the Commission is not

[15] I.e. including non-environmental cases.

[16] EC Commission, *supra* n.7, pp. 9, 50.

[17] Case C–45/91 *Commission* v. *Greece* [1992] ECR I–2509.

[18] Court of Justice, Press Release No. 45/99, 22 June 1999. The case has, so far, only proceeded as far as the AG's Opinion (see Press Release No. 71/99, 28 Sept. 1999), which recommended a reduction in the penalty payment to Euro 15,375 per day.

clearly separated from the day-to-day political activity of the Commission. As Williams notes, Commissioners involved in decisions on whether to commence or discontinue infringement proceedings are also involved in overtly political matters such as legislative proposals.[19] While trade-offs are an acceptable part of the political arena, they are not acceptable in the enforcement arena[20]: it is inappropriate, for example, for enforcement action to be dropped in return for Member State co-operation on political action which the Commission wishes to push through.[21] If cases are dropped, it should be for legitimate legal reasons.

Williams suggests either fencing off the enforcement function within the Commission, insulating it from the Commission's political functions, or taking enforcement away from the Commission altogether and giving it to an independent agency like the European Environment Agency.[22] Another solution would be to allow the public access to Article 226 letters, reasoned opinions and other Article 226 documentation,[23] and to allow interest groups to challenge enforcement decisions under Article 230 or 232.[24] At present, the only real form of accountability that exists is through the European Ombudsman, who has investigated a number of complaints about the Commission in relation to specific, environmental Article 169 (now Article 226) cases.[25] However, none of these particular investigations have concluded with a finding of maladministration—a finding which would inevitably follow if the Ombudsman were satisfied that a case had been avoided or dropped for political rather than legal reasons. In addition, the Ombudsman has looked at enforcement under Article 169 (now Article 226) on an "own-initiative" and general basis. As a result of this inquiry, he proposed that the Commission should seek the opinion of complainants before closing a case. The Commission accepted this recommendation and

[19] *Supra* n.7, p. 353.

[20] *Ibid.*

[21] As was the case with e.g. the decision to drop Art. 169 (now Art. 226) action on Twyford Down for breach of the Environmental Impact Assessment (EIA) Dir.—see further Williams, *supra* n.7.

[22] Which, at present, has mainly information-gathering powers.

[23] As advocated e.g. by Williams (*supra* n.7) and L. Krämer, "Public Interest Litigation In Environmental Matters Before European Courts" (1996) 8 *JEL* 1, p. 18. At present, the Commission can legitimately exclude access on confidentiality and public interest grounds—see Commission Decision 94/90 on public access to Commission documents [1994] OJ L46/58; and Case T–105/95 *WWF* v. *Commission* [1997] ECR II–313, [1997] 2 CMLR 55. Although the CFI annulled the Commission decision refusing access to Art. 169 (now Art. 226) documents in that case on the ground that insufficient reasons had been provided for the refusals, this did not lead to WWF receiving the documents. The *Interporc* case (Case T–124/96 *Interporc* v. *Commission* [1998] 2 CMLR 82) makes it clear that all that the ECJ has jurisdiction to do in Art. 230 proceedings is to rule that the institution has acted unlawfully; it cannot order the Commission to act in a particular way and to hand over the documents sought. The Commission thus receives another chance to refuse access "correctly".

[24] Which they cannot do at present—Case 48/65 *Lütticke (Alfons)* v. *Commission* [1966] ECR 19; Case 247/87 *Star Fruit* v. *Commission* [1989] ECR 291; Case C–107/95P *Bundesverband der Bilanzbuchhalter* v. *Commission* [1997] ECR I–947.

[25] See e.g. the Obudsman's Annual Report for 1996 [1997] OJ C272/1. One of his investigations involved the decision of the Commission not to bring Art. 169 (now Art. 226) actions for the UK's alleged breaches of the EIA Dir. in relation to the Newbury bypass and the M40.

agreed that in most cases it would inform complainants of its intention to close cases.[26]

Another notable aspect of accountability which is missing is a public enforcement policy. The Commission does issue an annual report on the application of Community law, but this does not provide the same degree of accountability as a proper public enforcement policy. In fact, the Commission does have a manual of operational procedures which provides internal guidance on the Article 226 procedure. While this is not a generally available public document,[27] there are strong arguments for saying that it should be.[28]

In the previous chapter on national regulation, it was suggested that the ability to bring private prosecutions is another means of keeping agencies to account for their enforcement decisions. What then is the equivalent in the Community context? At first sight, it might be thought that the answer is an ability to bring an action in the national courts. However, while this arguably provides Member States with an additional deterrent from breaching their Community law obligations,[29] it is not really the direct equivalent of a private prosecution, which involves using the "public" procedure in place of the public enforcer, not using an alternative "private" one. The equivalent would be for interest groups to be able bring Article 226 actions themselves where the Commission has been given an appropriate amount of time but has decided not to proceed.[30]

ENFORCING ALTERNATIVE INSTRUMENTS

Enforcement of economic instruments by national regulators

Pollution taxes

Monitoring of emissions is still necessary under a pollution tax or charging system. However, this monitoring would not appear to be any more difficult than monitoring of emission standards under a command-and-control system.[31] If continuous monitoring equipment is used, firms can vary their emissions as they wish and be charged accordingly. In other words, they will be charged on actual

[26] EC Commission, *supra* n.7, pp. 9–10.

[27] Although Williams (*supra* n.7) received individual access to it under the Commission's access to documents rules.

[28] *Ibid.*, pp. 360, 397.

[29] Particularly after the introduction of state liability in Cases C–6/90 & C–9/90 *Francovich and Bonifaci* v. *Italy* [1991] ECR I–5357, [1993] 2 CMLR 66. However, given the poor record of EC-based environmental actions in the UK national courts (see e.g. C. Hilson, "Community Rights in Environmental Law: Rhetoric or Reality?" in Holder, *supra* n.9, p. 51), it is arguable whether the UK government has any real grounds for feeling deterred.

[30] See Krämer, *supra* n.23, pp. 12–14.

[31] OECD, *Improving the Enforcement of Environmental Policies*, Environmental Monographs No. 8 (Paris, OECD, 1987), para. 4.2.

output. Enforcement is not a problem here, as there is no limit to be breached.[32] If continuous monitoring is not used, then firms will have to choose an emissions limit upon which they will be taxed. In other words, they will be charged on projected output. Monitoring and enforcement action will then be needed to ensure that they keep within this chosen level. Enforcement here involves ensuring that firms are paying what they should be for their emissions.[33]

With projected output cases, a charging system could lead to an improvement in monitoring and enforcement levels. If the agency were allowed to keep some or all of the charge revenue, a charging system would provide an increased incentive for the agency to monitor and enforce emissions because they would be keen to ensure that firms were not under-estimating their output levels. However, there would be no such incentive if revenue from the charging system were to go to central government, which then guaranteed the agency a certain amount. Industry too, would be keen to ensure effective monitoring and enforcement: charges would very likely make up a significant proportion of their expenditure, and selective non-enforcement of competitors might affect their market position. Of course, at the moment, non-enforcement of command-and-control standards enables certain firms to avoid pollution control costs; however, under a charge system, they would be avoiding these and the additional, significant cost of paying the charge on the each unit of pollution emitted. Charges in other words could give rise to a third enforcement arm—agencies and environmental interest groups would be joined in monitoring and enforcement activities by industry "vigilantes".[34]

At present, a "mixed-economy" of charges and command-and-control standards, seems more likely than the "pure" charges considered in the previous paragraph. Commenting on a mixed approach, the OECD has suggested that charges may improve enforcement because they act like an additional civil penalty and therefore increase deterrence:

> In the absence of an effluent charge, the reward for violating a standard is the expected gross profit of the actions, less the expected costs associated with being caught. If it is reasonable to assume that in a combined charge and standard system, those caught accidentally or intentionally exceeding the legal standard would have to pay fines plus charges which vary with the unreported quantities discharged, then the charge system reduces the expected net benefit of violating the standard.[35]

[32] Note of course that continuous monitoring may also improve the monitoring and enforcement of command-and-control regulation.

[33] However, with a charging system, there is another type of enforcement, which applies to both continuous monitoring and projected output cases. And that is enforcement in the sense of tax collection, with the need for criminal and/or civil penalties for non-payment (see A. I. Ogus, "Corrective Taxes and Financial Impositions as Regulatory Instruments" (1998) 61 *MLR* 767, p. 782).

[34] For a similar argument (but made in relation to tradable permits and considered further below), see B. A. Ackerman and R. B. Stewart, "Reforming Environmental Law" (1985) 37 *Stanf. LR* 1333, p. 1346.

[35] OECD, *supra* n.31, para. 4.2.

In other words, recalling the economic model of compliance, charges add to the costs of being caught (D). One might add that charges may improve enforcement even where there is no prosecution, and hence no fine. The Royal Commission on Environmental Pollution (RCEP), in its sixteenth report, cites the German system where higher charges are levied if monitoring reveals a breach of consent. This may deter infringements of consents which might not currently be thought significant enough to attract prosecution, and resembles the concept of a civil penalty which was discussed in the previous chapter. Ideally, this civil penalty would reflect the actual quantities discharged in breach of consent, but it would have a similar effect even if levied as a flat-rate. The RCEP refers to this as being a "powerful reinforcement of consents".[36]

Although the OECD and RCEP above are commenting on a mixed command-and-control/charge approach, the same will be true of a pure charging scheme—a company should expect not only to be prosecuted and fined for exceeding the level it has chosen,[37] but also to be charged on this extra amount as well as on its chosen amount. Alternatively, if no prosecution were brought, the firm could simply be charged extra for the amount beyond its chosen limit.

Finally, Beckerman has implicitly suggested that a charging system would improve enforcement because while standards may be selectively enforced, taxes are collected. He states that:

> [t]he collection of the charge or tax is then a routine matter unaffected by changes in the winds of fashion or local pressures. Tax collectors collect their taxes year in, year out, and in the same way from one part of the country to another.[38]

However, while this argument is superficially attractive, it ignores the fact that taxes can also be selectively enforced: the forces that lead to non-enforcement of command-and-control standards may simply be transferred into non-enforcement of pollution taxes.

Tradable permits

In one sense, monitoring under a tradable permit system would be different from monitoring of emission standards, in that the agency would have to monitor trades closely to avoid pollution "hot spots" and also, presumably, fraudulent trading. However, in another sense it would be much the same, in that the agency would still have to check emissions to make sure that firms were not emitting without a permit or in breach of their permit entitlements. It has been argued that tradable permits may improve enforcement incentives of the latter

[36] RCEP, Sixteenth Report, *Freshwater Quality* (Cm 1966, London, HMSO, 1992), paras. 8.45–8.48.

[37] And perhaps be given a rebate if monitored emissions are at or below projected levels—see J. Swierzbinski, "Guilty Until Proven Innocent—Regulation with Costly and Limited Enforcement" (1994) 27 *Journal of Environmental Economics and Management* 127, p. 128.

[38] W. Beckerman, *Pricing for Pollution: An Analysis of Market Pricing and Government Regulation in Environment Consumption and Policy* (2nd edn., London, IEA, 1990), p. 56.

kind, in that firms with credits are likely to be keen on effective monitoring and enforcement, lest cheating companies drive down their value.[39] The agency will therefore be under some pressure to take a strong enforcement line. If trading prices are very high, firms may also be more inclined to monitor and take enforcement action against competitors themselves, because cheating may confer considerable competitive advantage.[40] If permits are re-allocated through annual auctions and the revenue from these auctions comes to the agency, then the agency too may have an extra monitoring and enforcement incentive. If on the other hand there is only a one-off auction, or if permits are grandparented, then the agency will have no such incentive.

The OECD comments that emissions trading does not contain the same civil penalty-type sanctions described above in relation to a charging system. For this reason, it concludes that a trading system will require the same range of sanctions as traditional regulatory schemes.[41] Are there nevertheless any other ways in which tradable permits may improve enforcement? The literature on enforcement suggests that one reason officers fail to enforce command-and-control pollution laws is that they wish to avoid the consequences on local employment of forcing firms to comply with expensive standards.[42] It has been suggested that firms which were "let off" for this reason under a command-and-control system are more likely to be forced to comply under a tradable permit system; this is because they can now afford to do so by selling the pollution credits acquired by reducing pollution below the level specified in their permit.[43] However, this rather assumes that their abatement costs are low; and if they are so low, then they should be able to comply without too much trouble under a command-and-control system. Nevertheless, even if a firm facing insolvency could not now afford to comply by selling credits, it may be that a tradable permit scheme would still improve enforcement. Stewart, for example, has suggested that:

> The use of a permit system would not eliminate concerns over plant shutdowns and unemployment resulting from pollution control policies. But such shutdowns as might occur could be more readily seen as the product of impersonal market forces rather than a particular government decision.[44]

However, while this may be true at a macro level, it is unlikely to affect enforcement decisions at a micro level. If fear of creating unemployment is one of the reasons for non-enforcement of command-and-control regulation, then it seems unlikely that enforcement officers would feel any differently disposed towards enforcing a tradable permit (by penalising anyone who does not have sufficient

[39] Ackerman and Stewart, *supra* n.34.

[40] *Ibid.*

[41] *Supra* n.31, para. 4.3.

[42] Of course, this may be used as a threat by a firm when it can in fact comply.

[43] See T. Tietenberg, "Economic Instruments for Environmental Regulation" (1990) 6 *Oxford Review of Economic Policy* 17, pp. 28–9.

[44] R. B. Stewart, "Economics, Environment, and the Limits of Legal Control" (1985) 9 *Harv. Env. LR* 1, p. 15.

permits to cover his emissions). It could however become an excuse when they do feel compelled to enforce: rather than blaming "the law", they would now have the opportunity to blame "the market".

Finally, if, as Breyer suggests in a US context, enforcement is primarily targeted at large firms and leaves smaller firms free to continue with their non-compliance,[45] could one say that either a charge system or a system of tradable permits would improve enforcement because all firms, large and small, would have to pay the tax or buy permits? The answer, as Breyer implicitly recognises, is "no", because selective enforcement is just as much a feature of revenue and economic laws as it is of command-and-control standards. Just as the risk of unemployment may lead to the non-enforcement not just of standards but also tradable permits—so small firms may be pressured less for payment of their charges or to buy more permits.

Community law and the enforcement of alternative instruments

Alternatives to command-and-control instruments, such as taxes and environmental agreements, raise particular problems for enforcement of Community law. The instruments may be applied in two separate contexts. First, taxes or environmental agreements may be applied at Community level *as* Community laws. Secondly, they may be applied at national level by Member States *to implement* Community laws.

With national-level agreements, the Commission's Communication on Environmental Agreements[46] notes that monitoring of industry by Member States will be necessary to provide data on which to assess whether agreements are working, and suggests that details on how monitoring will take place should be included in the agreement. Member States themselves will be expected to notify agreements to the Commission and to report these monitoring details to it, so that the Commission can monitor Member States. With Community-level agreements, the Commission will monitor them and report periodically to the Council and European Parliament on their effectiveness.

On enforcement of national level agreements by national authorities, the Communication states that with unilateral agreements, the threat of replacement legislation combined with public pressure should discourage non-compliance by industry. With binding, bilateral agreements it states that these can be legally enforced by Member State authorities and may include sanctions for breach. Assuming that any problems concerning appropriate enforcement fora and causes of action can be overcome, it does indeed seem that bilateral agreements should pose few problems for enforcement by the relevant national

[45] S. Breyer, *Regulation and Its Reform* (London, Harvard UP, 1982), pp. 277, 280; *cf.* P. Yeager, *The Limits of Law: The Public Regulation of Private Pollution* (Cambridge, CUP, 1991), pp. 45–6, 292, 311.

[46] COM(96)561 final.

authorities. In addition, there is no problem posed by non-binding or binding national agreements, or by taxes for public enforcement by the Commission: if the agreements or taxes fail to reach the necessary result, then the Commission can bring an Article 226 action against the Member State. It is unlikely that the Court of Justice would regard instrument failure as a legitimate excuse for failure by a Member to meet its Community obligations. As for Community-level agreements, these are for the moment non-binding and thus, as with unilateral national agreements, the only real means of ensuring compliance is the threat of replacement, binding legislative action.

Non-binding agreements at national level enfeeble private enforcement as well as enforcement by national authorities, and non-binding agreements at Community level also enfeeble private as much as public enforcement. However, even with *binding* national agreements, private enforcement will be difficult in a number of Member States whose contract law contains the doctrine of privity. The Commission's Communication thus states that agreements should not be used by Member States to implement directives that are intended to create rights for individuals. The Court of Justice's case law makes it clear that, where directives are intended to create such rights, implementation must generally be in a legislative and not an administrative form, so that individuals have rights which they can enforce in their national courts.[47] Given the problems that privity may pose for enforcing rights, implementation in a contractual form would fall foul of this jurisprudence. While the Communication focuses here on *agreements* at the *national* level, much the same will be true of agreements at Community level, and of taxes at both national and Community level: where the Commission intends Community rights to be created, it should not choose a tax or *a fortiori* a non-binding agreement as an instrument; and where provisions of a directive are intended to create rights for individuals, a Member State should be careful in using taxes to implement it, as this may prevent individuals from relying on their rights in their national courts.[48]

The Communication states that Community level agreements are likely to be most appropriate for programmes and general targets.[49] It similarly notes that provisions of directives providing for the setting up of general programmes or the achievement of general targets are likely to be the most suitable for implementation via national level agreements.[50] However, with national agreements, the Communication goes on to suggest that even in these cases—on grounds of legal certainty and in order to deter free-riding—agreements should be supported by national legislation. It states that legislation should be used in all cases

[47] See e.g. Case C–131/88 *Commission* v. *Germany* [1991] ECR I–825, and see further Hilson, *supra* n.29.

[48] E.g. if a tax was to replace a limit value.

[49] E.g. targets for CO_2 reduction from cars, and reduction of energy loss from electrical goods on standby mode.

[50] Suggestions provided include targets for CO_2 reduction, waste reduction, recycling and energy efficiency, and (more controversially) environmental quality objectives.

where environmental agreements are used by Member States, but that the legislation should exempt parties to an agreement, as long as they are complying. This, it is stated, will deter free riders: those not covered by the agreement will be subject to legislation; and those in breach of the agreement will also have to comply with the legislation.

9

Pollution Regulation and Growth

DEBATES OVER GROWTH

Economic growth is sometimes used to describe an increase in the *aggregate* level of economic output or gross domestic product (GDP)—in other words, an increase in the total value of goods and services consumed. However, it is arguably more meaningful to use economic growth to describe an increase in economic output or GDP *per capita*. Field refers to the former as economic growth and the latter as economic development. Using this terminology, a country can experience economic *growth* fuelled by a population explosion; but if this were to occur with no increase in GDP *per capita*, there would be no economic *development*.[1] While this terminology is useful for heuristic purposes in the context of the above example, the term economic growth will generally be used below to refer to an increase in economic output or GDP *per capita*.[2]

The 1960s and 1970s saw the first sustained criticism of economic growth as one of the central goals of government policy—criticism that continues to this day. Essentially, there are two strands to this criticism.[3] The first denies the positive link made between economic growth and human welfare. Under standard economic theory, if GDP is increasing, then more and more preferences are being satisfied, and hence welfare is seen as increasing. However, environmentalists and others have been keen to point out that increasing GDP does not necessarily equate with increasing welfare. Some have made the common sense point that the materialism inherent in GDP does not lead to human happiness.[4] Others observe that GDP fails to measure some bads and even counts some bads as goods.[5] For example, a product from a polluting factory will be included within GDP, but the non-priced, welfare reducing pollution from that factory will not be. And money spent on cleaning up the pollution will boost GDP figures still further.[6] In recent years, a number of economists have sought to develop "alternative indicators" in order to capture the overall welfare picture,

[1] B. Field, *Environmental Economics: An Introduction* (London, McGraw-Hill, 1994), pp. 398–9.

[2] I.e. what Field would term economic development.

[3] For counter-arguments in relation to both strands, see W. Beckerman, *Small is Stupid: Blowing the Whistle on the Greens* (London, Duckworth, 1995).

[4] See e.g. E. J. Mishan, *The Costs of Economic Growth* (Harmondsworth, Penguin, 1969).

[5] See e.g. C. Cobb, T Halstead and J Rowe, "If the GDP is Up, Why is America Down?", *The Atlantic Monthly*, Oct. 1995.

[6] *Ibid.*

where increases in welfare stemming from rising GDP may be cancelled out by decreases in welfare caused by pollution and other social problems.[7]

The second strand of criticism levelled against economic growth was that, if left unchecked, it would take us beyond the physical "limits to growth" imposed by a world with finite resources and pollution absorption capacity.[8] However, limits to growth theories were themselves criticised by cornucopians, who argued that such theories failed to take sufficient account of the potential for technology to solve both resource and pollution problems.[9] In essence, the debate could be characterised as one between technological pessimists and technological optimists.

More recent versions of Ehrlich and Ehrlich's environmental impact formula[10] provide the key to understanding the role that technology can play in decoupling or delinking economic growth from environmental impact. The formula states that I = PAT, where I represents environmental impact, P population, A the level of affluence (output consumed *per capita*), and T technology (impact *per* unit of output). What this formula helps to demonstrate is that economic growth (an increase in A) can take place without harming the environment as long as technology (T) is acting to decrease the impact *per* unit of output sufficiently.

SUSTAINABLE CONSUMPTION

Historically, pollution regulation has focused on T rather than on P or A. Regulation has invariably been about making production processes and products less polluting—either by directly mandating cleaner technology or techniques or by requiring improved emission levels that can be achieved only by the use of such methods. The aim of this approach is often described as "eco-efficiency": to allow the consumption of the same or a greater number of products and services, using fewer environmental resources.[11] Nevertheless, the limitations of such an approach have become increasingly apparent, the car being an obvious example. Regulation of vehicle pollution has principally been directed at T, with product standards requiring, for example, catalytic convertors on new cars and changes in fuel content. However, while these technological improvements have led to a reduction in pollution from each individual car, the overall growth in the number of cars on the road means that environmental impact—far from improving—has in fact deteriorated. Those on the more rad-

[7] *Ibid.*

[8] See e.g. D. H. Meadows *et al.*, *The Limits to Growth* (New York, Universe Books, 1972). More recently, see D. H. Meadows *et al.*, *Beyond the Limits: Global Collapse or a Sustainable Future* (London, Earthscan, 1992).

[9] See e.g. J. Simon and H. Kahn, *The Resourceful Earth* (Oxford, Basil Blackwell, 1984).

[10] P. R. Ehrlich and A. H. Ehrlich, *The Population Explosion* (London, Hutchinson, 1990).

[11] See further OECD, *Eco-Efficiency* (Paris, OECD, 1998).

ical end of the "sustainable consumption" spectrum thus emphasise not just efficiency, but also the idea of sufficiency or "having enough".[12] The suggestion is that consuming products and services rendered less polluting by T is no longer sufficient: we also need to tackle A by consuming less.

This emphasis on sufficiency takes us back to the topic of choosing goals analysed in Chapter 5. If (strong) sustainability is seen as imposing physical constraints on pollution which it is immoral to breach, then economic growth must either be decoupled or delinked from environmental impact via T, or else reductions in A or P *must* be achieved.[13] However, if one analyses it from a welfare economics or even a democratic perspective, then if T cannot ensure that growth can take place while maintaining the same or reduced levels of environmental quality, environmental quality may simply be allowed to decline. On this view, there are no physical constraints that *must* be respected: society is free to trade off the increased welfare arising from increased consumption (A) and population (P), for the decrease in welfare brought about by a lowering of environmental quality (I).

INSTRUMENTS FOR TACKLING A AND P

Voluntary and market approaches

Assuming that the former constraints model is accepted, and that T is not sufficient to achieve the requisite level of environmental impact, the question then arises what regulatory techniques could in theory be used to control A or P. Essentially, those available mirror the ones that can be used to tackle T which were discussed in Chapter 6. First, there are voluntary approaches—extolling people to have fewer children, and to "downshift" or to adopt voluntary simplicity. However, the same rational choice dilemma exists here as we saw with firms and voluntary pollution control: many people will be tempted to free-ride. State regulation is thus necessary to ensure that everyone is contributing. This regulation could take the form of economic instruments. Thus, families could be taxed beyond a certain number of children, or a tradable quota system for children could be instituted, so that those who wanted more than the allocated

[12] See e.g. D. McLaren, "Achieving Sustainability Through the Concept of 'Environmental Space': A Trans-European Project" (1996) 6 *European Environment* 69. For a more conservative approach to sustainable consumption, which emphasises eco-efficiency and is dismissive of the need for sufficiency, see OECD Proceedings, *Sustainable Consumption and Production: Clarifying the Concepts* (Paris, OECD, 1997).

[13] This is essentially the premise shared by a number of similar theories such as environmental space (on which see McLaren, *supra* n.12, and D. McLaren, S. Bullock and N. Yousuf, *Tomorrow's World: Britain's Share in a Sustainable Future* (London, Earthscan, 1998) and ecological footprints (on which see M. Wackernagel and W. Rees, *Our Ecological Footprint—Reducing Human Impact on Earth* (Gabriola Island, BC, New Society Publishers 1995).

number of children could purchase quotas from those in credit.[14] Similarly, products and services could be taxed much more than at present in order to decrease consumption levels. However, given existing experience with tobacco and vehicle fuel, tax levels would have to be *extremely* high in relation to certain products where demand is relatively price-inelastic. In addition, careful thought would need to be given to whether such taxes should be based on the pollution associated with the product or service, or on a flat rate, as with value added tax (VAT). If the former approach were adopted, society could find that certain valued, but polluting, goods were all but priced out of the market, while numerous less valued, but less polluting, goods remained. A collective choice might well prefer the ecological space taken by the latter to yield to that of the former. A flat-rate, VAT-style tax on "non-essential" items would therefore be preferable, because this would enable such a preference to be expressed.

Command-and-control

A tax system of the above kind would already begin to impinge on certain cherished values of liberal market economies, such as consumer sovereignty, freedom of choice and liberal neutrality. However, command-and control approaches to regulating A and P would take this one step further. Population controls would inevitably be authoritarian—families would be limited to a certain number of children, and such limits would have to be enforced by sanctions of some kind.[15] China's one child per couple policy is allegedly of this nature and has been criticised for infringing female reproductive rights.

As for controls on A, one version of command-and-control would involve not just firms being told *how* to produce in pollution terms, but being told *what* to produce: in other words, a planned economy. In such an economy, the allocation of goods and services proceeds via the plan rather than through millions of individual market decisions. There are two ways of determining what is allocated through the plan: either one has an authoritarian body of planners—as was the case in the Soviet Union—or the contents of the plan may be decided upon democratically.[16] In theory, in a market system, what is produced depends on the preferences of the consumer—consumer sovereignty is the ideal.[17] In the first type of planning, consumer sovereignty is non-existent and a dictatorship

[14] On transferable birth quotas, see e.g. H. E. Daly and J. B. Cobb Jr., *For the Common Good: Redirecting the Economy towards Community, the Environment and a Sustainable Future* (London, Green Print, 1990), pp. 244–6.

[15] Though this would also be necessary with transferable birth quotas (*ibid.*, p.245).

[16] See e.g. E. Mandel, "In Defence of Socialist Planning" (1986) 159 *New Left Review* 5 (and *cf.* the comment by Nove (1987) 161 *New Left Review* 98, and the counter-comment by Mandel (1988) 169 *New Left Review* 108); *cf.* also C. Castoriadis, *Le Contenu du Socialisme* (Paris, Union Générale d'Editions, 1979), pp. 164–5.

[17] Though *cf.* J. K. Galbraith, *The New Industrial State* (Harmondsworth, Penguin, 1969), pp. 216–23.

of needs prevails. With the second, democratic, type there is some attempt to mimic consumer sovereignty, and the people decide their own needs.

There are effectively two separate issues concerning state economic planning and the environment. The first is how it affects levels of consumption (A). The second is whether planning can create the right incentives so that pollution control technology (T) is installed and maintained. Most of the literature on environmental policy in the Soviet Union has focused on the latter—highlighting, for example, that the incentive to meet one's production quota usually took precedence over environmental protection measures.[18] However, the former issue of how planning affects consumption is of greater concern to us here. In theory—unlike Capitalism, which requires growth for its survival[19]—planning need not be growth-centred. However, in practice, the Soviet Union was as obsessed by increasing economic growth as countries in the West. Nevertheless, it had much lower levels of GDP. The popular Western image of the Eastern Bloc as a society of shortages and queues was thus not without foundation. The question is what is it about central planning that made such shortages inevitable, even with growth as a goal? The answer is that authoritarian planners have inadequate information about the preferences of consumers,[20] and are therefore bound to produce less than a market system where these preferences are allowed free reign. Even under democratic planning, if people were to sit down and think about they wanted, it would almost certainly come to less than that which obtains in current market-based societies.

However, even if this absence of conspicuous consumption is accepted as an environmental advantage of planning, it is outweighed by myriad disadvantages. From an environmental perspective, poor controls on T in the Soviet Union in practice more than cancelled out any advantage gained through low levels of A.[21] But more importantly, few would accept the absence of competition and resulting poor quality of goods and services as a price worth paying for the environment, given that the worst excesses of the market can in theory be controlled without such a wholesale change in economic system. One could, for example, simply ban certain trivial and luxury items, and perhaps even place quantitative limits on the number of other items that individuals are allowed to

[18] See e.g. D. J. Peterson, *Troubled Lands: The Legacy of Soviet Environmental Destruction* (Oxford, Westview Press, 1993), pp. 17–18; C. E. Ziegler, *Environmental Policy in the USSR* (London, Pinter, 1987), esp. pp. 114–30; B. Komarov, *The Destruction of Nature in the Soviet Union* (London, Pluto Press, 1978), pp. 66–7. *Cf.* R. J. McIntyre and J. R. Thornton, "On the Environmental Efficiency of Economic Systems" (1978) 30 *Soviet Studies* 173; the reply by Ziegler (1980) 32 *Soviet Studies* 124; the reply to Ziegler (1981) 33 *Soviet Studies* 146; and Ziegler's rejoinder (1982) 34 *Soviet Studies* 296.

[19] See D. Pepper, *Eco-Socialism: From Deep Ecology to Social Justice* (London, Routledge, 1993), pp. 78–97; M. O'Connor (ed.), *Is Capitalism Sustainable? Political Economy and the Politics of Ecology* (London, The Guilford Press, 1994).

[20] A. Nove, *The Economics of Feasible Socialism* (2nd edn., London, Allen and Unwin, 1991); F. A. Hayek, *The Road to Serfdom* (London, Routledge, 1944).

[21] However, as Peterson points out, this is not an *inevitable* feature of planning. With the correct incentives and institutional arrangements, planning could in theory operate without causing significant environmental harm (*supra* n.18, pp. 171–4).

purchase. However, even having the state commanding what *must not* be produced in this way (rather than—as with planning—what *must* be produced) would be regarded by many as unnecessarily draconian and too great an interference by the majority with the freedom of minorities to choose particular products or services.[22] An increased VAT-type tax on non-essential items as discussed in the previous section could provide a compromise solution. As with taxes currently imposed on cigarettes and alcohol, people would still be relatively free to choose non-essential items, but consumption levels would be reduced.

CONCLUSION

Given that economic growth is a key aspect of both UK and EU policy,[23] it is surprising how little the impact of growth on the environment has been discussed in official policy documents. However, with the recent emphasis on integrating environmental concerns into all areas of policy, there have been signs of change in this regard—at least at EC level. There are now one or two EC policy documents that explicitly tackle the question of growth and the environment[24]—though there are equally some where such discussion is surprisingly absent.[25] However, even where it is discussed, the issue of whether controls on affluence or levels of consumption are needed is seldom broached. Instead, such documents assume that technology will be able to decouple growth from environmental impact. That policy-makers should choose to avoid discussion of affluence is less surprising. They are likely to be wary of re-opening politically controversial debates on limits to growth, which many regard as having been fully aired and put to rest. Environmentalists are no doubt aware of this—and this may explain the shift towards other explanatory paradigms such as environmental space and ecological footprints. These are, of course, essentially limits to growth arguments in another guise. The key issue of affluence will thus continue to be debated, but in a rather less explicit manner.

22 On which see Castoriadis, *supra* n.16.

23 In relation to the latter, economic growth is one of the main tasks of the EU listed in Art. 2 of the EC Treaty.

24 EC Commission, *Growth, Competitiveness, Employment: The Challenges and Ways Forward into the 21st Century*, COM(93)700 final, (1993) Bull. EC. Supp. 6–93; and *Economic Growth and the Environment: Some Implications for Economic Policy Making*, COM(94)465 final.

25 E.g. the *Commission Communication on the Single Market and the Environment*, COM(99)263. However, the Commission is not alone in failing to discuss the growth implications of the single market for the environment. Many academic environmental lawyers also appear happy to discuss the tensions between the single market and the environment in terms of conflicts between Member State environmental regs. and EC trade law, but not in terms of a conflict between the environment and one of the main aims of the single market (growth).

Index